Making Peace with God

ALSO BY PAULINE EDWARD

Astrological Crosses in Relationships

The Power of Time

Leaving the Desert: Embracing the Simplicity of A Course in Miracles

Praise for *Leaving the Desert*

"*Leaving the Desert* is one of the most practical spiritual
books ever written. I highly recommend this book."
Gary Renard, Best-selling author of
The Disappearance of the Universe

"I thoroughly enjoyed *Leaving the Desert* by Pauline Edward.
It is an excellent description of the basic metaphysics and
psychology of *A Course in Miracles* and its practical application
in daily life, written in a clear conversational style."
Jon Mundy, Ph.D., author of *Living A Course in Miracles*

"*Leaving the Desert* will inspire Course newbies and veterans alike with
its profound, comprehensive understanding and specific examples
fearlessly and generously drawn from the classroom of the author's life."
Susan Dugan, author of *Extraordinary Ordinary Forgiveness*

"Written with humor and courageous self-disclosure, Pauline
Edward's *Leaving the Desert* is a delight. You will read
this book with a smile of recognition and gratitude."
Carol Howe, author of *Never Forget To Laugh*

"This book is wonderful. It offers a deep and much-needed
exploration of the core message of *A Course in Miracles*."
Robyn Busfield, author of *Forgiveness is the Home of Miracles*

Making Peace with God

The Journey of a
Course in Miracles
Student

Pauline Edward

Desert Lily Publications
Montreal, Canada

Cover design and photography: Pauline Edward
Editorial consultation: Veronica Schami, Traci Williams

V1.02

Library and Archives Canada Cataloguing in Publication

Edward, Pauline, 1954-
  Making peace with God : The journey of a *Course in Miracles* student /
  Pauline Edward.
  Includes bibliographical references.
  ISBN 978-0-9810433-0-2
  1. Edward, Pauline, 1954-. 2. Course in miracles. 3. Spiritual life.
  I. Title.
BP605.C68E39 2009   299'.93   C2008-905932-8

www.DesertLilyPublications.com

*For Maman
with love*

I was a stranger and you took me in, not knowing who I was.
Yet for your gift of lilies you will know.

A Course in Miracles

CONTENTS

FOREWORD

I have known the author since 1976 and, indeed, more intimately through her hands and astrological chart. It seems fitting that, as a practising palmist-astrologer for over forty years, the most authentic preamble I could give in commending Pauline and her work would be, in part, through the language of these sublime sciences. I am confident and pleased to offer this brief testimonial to the sincerity and genuine truth seeking that permeates throughout *Making Peace with God*, making it a truly enjoyable read and a revealing and insightful journey of self-discovery.

To begin, Aquarius is the ascending, or rising, sign, in Pauline's chart, signifying her serious, humanitarian nature, and one that is seasoned with an innate sense of life's ironies. Saturn, the planet ruling (closely associated with) Aquarius, is exalted in Libra. Pauline can use her powers of discrimination and wisdom to perceive circumstances clearly and extract meaning that can be conveyed to others in a down-to-earth, articulate manner. Moreover, Saturn occupies the ninth house of the chart, the house of dharma (ethical behaviour) and higher learning. Together, these auspicious placements show that Pauline was born to explore the world of the Infinite.

Significantly, and confirming the previous astrological observations, Pauline's handprints over the years have changed considerably for the better. In a handprint taken in September 1976, Pauline has a Ring of Saturn—indicating a more isolated and guarded nature. In handprints taken in September 2008, this line has been transformed into a Girdle of Venus. This auspicious sign indicates an intuitive, inspirational nature in addition to a creative and caring desire to help humanity.

Additionally, the angle of Pauline's thumb in relation to her hand is much wider than before, showing that she is a freer spirit, unencumbered by self-limiting inhibitions. This, combined with an improved Mercury line, the line of self-expression and the Girdle of Venus, points to an ardent desire to attune to the metaphysical mysteries of life and to share with others the knowledge gained through these experiences. This she does to a high degree from the first chapter, "I Want to Go Home," to the last, "The Journey Begins."

On February 1, 2007, Pauline entered a major astrological period associated with expressive, communicative Mercury that will last twenty years. This corresponds to the house of creativity—the fifth, and the house of occult wisdom, transformation and karmic obligations—the eighth.

Therefore, both hands and chart signify this to be a time of deep personal discovery and spiritual connectedness. These observations have simply confirmed my long-ago suspicions that Pauline would one day author books such as this one—works that are timely and speak intelligently and warmly to the hearts and minds of her readers.

Pauline herself wished she could have had a book such as *Making Peace with God* when she first encountered the teachings of *A Course in Miracles* to strengthen her courage and perseverance to pursue its study with greater conviction. I am sure that this heartfelt account of her journey, substantially enriched by *A Course in Miracles*, will provide an immensely useful stepping stone for those truth seekers also looking to find their way home.

Much success, lovingly,
Ghanshyam Singh Birla
Director, The Birla Centre for Hast Jyotish
September 2008

ACKNOWLEDGMENTS

Although this book is very much the result of a process of inner healing, it was also written in response to the many questions asked by clients, students, friends and, in particular, the members of our *Course in Miracles* study group. This work is dedicated to all who have crossed my path, nudging me steadily in the right direction.

I wish to express my deepest appreciation for two very busy ladies for providing invaluable editorial feedback—Traci Williams for an initial cleanup, and Veronica Schami, whose perspicacity prevailed over my perennially perverted punctuation.

Thanks also to Epp Luik, Helena Basso, Tina Brooks and Karen Ripplinger Wylie for their comments on the manuscript and to Ronnie Kellner and Lisa Lajoie for their help with cover design and graphics.

I will remain forever grateful to Kenneth Wapnick, founder of the Foundation for *A Course in Miracles,* for his dedication to the teachings of the Course. Without the help of his books and CDs, I can assure you that this journey would not have been as rich and rewarding.

Of course, a very special thank you to Gary Renard, author of *The Disappearance of the Universe,* the work that, after a lifetime of searching, finally pointed me in the right direction, thus ending a very long quest for truth and peace.

No words can adequately express the depth of my gratitude for the gift of *A Course in Miracles.*

Thank you, Jesus.

God is no enemy to you. He asks no more than that
He hear you call Him "Friend."

A Course in Miracles

Only in a Dream

Only in a dream
Can a world be made up
That is not true.
It not being true,
It cannot create
It cannot last.
It has no power.
And, therefore,
Must have no value.

How can a world that is
Outside the Truth even exist?
It be but a thought
In a dream
Hence it must be unreal.

And what is unreal
Cannot harm me
Cannot destroy me
Cannot cause me pain
Cannot cause me sorrow
Cannot take away my peace.

What is only a dream
Cannot be real.
So it is that I seek
To awaken from the dream
And remember what is real.

PAULINE EDWARD, 2006

INTRODUCTION

The journey that we undertake together is the exchange of dark for light, of ignorance for understanding. (T-14.VI.1:1)

*U*nlike the many books that recount the astonishing spiritual quests of extraordinary individuals, this is a simple story of one ordinary person's sacred journey. Like most people, over the years I have cultivated countless hopes, dreams and expectations, set goals, worked hard, struggled to overcome obstacles, won and lost battles. I have met with joys, successes and triumphs as well as failures, heartaches and disappointments. I have experienced fulfillment and longing, laughter and tears, gains and defeats, abundance and scarcity. I have attained the heights of ecstasy and sunken into the abyss of heart-wrenching grief. I have loved and been loved, given and received, nurtured and been nurtured, but, most importantly, I have lived and I have learned. Such is the normal stuff of life.

Many people know me as an astrologer. Given the unusual nature of my profession, I worked hard to develop a credible business persona so that I could earn a proper living. This enabled me to build a solid client base and, in the process, I became a successful businesswoman, even winning a Chamber of Commerce award for my efforts. Though in itself a noteworthy accomplishment, that is not the story that needs telling.

More precisely, this is the story of the life not seen—my inner life, the part of the journey that has lain mostly hidden from the world. It is my quest for spiritual fulfillment, and, by all accounts, it is a modest journey. There were no extraordinary spiritual encounters or travels to ashrams in faraway places or initiations by teachers possessing remarkable powers. There were no voices from beyond or visits from ascended beings, angels or spirit guides from other times or places. The truth of the matter is that, although my journey has had its unique twists and turns, I have, all in all, lived a charmed life, surrounded by love, support and abundance, no doubt with more than my fair share of luck and opportunity, never really wanting for anything.

There would be no story were it not for the fact that, despite these favours, since a very young age there brewed beneath the surface a subtle, yet prickly divine discontent that would gnaw away at any chance of lasting peace, making it difficult to simply be content with what I had. There would inevitably be something that was not quite right. On occasion, I had a strange feeling of being blind, with a disturbing sense that there was something out there that I needed to see, something I needed to know, something I was missing. Unanswerable questions disturbed my sense of order: What was it all for? Why were we really here? What else was there, if anything? What happens when we die? Do we just keep returning over and over again? If so, why? For what purpose? Is there a God? If so, where is He? What was He thinking when he created heaven and earth? Why couldn't we simply have stayed in heaven? Why does He allow suffering? Why does He not answer my prayers? Variations of these and similar questions would arise in times of difficulty and crisis, simmering down and fading into oblivion during periods of relative peace and contentment.

In the hope of finding answers to my burning questions, I read books—many books. I delved into the teachings of the faith of my early upbringing and explored a variety of religious and spiritual thought systems, always remaining hopeful that one day answers would come. If anything, my journey resembles a trek down a long and winding spiritual buffet line,[1] with occasional pauses

1. A term aptly coined by Arten in *The Disappearance of the Universe* (DU) by Gary Renard, page 93.

when interest was piqued and needs were temporarily satisfied, but ultimately always failing to fully satisfy my hunger for truth.

Although I have sought knowledge for as long as I can remember, I have never considered myself to be in any way scholarly or even remotely holy, though I did entertain the notion that I was a spiritual seeker. I'm certainly not an academic; I don't even have a college degree. It may also seem somewhat odd that I have maintained a spiritual quest for so long, since I am in fact a practical and down-to-earth person, preferring the tangible to the abstract. And though at times I may seem to be creative and even inspired, I have said more often than I can remember, "I'm just a mechanic."

Interestingly, sometimes it is the seemingly inconsequential comments made in passing by ordinary people that turn out to be among the most significant, leaving behind words that resonate over and over in the back of one's mind. One day, while lamenting my lack of academic savoir-faire to my academically inclined daughter Caroline, she said simply, "That's because you're a gist learner."

"Humph," I replied, replaying the words in my mind. And although I had never before heard the expression, I got the *gist* of what she was saying. In one very simple statement, I felt profoundly vindicated. After years of reading and trying unsuccessfully to acquire an intellectual grasp of the issues that had plagued my existence for far too long, I had just been told that I was okay. I was a *gist learner*. Somehow, I took that to be a good thing. I was no longer just a struggling, non-academic seeker drowning in a sea of unanswered questions. To this day, I remain a proud gist learner.

In the end, my lack of rigid academic attachments may have been my saving grace, allowing me to navigate the spiritual buffet line in an open-minded, naive and ultimately perhaps even more effectual manner. My search was for a truth that would lead to an experience of lasting peace and wholeness rather than for a truth that would satisfy my intellect and allow me to debate with eloquence the age-old mysteries of the meaning of life. Over the years, guided by this inner urge rather than by rational motives, I was eventually led to a teaching in which I found the answers I was seeking, a remarkable work called *A Course in Miracles*.

It is the winding journey that led to the Course and the subsequent discovery of its powerful and profound message that I share in the pages that follow. I consider myself a student rather than a teacher of the Course, and this book is meant as an example of one student's process—my process—as I studied and struggled to put into practice its incredible teachings. This book is *not* a course on *A Course in Miracles*. A list of Course-related resources is provided at the end of the book for those who wish to learn more.

While my journey began the day I was born, it only started to truly make sense once I chose to become a student of *A Course in Miracles*. I say *chose* because the Course is very much about making choices. It was without a doubt the most provocative material I had ever encountered and it soon became clear that its learning and integration would require serious dedication and application. A casual reading of the book would not suffice. Not having the theological or academic background to approach this complex work in an analytical and intellectual manner, I needed help before I could even begin to make sense of what it said. And help came. And with that help, despite being faced with a seemingly impossible thought system, I did eventually acquire enough of a gist of what it was saying to know that for the first time ever, I was being told the Truth.

Our journeys may appear to differ in form, but we all share the same desire to return home to that place where we are eternally safe, forever and unconditionally loved, experiencing everlasting peace, where scarcity is forever replaced by wholeness and abundance. Although for the most part unconscious, all of our actions are witness to this fact. As the Course sets forth, it is given to us to awaken from the dream and return Home, to the peace and love that is our natural inheritance.

In a way, this is the book I wish I could have read when I first began to study the Course, for it would have reassured me that persistence leads to the gift of answers. Many of my friends and clients are trying to understand the Course's teachings. In search of inspiration and support, some have asked how I came to the Course, they too, struggling to get the gist of its meaning. HOW DO YOU DO IT? An exasperated friend wrote in the subject line of an e-mail. Although I wrote this book in large part for my own sorting out, it is also their questions and pleas that kept me focused on completing the task.

This book does not recount all the events of my life, but focuses rather on those experiences that reflect the inner struggles and progress of my spiritual quest as well as some of the circumstances that served to establish the patterns and motives for the choices made along the way. What is important is the process, the experiences that led from one level of understanding to the next, rather than the details of my everyday life. In the end, at least on the level of form, it is our perception of the journey and our interpretation of these perceptions that matter.

(Note: Although this account is true, as told from my recollections and journal entries, some of the names have been changed.)

REFERENCES

References to *A Course in Miracles* (ACIM) correspond to the numbering system of the Text (T), Workbook (W), Manual for Teachers (M) and Clarification of Terms (C) used in the Second Edition. For example:

T-27.VIII.6:2–5 corresponds to Text, Chapter 27, Section VIII, Paragraph 6, Sentences 2 to 5.

W-pI.132.5:1–3 corresponds to Workbook, Part I, Lesson 132, Paragraph 5, Sentences 1 to 3.

M-16.4:6 corresponds to Manual for Teachers, Question 16, Paragraph 4, Sentence 6.

C-3.4:1 corresponds to Clarification of Terms, Term 3, Paragraph 4, Sentence 1.

PART I: SEEK BUT DO NOT FIND

"Seek but do not find" remains this world's stern decree,
and no one who pursues the world's goals
can do otherwise. (M-13.5:8)

Chapter 1

I WANT TO GO HOME

My home awaits me.
I will hasten there. (W-pII.226)[1]

From *A Course in Miracles*, we learn that time is but an illusion, that even though we seem to be moving forward in a linear fashion, we are in fact reviewing a journey that has already ended and, furthermore, it is a journey that was never real. When first introduced to these concepts, I felt shock and confusion. I couldn't even get the gist of what was being said. I had spent the better part of my life in pursuit of a better future, and, through my work as an astrologer, had counselled thousands of people on creating better futures for themselves—or at least that's what I earnestly believed I was doing. "Helping you create a better future, Pauline Edward, Astrologer" was my memory hook at networking events. My business name and tag line, A Time for Success, Trends, Cycles and Lifestyle Planning—in fact my entire professional identity—suddenly went into a tailspin.

Time is a trick, a sleight of hand, a vast illusion in which figures come and go as if by magic. Yet there is a plan behind appearances that does not change. The script is written. When experience will come to end your doubting has been set. For we but see the journey from the point at which it ended, looking

---

1. Interestingly, Lesson 226 of ACIM corresponds to the 226th day of the year, the day of my birth.

back on it, imagining we make it once again; reviewing mentally what has gone by. (W-pI.158.4:1–5)

Here I was being confronted with the radical idea that in reality, there is no future, that we are simply watching an old movie, that we do not actually create anything, that there is no world and that we are not really here at all. My beliefs about time and the future, and what now seemed like romantic notions about our creative abilities, were severely compromised. As I stood back and watched the dissolution of my entire belief system, I felt as though reality as I knew it had been suspended. For a moment I hesitated, perched on the precipice of a drastically new alternate view of reality. But I wanted answers. I wanted to know that there had to be more than what I had been taught and what I had learned. Disoriented yet intrigued, I did as I have done with most things in my life—I jumped right in.

It took a bit of time, actually *lots* of time and especially loads of persistence, but once I began to grasp the truth of these far-reaching notions, I understood that if I were ever to reach my goal of returning home, I would have to take a long hard look at the movie, *my movie*, with the right mind, something I would learn to do, as taught in the Course, with the help of the Holy Spirit and Jesus. Only then could I begin to remove the blocks that prevented me from awakening to the truth of who I really was; only then could I begin the journey home. That's when it occurred to me that I should take a trek down memory lane, re-examine my life in light of this new learning, and, in the process, perhaps hasten my return home.

Coincidentally, shortly after having begun to work on this book, I listened to a lecture by *A Course in Miracles* teacher Ken Wapnick in which he refers to a workshop exercise where he invited partici-pants to try to remember their earliest memory. That early memory, he explained, would become like a theme in a symphony that was their life, and everything that took place in their life could be seen as a variation on that theme.[2] This story begins with my early memories and covers those events that established the themes that would play out thereafter.

Some people can recall their past in great detail, while others remember barely a scrap here and there. I am definitely among the latter. What I do recall is looking forward to the future a lot, in anticipation of what—I don't think I ever really knew. All I know is that I spent a lot of time longing for that time when I would finally experience total peace. When I gather up all the tiny scraps of memory from my early life, somehow they paint a cohesive picture—they paint the portrait of the hero of my dream. I'm sure that my mother would paint a different picture, as would my brothers, or my dad, were he still with us. But this is the portrait that lives in my mind and, in the end, it is this mind that seeks healing. Although the few memories I did manage to retain have remained relatively intact, since my introduction to the thought system of *A Course in Miracles*, something in my perception of those events has changed. Where not so long ago remembering might have stirred up feelings of sadness, loneliness or resentment, now I can look back with a whole new understanding of their meaning. Something in the way I see things is changing; somehow, I am changing. Perhaps the healing has begun.

Nothing in my childhood—in fact, nothing in all of my life—can adequately explain the divine discontent that, for the longest time, came to define my existence. So why this journey? All I can say is that it just was. At the same time, I can say that I am as grateful for the divine discontent as I am for the blessings, without either of which this journey would not have been.

I was born August 14, 1954[3] in the beautiful Saguenay, at forty-eight degrees north latitude, where snow in June was not unheard

2. *Living in the World: Prison or Classroom*, Workshop on *A Course in Miracles*, Kenneth Wapnick, Ph.D., Atlanta, GA, July 2003.

3. For the benefit of readers of *The Power of Time* and *Astrological Crosses in Relationships*, occasional numerological and astrological references have been included. My chart has the Sun in Leo; ascendant and Moon in Aquarius.

of. Being a lover of sun and warm weather, I once considered this to be one of those queer twists of fate, perhaps a fitting punishment for some misdeed perpetrated in a past life. Isle-Maligne, the town where I spent my first six years, sat on a jagged island rock where Lac Saint-Jean pours into the Saguenay River. To this day, the thought of my birthplace evokes images of a nature and geography of unparalleled beauty, no doubt a contributing influence to my lifelong love of flowers and gardening. In the early sixties, Isle-Maligne merged with Alma, a slightly larger town that, to my chagrin, eventually grew to have its very own set of golden arches and a Walmart, symbols of the impermanence of the world of form.

On the surface, my early life boasts nothing out of the ordinary. Like most young couples just starting out, my parents had to count their pennies, but we were always provided with everything we needed to grow and thrive. We lived in a tiny two-storey, semi-detached house built for the employees of the aluminum company for which my dad worked. Aluminum and pulp and paper were the main industries of the region. My mother was the consummate homemaker, completely devoted to the care of her family and home. Everything was always well ordered and organized, and I would not hesitate to wager that our house was the cleanest house in all of Alma. My dad was an electrical engineer; he had a job that was guaranteed to provide stability and growth for years to come. I had my own room, toys to play with, clothes for all seasons and home-cooked meals. It was a simple existence for a small-town family in the peaceful mid-fifties. In most ways, it was idyllic.

One has to dig a little deeper to uncover the seeds of unsettling that would eventually surface and fuel my quest for the meaning of life. The first indication that something was amiss came very early when, like everyone else born into this world, after being thrust from the safety and nurturing abundance of my mother's womb, I found myself gasping for that first scorching breath of air, without which I would have died. A distinct being, separate from my source, I was now required to fend for myself. I had very specific needs: air to breathe, food and water for sustenance, and shelter from the life-threatening dangers of the outside world. I needed warmth, comforting and reassurance. I needed love. In that one fateful moment, the stage was set for my eventual experiences of fear and scarcity, two of the major themes of the symphony of my life.

> A sense of separation from God is the only lack you really need correct. This sense of separation would never have arisen if you had not distorted your perception of truth, and had thus perceived yourself as lacking. (T-1.VI.2:1–2)

My next hurdle came when it was discovered that, not only was my mother anaemic and incapable of breastfeeding, but I was also allergic to conventional formulas. Hungry, I cried. Apparently, despite my inability to keep foods down, I had a healthy set of lungs, which I shamelessly used to express my displeasure. The loudness of my cries was disturbing to my fellow nursery mates, and so the staff, unable to soothe and cajole me into being quiet, and by then no doubt at their wit's end, placed me in a room by myself. In those days, babies were not picked up and held for it was believed that nasty, deadly germs could be transferred to the infant causing illness or, worst, death. Even my parents were allowed only limited contact. So, alone, I cried some more. Here I learned my first two biggest life lessons: one, you cannot count on others to tend to your needs, so you better learn to do things yourself, and, two, no matter how loud you cry, no one will listen.

The greater part of those first weeks of my life was spent in my own little crib in my own little hospital room while my caregivers searched for a formula I could keep down. I was now a unique and distinct little being, with very special needs, struggling to survive. It doesn't take a seasoned psychologist to see how these circumstances set the stage for the feelings of abandonment, isolation and special-ness I would harbour for many years to come, the next big theme in my personal symphony. In those early experiences, the foundation for a lifelong quest for wholeness, a deep need for self-reliance and a preference for solitude were firmly established.

It took about six weeks before a suitable formula was found and my parents were finally allowed to take me home, thus putting an end to my initial trauma. With a food I could keep down, I settled contentedly into my new home life, forever leaving the past behind. Those were the days of stay-at-home moms and home cooking. What more could a newborn infant ask for? My father came from the big city, Montreal, but he had nothing of the harried urban pace of life. He was a calm and peaceful man, typical of his earthy Taurus Sun sign. He was a rock; strong in his values, steadfast and infinitely patient. My mother was a small-town French-Canadian girl, but her heart was aimed at the big city. A fiery Sagittarian with three Capricorn[4] planets, another earth sign, she remains to this day idealistic and energetic, highly intelligent, ambitious and inquisitive.

Taurus and Sagittarius—my parents were as different as peaches and peppers, but, somehow, they made it work. In those days, you made it work. Just like your job. My dad would stay with the same company for thirty-five years. Of course, *Maman* and Daddy had their differences of opinion, major differences from what I saw occasionally, but in all my life I never heard either express anger or a mean word toward the other. Neither did they raise their voices at us, although my mother's frustration and displeasure with some of my adolescent moods would push her buttons some. My dad spoke French and English, the languages of his mother and father, while my mother spoke French. Maman and Daddy were my first outward symbol of duality, and, from what I could see, they managed to make it work quite well.

My brother Donald was born when I was sixteen months old. That would make him a Capricorn. He also has a Taurus Moon, establishing one of the relationship themes in the symphony of my life. I was surrounded by earth types and would continue to attract Capricorns, the sign associated with power and authority, into my life for a very long time. The fact that there is a total lack of earth

---

4. For astrology buffs, my 12th House cusp falls in Capricorn.

in my own chart is significant, somewhat like being born with a missing limb or with only one lung. A missing element acts like a cosmic handicap of sorts, and, with an absence of earth, it is as though the spirit is born, but there seems to be no connection to the physical realm. Until my first pregnancy, I would experience this lack of earth element as an awkward sense of my physical being, as though being trapped in a foreign body. This feeling of confinement may have been one of the driving forces behind the many years I would spend seeking to escape from the bondage of the world, looking for liberation from all things material.

During those first six years, my playground was the forest against which our backyard was tucked. I can still clearly recall the scent of fallen pine needles blended with the rich aroma of maple leaves slowly decaying into the soft, spicy loam that covered the forest floor. I remember my eyes burning against the glare of the late afternoon January sun, mercilessly blinding as its rays ricocheted off the pure white snow-covered ground. There was the unmistakable sweet and musky scent of burning leaves and grass clippings in the spring and fall. Whenever a grass fire burned, I would stand there and enjoy the scents breath after breath after breath.

My fondest memories include days at the beach at Lac Saint-Jean, with its rolling white sand dunes undercut with shiny black mineral-rich patches. We would use runaway logs from the paper mill as floats and, on lucky days, abandoned truck-sized tire tubes, which were much smoother and more fun. I remember sipping Coke through a straw while trying to avoid the sand that would invariably make its way to the bottom of the curvy glass bottle. It was the tastiest drink of all. As I ran to the blanket where my mother had laid out the picnic, I would try very hard to slow down so as to avoid kicking up too much sand. But the fine grains always found their way into our food. And there were chips too. Generally, my mother was very mindful about healthy eating, but we were allowed chips to go with our Coke when we went to the lake. The chips too would be covered in sand, but the grains of sand blended in with the grains of salt, which made them the best tasting chips in the world. For the main course, my mom always made sandwiches with the crusts cut off: neat little egg salad triangles, salmon salad rectangles and ham squares, just as my brother liked, and he was right—I was certain that they were the best tasting sandwiches in the universe.

Of course, there was blueberry picking. Lac Saint-Jean is blueberry country, and its natives are known as *bleuets*. That makes me a genuine *blueberry*. I recall one sunny summer afternoon, when, in a burst of adventurous spirit, my brother and I ran over the dunes in search of the dark, sweet berries. The scent of blueberry bushes was thick in the air as we wandered off to the top of the hill above our picnic spot. And there it was—what we believed must have been the biggest blueberry patch in the universe—and big berries too! There were so many that once we had filled all our empty picnic containers, we began to fill our sun hats. We even pried my doll's head off so we could fill it with berries! To this day, even in a car speeding along the highway with closed windows, I can always tell when a blueberry patch is nearby, recognizing the delicate woodsy aroma in the air.

Apparently, I was quite content to play by myself for hours on end. My mother once told me of the time I disappeared. In a panic, she tore the house apart, room by room, until she found me, fast asleep, curled up inside my toy box snuggled with one of my dolls.

Given my relatively sheltered and isolated life, I was very shy—actually—painfully shy. I recall visits to my aunt's house nearby. *Matante* Irène was also my godmother. Not wanting to attract attention, I would melt my little body into the huge rocker in the corner of the dining room that also looked over the living room and sitting room. From my vantage point, I could see everything and hear everyone, but, given my small stature and the engulfing size of the chair, I felt safely invisible. Occasionally, someone would turn to me, perhaps say a kind word or two, and I would smile. Everything was fine, just fine, the silent smile said, while inside, I patiently awaited our return home, where I could feel safe and comfortable again.

I do remember one evening returning home from *Matante* Irène's, heading straight for the kitchen drawer filled with cooking utensils and plunging the bread knife down my throat in an attempt to imitate a circus performer I had seen on the television. I have a vague recollection of my mother's scream, which of itself was a most unusual occurrence. But I think I was more perplexed by the fact that I just didn't understand what I was doing wrong. For some reason, the knife wasn't going down the way it was supposed to.

My initiation into the greater world that existed beyond my backyard paradise began at the tender age of four. In order to fulfill my pedagogical agenda, it was decided that I should attend an English pre-kindergarten. Problem was I spoke not a word of English. At home, we spoke my mother's language. Even my father spoke to us in French. In kindergarten, everyone spoke only English. There was a strict rule in place: in order for me to learn English, I was not permitted to use any French. I didn't understand what anyone was saying and no one could understand me. I was an outsider, a hostage to the prison of my mother tongue, and there was no rocking chair in the corner of the room with which I could merge. The theme of specialness in the symphony of my life had developed its first variation.

What I recall from those two years is scant and seemingly disconnected and unrelated. I remember one day, as I was being readied for school, telling my mother that I was feeling *pas bien*. I was nauseous and feared that I couldn't make it through the morning without throwing up. Not a big fan of missing school, my mother told me that I would be fine, and if I didn't feel well, I could simply tell the teacher I wasn't well, or I could ask the bus driver to stop the bus. In which official language, I wasn't sure, since I knew one, and the teacher used another, and she had made it very clear that under no circumstances was French ever to be used in her class. Since I couldn't explain that I was feeling *pas bien* in English, I did my best to keep it down. And I was successful, until the bus ride home at lunchtime. I would later wonder if the bus driver ever knew which little brat had heaved beneath the second-to-last seat of the bus. At least I had had the instinct to lean my head way down low. That way I hadn't soiled my pretty clothes, nor left any visible evidence. As for asking the bus driver to stop so that I could puke my guts out on the side of the highway while the other kids watched, well, even if he did speak my mother tongue, that was a no-brainer. At the age of five, I did have my dignity.

One thing I recall from my kindergarten years was a feeling of being small and powerless. The teacher loomed tall; her mouth seemed to be in constant motion, uttering sounds that made no sense. I would laugh heartily years later while watching Charlie Brown cartoons on the television, where adults were depicted as towering, squawking creatures … wah, wah, wah, wah, wah … That was how I had perceived my kindergarten teacher.

The only other incident I recall from that time was a brush with humiliation. I had gone to the upstairs toilet, and must have had a good dump. Maybe I didn't flush the toilet properly, no doubt not wanting to make noise and attract undue attention, but, shortly after, feeling refreshed and having returned to my corner downstairs, I was struck with panic as I heard the teacher cry out in indignation. Judging from her gestures and, most likely because she was coming down the same stairs I had just descended, she must have been referring to the gift I had left in her toilet. Somehow, it hadn't been that big, but it occurred to me that I might have blocked her toilet. Perhaps this was the seed of the constipation problems I would suffer through adolescence and again, during my menopausal process. Clearly, I was finding it difficult to remain off the radar.

One thing was certain, throughout my youth, I was very anxious to be grown up. Grown-ups were allowed to do what they wanted. They didn't have to ask for permission, and, most of all, they didn't have to be silent. Grown-ups were tall, too, and they got to see things from higher up. When I was small, I wanted to be tall. I remember one day standing by the checkout counter in the grocery store while my mother processed her order. I so much wanted to see what was on top of the counter, but I was too short. I stretched onto my tiptoes until my eyeballs barely made it to the edge. One day, I told myself, I'll be tall and I'll be able to see everything.

One of the great things my mom did for us right from the start was to encourage the development of our minds through open discussions of most any subject, as well as through reading and education, which she held in the highest regard. Although her own schooling had been cut short, or perhaps because of that fact, my mom remains to this day an avid reader. I recall her always with a book on the coffee table next to her chair. Apparently, my brother and I became well known for our own natural inquisitiveness, which found expression in the local general store. It seemed that we liked to touch things and, in our eagerness to discover what the world had to offer, we occasionally made displays come tumbling to the floor. My mom jokingly tells of how quickly the sales staff would come to her assistance when we walked into the store; the faster we were served, the sooner we were gone, the safer the displays. "You can't find service like that today!" she would say.

Maman was also a huge fan of classical music, another great gift that she shared with us. From the classical shows on the CBC or the hi-fi system built by my father, our house was always filled with the sounds of Mozart, Chopin, Puccini or Beethoven. In his spare time, my dad played the guitar and, having graduated from the rock and roll of his college days to classical Spanish music, our musical ears were treated to a rich range of sounds. Understandably, music would become an important aspect of my life and, in fact, during the most difficult moments, it would serve to light up the dark recesses of my soul and, in a way, even act as a buoy keeping me from sinking into the deepest pits of depression.

All in all, this was a simple time, in a quiet town, in a relatively peaceful window of history, the ideal setting for firmly establishing a deep desire for peace of a lasting kind.

Chapter 2

THE SEEDS OF SPIRITUALITY

You are at home in God, dreaming of exile but per-
fectly capable of awakening to reality. (T-10.I.2:1)

*I*t would appear that language was not a required skill for admission to Riverbend Catholic Grade School, because I graduated from kindergarten and made it to the first grade with a very meagre knowledge of the English language. Stepping off the school bus, wearing my brand new, freshly pressed ink-blue, box-pleated wool tunic one bright September morning, I met my first grade-one teacher, a nun whose name I no longer recall.

I do remember sitting and watching my teacher for hours on end, fascinated by the complex layers of the enormous habit that fanned outwards from a tight band around her head. I wondered if it ever fell off, if it were heavy or if it hurt. I tried to imagine what she might look like without her huge white halo when she removed it at night, for I had gathered that no one could possibly sleep in that gargantuan head gear. There were layer upon layer of black fabric sewn into her dress, and a stiff white collar that looked like a huge bib. And then there was the smell of clean; nuns were especially clean and tidy beings. They never got messy like normal people, not even when they wrote on the blackboard.

What struck me most during my brief time at Riverbend was the enormous fresco drawn in coloured chalk on the blackboard. Although in my mind I have pictures of it being in full colour, I wonder now if it really was, since at that young age, the imagination can fill in a lot of details. I say this because, one day, while watching television, my brother and I had a disagreement over the colour of a woman's outfit. I saw it as one colour, perhaps red, I can't remember now, while my brother saw it as an entirely different colour, maybe blue. The interesting thing about the incident was that in those days, colour television was not yet available. Adding to that the fact that my brother is severely colour-blind, we have a perfect example of childhood imagination stepping in to fill the gaps of perception.

According to my memory, which no doubt was also influenced by some form of childhood imaginings, the fresco that almost completely covered the four-paneled blackboard was a detailed rendition of the Biblical scene of the Garden of Eden, complete with requisite serpent wrapped tightly around the trunk of a very large tree that was loaded with bright red apples. Adam stood tall, private parts hidden by a bush, and Eve, clad in long thick, black hair, was passively accepting a beautiful apple from the serpent. Being a visual person, and very imaginative, that scene alone pretty much summed up the start of my religious education.

Being in a Catholic school run by nuns, it wasn't long before I learned that the woman, Eve, had accepted the forbidden fruit from the fallen angel, Satan. Being impressionable and eager to learn, I took these teachings quite literally. This was the birth of my meta-physical foundation: I was a girl, and would one day be a woman. Eve was the first woman. Eve had sinned and, furthermore, she had been a very bad influence on poor innocent Adam, the first man. This displeased God, the Father of Adam and Eve and everyone else on earth, and so He punished both her and Adam for her sin by banishing them from the safety and abundance of the beautiful Garden of Eden. God was a serious guy who meant what He said. He was angry and no one had better mess with Him.

As a woman in the making, I figured that I had better tread lightly, or else, as a descendant of Eve, I too might piss off God, and that is one thing I did not ever want to do. Profoundly fearful of authority, I decided right then and there that I would do every-thing in my power to be a good girl. That would be best. Despite this bleak metaphysics, I wasn't overly concerned for myself, as I believed I actually was a good girl. At least according to my mother, I was a good girl.

When my teacher learned that we were moving away, she took me under her wing and prepared me for my new school in the big city. With a privileged seat on her lap, she gave me extra reading lessons. I liked her very much. She was gentle, sweet and caring, and I sensed that she wanted me to make her proud. She made me feel special, so I worked extra hard so I could read "See Spot run." This was a joyful interlude in my theme of isolation.

At the time, I don't think I really understood what *moving away* meant, at least not until we made the actual move. I would later miss the peaceful simplicity of life in a small town, especially the forest and the open farm fields and the sand and the lake—my very own Garden of Eden. We moved to Montreal when I was six, barely a couple of months after I had started school at Riverbend. With a whole new life to contend with, the kind sister with the huge habit quickly slipped from memory.

For the next five years, we lived in an upper duplex, something to which I would never really get accustomed. The thought of walking over people's heads or hearing voices below would always give me the creeps. But my brother and I each had our own room, which made living in an apartment rather than a house almost okay.

We also lived at the outermost limit of the school district, which meant that I had to be bussed to school. There were nuns at Immaculata too, but my new first grade teacher was not a sister. Miss McFee was grey-haired, stocky, mean-looking, English and, for some reason, she hated me from the first day I entered class. I was French and, having moved in October, I joined the class late. I suspect that my tardy arrival may have disrupted her rhythm.

I recall being told to stand in the corner of the classroom for having used a French word instead of the correct English word. And it wasn't even a bad word, since, in those days, cursing and profanity hadn't yet been invented. Not having done anything wrong, I felt unfairly treated. Still painfully shy and fearful of almost everything outside the safe confines of home, standing in the corner of the classroom that day, engulfed by a thundering refrain from my theme of specialness, I reaffirmed my commitment to work harder at being good.

The day came all too soon when I missed being short, as suddenly, I began to sprout to my full height. I would eventually grow to five six, which isn't by any means unusually tall, but I seemed to be growing faster than everyone else so that, throughout grade school, I never got to stand at the front of the line for any event. Being tall placed me at the back. In those days, things were done in an orderly fashion. Students lined up, two by two, in silence and by order of height. Once short, now tall; it was a losing battle!

My early spiritual education was about as uneventful as my early life. There were no angelic voices, no messages from beyond, nor did I manifest any special gifts. We attended church on Sundays and Holy Days, something I found for the most part boring. From what I recall, not too many people seemed to actually enjoy Mass. In fact, if they didn't have to, I believed that most people would have stayed home and slept in. Attendance at Mass was a requirement for Catholics.

In those days, most of the ceremonial segments of the service were spoken in Latin and the sermons, although in French, were way over my head. As instructed, I sat still. Unless in response to a prayer, no one but the priest spoke in church, and when he did his voice echoed and bounced around the vast space in long waves so that the words seemed to catch up with each other like a pile-up of cars in a traffic jam.

When I did manage to pick out a few words, I would turn them over in my mind like curios at an antiques shop: *La parole de Dieu, le péché, le pardon, la résurrection, l'amour de Dieu.*[1] Priests had a special way of saying words like *péché* and *Dieu* so that there was no doubt that you knew you were a *sinner* and that God knew it, and He was watching and if you wanted to be forgiven and eventually

---

1. Translated from French meaning: the word of God, sin, forgiveness, resurrection, the love of God.

be saved so you could go to heaven instead of hell, you had better not screw up. It was also stressed that Jesus Christ, the very special, one and only Son of God, had died on the Cross for our sins, and it was up to us now to do our share by atoning for our sins through prayer and sacrifice.

If we obeyed the Ten Commandments, accepted the sacraments, attended church as required and went to confession, we would be allowed back in heaven when we died, that is, if we stayed away from mortal sins. Venial sins, like occasional fibs or disrespect for a teacher, were okay as long as you prayed for forgiveness and did your penance, but mortal sins—these were to be avoided at all costs. Mortal sins like murder and other wilfully executed unconscionable acts led straight to hell. One thing was very clear to me: I wanted to go home to heaven when I died. Since on that point, there was no question, I would steer clear of the mortal sins and try as much as possible to avoid the venial sins, just in case I messed up in my bid for forgiveness.

Priests had a direct line of communication with God. They were God's link to us. I wondered what it would be like to be a priest, to stand in front of the church and talk to God. Did God understand only Latin or did He also understand French? What about English? What about Polish and Italian and Spanish, the languages spoken at home by many of my classmates? Since we were taught that the Catholic Church was the one and only true church, I would also wonder how it was that Latin was God's language, instead of one of the much older languages like Hindi or Mandarin. If God was eternal, He must have been around for a long time. Why wasn't He Hindu or Chinese? Where was God in ancient times?

Benches in churches were almost always uncomfortably hard and narrow, fitting punishment for the wayward sinners that we were, whereas the priest's chair was large, gilded and quite heavily padded. I surmised that priests must be doing something right. Being a priest was special. Despite that much of what was being said during services was beyond my appreciation, there was some-thing about churches that always struck a chord with me. The smell of frankincense permeating wood and cement; exquisite carvings on walls and stained glass windows depicting dramatic scenes of punishment, sorrow and revelation; an intrinsic hopefulness and longing for a better world through a promise of salvation; the deafening quiet or the thundering voice of the priest—no matter the denomination, I was always inspired by the vastness and beautiful architecture of traditional places of worship, a true symbol of our collective belief in and yearning for something greater than this world in which we live.

Although I did not understand the sermons much, I did enjoy many of the readings from the Bible. Over the years I grew particularly captivated by the stories of the New Testament, and developed a special bond with Jesus. I imagined myself alongside him two thousand years ago, walking the dusty roads that took him on his healing and teaching missions, breathing the hot, dry salt air, touching the sick, comforting the desperate. I was in awe of Jesus. Unlike me, he did not seem to have any questions or any doubts. Only answers. He was kind and loving and, above all, forgiving, even in the face of the most inhumane acts. He was always in a state of peace, something I wished to attain one day too.

On occasion, my father would take us up to Saint Joseph's Oratory for Sunday mass. Despite the very long service, I very much enjoyed these outings. The Oratory is a huge, cavernous cement structure built into the side of Mount Royal. It had nothing of the traditional churches of the time. Here the voice of the priest really bounced around and I had to strain to sort through the pile-up of words that circled the dome. *La parole de Dieu* hovered above my head like a flock of large white gulls. There was also a colossal pipe organ that was played to punctuate the various parts of the service—like a scene right out of *The Hunchback of Notre Dame*—it was impressive and at the same time ominous, commanding immediate attention.

Tucked away behind the enormous structure that housed not only the high-domed basilica but also a chapel and a crypt, there stood a simple chapel devoted to the memory of Brother André, the driving force behind the shrine to Saint Joseph. It was during one of those visits that I was first struck with a deep admiration for the profound power of faith. Brother André was a simple man of limited education but with a heart of gold, true to his Leo birth sign. Through his unshakable faith in God and humble devotion to Saint Joseph, the patron saint of the working class,[2] he attracted some remarkable events in his life, including the enormous funds required for the construction of the Oratory. In the shrine built in his memory, there was a wall against which had been stacked and mounted hundreds of crutches, canes, wheelchairs and other medical devices, reminders of the remarkable healings that had occurred following visits to Brother André and prayer to Saint Joseph. Like Jesus, he had healed and comforted countless sick, but he had done so recently, in my city and in my church. During those brief visits, I was awed by a sense of closeness to true holiness.

But, what I really enjoyed about these special Sunday outings was our after-mass visits to the gift shop. There were rows and rows of wide tables filled with all manner of holy pictures, candles, incense, rosary beads, bibles and crucifixes. It fascinated me to think that all these holy things a person could purchase and take home. Everything was extremely well organized in appropriately sized display boxes and trays. From these visits, I gathered a small collection of plastic statuettes of the Holy Family that I displayed on an altar in the corner of my bedroom. My altar was an upside down cardboard box that I had covered with an old blanket. I wasn't allowed candles and incense, as they could be a fire hazard, but I imagined that my altar had all that it needed. Having it there in my room made me feel close to God, almost as I did at church on Sundays.

> Your sinlessness is guaranteed by God. Nothing can touch it, or change what God created as eternal. (W-pI.93.6:4–5)

The first Friday of the month, the sisters at Immaculata Grade School would set up a makeshift confessional in the gymnasium

---

2. Saint Joseph is also the patron saint of Canada.

that consisted of a pair of chairs separated by a narrow divider, con-spicuously laid out in the middle of the huge room. Class by class, we were called down and directed to line up for confession. One by one, we would walk to the confessional to profess our contrition for our sins. After confession, we would kneel at the stage steps to do our penance. Since I had stuck to my plan of being a good girl so as not to raise the wrath of God, I was at a loss as to what to confess to the priest. If I confessed no sins, I would stand out. If I confessed too many, I would stand out.

While standing in line awaiting my turn, I would plan my con-fession. Based on how long the others took at the confessional and then on how long they spent doing penance by the stage steps, I determined what I needed to say just to fit in. I would make up a series of sins, like, I lied to my mother three times, I was mean to my brother twice—none of which were true, of course—but it seemed to work. The priest would assign my penance, maybe three or four Hail Marys, I would take my turn at the stage steps, pace my Hail Marys to appear not too sinful, but sufficiently contrite, and, with as penitent a look as I could muster, I would return to class. It never occurred to me that to get through this monthly ordeal, it was necessary for me to lie to the priest, the spokesperson for God! I wonder how many Hail Marys I would get for lying to the priest all those years.

I don't know if the other girls in school thought about God much, or even at all, or if they wondered what heaven was like or where we came from or where we went after we died. I didn't have any real friends and I wasn't much of a talker. From what I heard at recess and in the schoolyard, these were not the types of questions that were important to my classmates. God remained in religion class and Sunday mass, so I never brought up the issue with my classmates or with anyone else, for that matter.

I recall when I was around eight or nine years old, lying in bed late at night, unable to fall asleep, pondering the nature of God. I don't remember how long these late night musings lasted, perhaps weeks or months, only that they were very real to me at the time.

They would occur after everyone had fallen asleep. The house was silent. Wide awake, I would let my mind wander out to the end of the universe, imagining myself flying through space, beyond the stars and the galaxies, to the other side of infinity. It didn't seem to matter that we had been taught that infinity went on and on forever and ever; for me, infinity had to end somewhere because where infinity ended, God began. In fact, the eternity issue was a bit bothersome to me, for, if God was eternal and living in eternity and He had made us in his image and likeness, how come our universe was outside of God? Why was He so far away?

While moving through space on my nightly voyages, I would hear a strange, high-pitched sound, not unpleasant to the ear, but definitely unlike anything I would ever hear in the regular world. The sound would accompany me, rising in intensity, as I travelled away from my bed, far from my home and city, further and further up through the blackness of the night sky, past the solar system, beyond the tiny white lights of the stars. When I reached what I thought must be the edge of the universe, where God lived, I stopped. Standing there, alone, feeling at peace, I waited for God. Although I couldn't see Him, I knew He must be there, somewhere. He just couldn't come and see me at that moment. He must be very busy, I told myself. Besides, there was no hurry. I was young and there was plenty of time before I would return home. There was simply no doubt in my mind that He was there. Standing patiently at the threshold of God's home, I believed that one day He would answer me and I would be welcomed home.

One night, I told myself that perhaps it wasn't such a great idea to wander so far out into the universe like that. It occurred to me that perhaps I should be afraid. Although I had not once felt the slightest twinge of fear as I stood by the gates of the home of God, I managed to convince myself that I should be afraid. That night, I went to my parents' room and crawled into bed next to my mother. She told me that I was too old to sleep in her bed. I told her I'd had a bad dream, although I knew very well that I hadn't and that there was really nothing to fear. I stayed there a minute, maybe two.

Not feeling particularly comforted from my imagined non-fear, I decided to return to my room. After that night, my late night visits with God came to an end.

The only event of significance during those years was the birth of my brother Michael. *Le Bon Dieu*[3] had sent me a little brother. I was thrilled. Michael and I established an instant bond, and, although I was only seven and a half, I became like a second mother to him. For many years, he would call me his *Petite Maman*.[4] I recall my second grade teacher, Sister Charlene, happily announcing to the whole class that Pauline had a new baby brother. For a moment, I felt very special. I liked Sister Charlene. She was nice to me.

I managed to get through grade school relatively unscathed. Vying for first, second or third place alongside Barbara Winston and Lorraine Street, I kept up my end of the bargain with God and was a good student, never stepping out of line—at least not consciously—always doing as I was told. Being that we lived at the outer limit of the school's territory, my opportunities for making friends were limited. Having no means of getting home other than by school bus, I was never invited to anyone's house after class. In 1965 we moved to a new development on the other side of the tracks, even further from the school. It would be some forty years before I would meet up with Lorraine Street again, only to discover that she too had been on an intense spiritual quest throughout most of her life. Lorraine had lived in walking distance of the school.

---

3. Translated from French meaning: the Good Lord.
4. Translated from French meaning: little mother.

Chapter 3

A ROAD LESS TRAVELLED

This is the road to nowhere, for the light cannot be given while you walk alone, and so you cannot see which way you go. And thus there is confusion, and a sense of endless doubting as you stagger back and forward in the darkness and alone... A blindfold can indeed obscure your sight, but cannot make the way itself grow dark. And He Who travels with you *has* the light. (T-31.II.11:4–5, 8–9)

Clearly unprepared for the social challenges of the teen years, I nonetheless entered high school with a certain feeling of enthusiasm. One thing that had begun to bother me in grade school was the stifling emphasis on discipline, limitation and order. I needed a little freedom and a little breathing room, and it looked like Holy Cross–Father MacDonald High School would afford me that liberty. And it did, at least relative to where I had come from, and also relative to my humble needs. Since I was now fully bilingual, I was exempted from French class. This gave me the opportunity to either take an extra class of my choice, or take time out in the library for study and homework. Enrolled in an enriched program that offered all the courses I thought I needed, I chose the library, a place where I could quietly disappear.

This was the late sixties, a time of free will and self-expression. Some assign this period to the birth of the Age of Aquarius. Aquarius is the zodiac sign associated with freedom, liberty and individuality, qualities that were certainly quite evident in the sixties and would become important influences for the youth of the time. One of the symbols of this change was a lessening of the church's influence on culture and education. As the Church was phased out of the school system, the nuns and brothers gradually retired, taking along with them their pervasive religious authority. Although a few of them would be missed for their true vocation as educators, for the most part they had served their time. To my relief, this also meant the end of first Friday confessions, hence the end of lying to the priest. Religious instruction was replaced with social and moral education, so that now communion with God and Jesus was limited to Sunday and Holy Day masses.

This was a time of social reform, revolution and the transcending of boundaries. Barely into my second year of high school, a small group of us staged a minor demonstration to express our stand on mandatory school uniforms. We boldly declared that we were individuals and should be allowed to express ourselves freely and wear whatever we wished. My mom was very cool about this; she even wrote a note stating that, as long as my grades stayed up, it did not matter what I wore. Of course, my grades stayed up. With surprisingly very little fuss, school uniforms were abolished and we were allowed to wear what we wished. Since almost everyone wore them, jeans became our new uniform, proving that we in fact remained far more conformist than individualistic.

Sex, drugs and rock and roll was the battle cry of the day, and, although initially intrigued by the music of my generation, I early discovered that I was more in tune with jazz, blues and the classics. While popular music never held my interest for very long, I developed a passion for the smooth and sensual bossa nova rhythms of the sixties, music that remains to this day my favourite. I would spend hours in my room reading or doing homework, listening to Astrud Gilberto, Stan Getz, Mozart or Beethoven, depending on my mood. Almost always, music soothed and uplifted my spirit. Many times I wondered what it was that determined a person's musical preference or any other, for that matter. Though raised under the same influences, my brothers and I have completely different tastes in music, one being a gifted classical musician in his own right, the other quite happy with the pop music of the day.

Television was limited to tame shows like *Father Knows Best* and *The Ed Sullivan Show*, so sex was not the overt commodity it is today. Although this was regarded as a time of sexual liberation, for most young people it remained common practice to wait for a life partner. Marriage was taken seriously and divorce was still frowned upon. For myself, I began to yearn for that special soulmate who would fulfill that most important function of making me feel whole. The challenge was to find someone with whom I could relate, someone who shared my interests and my desire to uncover the mysteries of life. The search for my soulmate would become another important theme in the symphony of my life.

In school, I did well with most subjects, and exceptionally well with mathematics. As I wrote in *The Power of Time*, unlike words, math was straightforward, clean and direct but, mostly, refreshingly logical. I developed an early love of mathematics because it was the easiest way to establish common ground with my dad. The infinite patience of his number 9 Life Path tamed the restlessness and anxiety of my 14/5 Life Path. Throughout the difficult years of high school, no other subject had the appeal of algebra and geometry. There was never any ambiguity with numbers, as there was with ideas, communications, relationships and the shifting values of the sixties. With math, there was always one answer, the right answer, even if it was a zero. Opinions, feelings, preferences or impressions didn't matter.

Math was like solving puzzles. I would stay up late at night just to attempt the advanced problems that were designed to really challenge our knowledge. If I couldn't get an answer, I'd go to sleep, and almost without fail, my brain would work out the solution during the night. Refreshed and clear-headed, I'd wake up the following morning and complete the equation. It was rewarding and validating. Here was something I could do right. Where everything else seemed confusing and often frightening, numbers never failed to come through. Mathematics was an oasis of order and logic in a world of chaos and uncertainty.[1]

I had no interest in history and took no pleasure in reading the books that were assigned in English class, clearly unable to relate to the subtleties of classical literature. In fact, I found reading to be painfully slow and arduous, and would one day wonder if I hadn't been slightly dyslexic. However, one work did stand out above all others: George Orwell's *1984*. I was in a state of shock for months after reading that book, and must have written an outstanding essay, for my English teacher made a point of telling me how great he thought it was. This was the only time I was ever praised for my writing efforts.

Although I no longer kept an altar in my room, my fascination with Jesus and all things mystical never waned. In fact, in spite of the absence of religious instruction in my life at that time—or perhaps because of it—my curiosity grew. I watched all the movies about Jesus that played on television, every year, watching the same old movies, over and over, never once tiring of them. I continued to enjoy our occasional visits to the Oratory, and grew more attentive during services and sermons. I listened hard and tried to understand but the teachings were harsh and the tone of the priest often accusatory and punitive. A constant theme was that we were sinners, destined to suffer until we were forgiven—ideas that were beginning to bother me. If Jesus had already died for us on the Cross, why did we still have to atone for Eve's sin? I didn't get it. In fact, I thought Eve was an idiot. Although I continued to work hard at being good and avoiding sin, I wanted to know whether there was something more I could do to ensure my redemption.

Next to the school where I took ballet classes, an occult bookstore opened. It was no surprise when I overheard my ballet teacher tell my mother that she should not hold too much hope for my dance career. I'm not sure why I took ballet; I think I just wanted to feel like I belonged somewhere, do the normal things other girls

---

1. Paraphrased from *The Power of Time*, pages 173–174.

did. The occult, however, was a whole other matter. The store was small and new and brightly lit, and with inquisitiveness winning over shyness, I dropped in one day on my way to ballet class. The owner of the new business was very eager to help with my budding quest for truth, even offering to lend me books if I didn't have the money to pay. Since I did a fair amount of babysitting, I always had the money to buy books.

The day I discovered the world of the supernatural and the occult, my appetite for books was unleashed. As it turned out, my innate dislike of reading was selective, since it applied mainly to those titles assigned as required reading in school. In those days, there were no New Age or Self-Help sections in bookstores and, of course, there was no Internet. Subjects that were hidden, secret and ancient intrigued me, igniting a profound passion for the mysteries of life. In fact, the more secretive the teaching, the more I was attracted. I was particularly fascinated by initiations and secret rites, and began to look for a secret society into which I could become initiated. Almost overnight, books became my best friends. In fact, books seemed to somehow magically *find me*. Throughout my life, whenever in need of answers or guidance, almost without fail, someone would recommend a book or I would be guided to the one I needed.

The work that had the most significant impact on me during that period was Jess Stearn's *Edgar Cayce: The Sleeping Prophet*. This book opened up a whole world of possibilities for me. It resonated with truths that lay deeply buried, inspiring me to search for more information about reincarnation, healing, the occult and spirituality. A cousin who was just passing through town left me her copy of *The Search for Bridey Murphy*, a book that further fuelled my fascination with reincarnation. Although I was aware that the Catholic Church was categorically opposed to the concept, rebirth made a whole lot of sense to me. In fact, when first introduced to the subject, I felt as though I was learning something I already knew. For the time being, I set aside the unsettling realization that the Catholic Church may not hold the whole truth. I was after all a member of the *right* Church, the one and only *true* Church, and felt safe under the assumption that my spot in heaven after my death was guaranteed, no matter what thought systems I explored. Nonetheless, I kept my new beliefs to myself. Besides, no one I knew was interested in spirituality, much less the occult.

When I was thirteen, on a family visit to Quebec City, I was introduced to my Aunt Colette. The eccentric of the family, Colette was divorced, living in a small apartment in a quaint, delight-fully renovated heritage home, but, most of all, she was an astrol-oger. Already familiar with the subject through the Cayce work, I was quite excited to gain first-hand knowledge of astrology. Aunt Colette was a bit ahead of her time, considering that the New Age was still many years from being born. We connected instantly, shar-ing thoughts on everything from astrology to religion and philoso-phy. That summer I learned how to draw my first astrology charts. The idea that it was possible to look into the future and know what was coming absolutely captivated me. I began to collect birth data from everyone I met and drew up as many charts as I could. However, I was far too young and immature to be able to interpret astrology charts. In time, I would learn that a certain amount of life experience and maturity are essential before one can expect to derive relevant information from the planets.

More and more, the teachings of the Catholic Church were posing problems for me. Reincarnation was a recurring theme in the works that interested me, an essential component of the more ancient philosophies of the Orient and India. Though flatly rejected by the Church, it made so much sense that I could not ignore it. What better explanation was there for the inclinations and talents a person was born with? My brother Michael had a musical gift from birth, but not I. However, I had a natural curiosity for all things mystical, something not shared by the other members of my family. My brother Donald shared neither of our interests. We had differ-ent tastes in everything from music to food, and each had his own philosophy of life. If, as the Church taught, we were all created in the image and likeness of God and, furthermore, born and raised by the same parents, then why were we so different from each other?

During that time, a sense of weariness with the world emerged—a sense of *having been there and done that*. This feeling reinforced my belief that I must have lived many times in the past. I felt old and sensed the stir of an ancient yearning deep inside, something I was unable to describe, and also something I could not share with anyone in my life at the time. Not being academically inclined and still too young for the more pithy works such as *Le Matin des Magiciens* or the writings of Gurdjieff that I looked at but set aside for later, I gravitated toward stories about people, particularly spiritual masters and teachers. Feeling isolated and alone in my spiritual pursuit, I longed to find a teacher of my own, someone who would guide me on my journey.

Books became my teachers. I read everything I could find about Jesus, my favourite teacher, and was constantly on the lookout for stories about spiritual quests and journeys. I eagerly devoured books such as *The Greatest Story Ever Told*, *The Third Eye*, *Siddhartha*, *Lost Horizon* and *Dear and Glorious Physician*. The subject of healing captivated me completely, and I imagined that, in a past life, I might have been a healer like Jesus or Edgar Cayce. While I read these extraordinary stories, the line between fiction and reality blurred and I felt my spirit lift higher than ever before in my life. In my mind, anything was possible. It was possible to heal, it was possible to travel into the past and it was no doubt possible to walk on water. One day, I fantasized, when I was much older and had something to say, I too would write a book.

My bedroom was my sanctuary, and I spent a lot of time alone there, drawing astrology charts, reading and listening to music, or sketching with pencil or charcoal. Because I enjoyed drawing, I became the favourite babysitter on the block. Kids would make a point to tell their parents that they would have none other than me. Sometimes, when parents wanted to go out together, I would sit for two households at the same time. We would spend entire evenings drawing silly characters, laughing and making up stories. For those few hours a week, I felt like a hero.

Throughout the high school years, still struggling with paralyzing shyness, I kept mainly to myself. For the most part, I tried to attract as little attention as possible. I let my hair grow very long and hid beneath the long thick mane. If anything, this device worked against me, since my ultra-thick strands attracted rather than diverted attention. I recall the high school janitor one day asking me why I always looked so sad. He was French-speaking, working in a predominantly English environment, and we had occasionally exchanged friendly chats. This time I had no answer for him. It had never occurred to me that I was sad; pensive, timid, desperately introverted, yes, but not sad, or so I thought.

Needless to say, I was not very successful at establishing significant relationships with my peers. Being in the enriched classes, a group of us shared the same teachers for a while, and there were a few classmates with whom I was friendly, but long-lasting connections eluded me. For the most part, my interests were just too unlike those of my classmates. I couldn't fully get excited about the things that brought the others together, nor could I share my true interests with them. It was as though I had been dropped onto this planet from another part of the galaxy. Generally, I preferred to spend time reading up on astrology and whatever I could find that was esoteric in nature.

I briefly dated a couple of guys, but struggled with a very strange feeling that I could and probably would destroy anyone who showed love for me. It was the oddest feeling, one that was difficult to ignore, considering that I did in fact destroy each of these early relationships. I did have a few passing friendships with marginal types, mostly misfits like myself. Allan, who had been left crippled by childhood polio, introduced me to jazz and blues. He played the saxophone. We enjoyed chats about music and about life. In his opinion, I had been very blessed in this lifetime. "Whatever you touch, turns to gold," he once said. But I did not see the light of gold, only the dark of lead. Another friend introduced me to the

Jehovah Witnesses. It was the first time that I actively explored a religion outside Catholicism. I attended a few meetings. Although I enjoyed the fact that the teachings seemed simple and straightforward and somehow accessible to the common person, in fact very unlike the more serious services I was accustomed to, having been thoroughly conditioned to believe that the Catholic Church was the one and only Church, I could not embrace this path.

Special relationships formed around me, while for the most part I remained alone. As a child, I had enjoyed spending hours playing by myself with my toys, but now, seeing my peers forming couples, being single was beginning to equal being defective. Having had no luck meeting people who shared my interests, and growing increasingly tired of my solitude, I set aside my fascination for the occult and dated one boy for a while. We shared no special interests and had little in common other than the fact that we lived in the same town and attended the same school in the same century. For those few months, I felt sort of normal, but by far remained unfulfilled. Longing for a deeper spiritual connection, I abandoned this relationship, promising myself that I would only embark in a partnership with someone who shared my spiritual quest. What I needed, I decided, was a very special relationship; I needed to find my soulmate.

I had little money for clothes, and my mother, coming from a childhood of scarcity, was very practical about her spending: if you don't need it, you don't need it. When we were young, she sewed most of our clothes, and wanting nice things to wear, I enlisted her help and learned to sew. Having plenty of imagination and creative energy, I sewed a lot. It was something I did well, something I did alone. Being self-sufficient was one of the major themes that would increasingly colour the symphony of my life.

I discovered Plato, Camus and Sartre, and, for a while, was comforted by the cold detachment of existentialism. My motto became: Expect nothing and you won't be disappointed. That way of looking at life was practical and seemed to give me a sense of control. I discussed these notions with one friend, an older boy who lived near my house and had already completed high school. We shared a mutual understanding of what it was to live in darkness. I believe he was my first real crush. He disappeared one day; some time later, I learned that he had committed suicide. In the end, existentialism did not fill the void that was beginning to take more and more space in the core of my being. The more I read, the more I questioned, the more I searched for answers, the more elusive the truth became and the more I grew apart from everyone around me.

During my final year of high school, I began to turn increasingly inwards. There was no outward reason for this condition. Blessed with a stable family environment, no real difficulties in school, excellent health—I should have been happy. Although the fire of discontent had begun to stir deep beneath the surface, I managed to pull myself up and hold on to hope for a better future. I was eager to leave the high school years behind and move forward with my life as a college student. The inscription in our high school yearbook beneath my photograph read: *Probable Destination: Happiness.*

The summer following graduation was an exciting time, filled with anticipation and promise, and, for a while, I was able to push back the dark clouds that had begun to hover around the edges of my awareness. I obtained my driver's license, an exhilarating rite of passage, giving me a sense of freedom such as I had never before experienced. No longer limited to the schedules of trains or busses, I was able to go where I wanted, when I wanted. Well, almost. Of course, I had to justify my need for the use of my father's car, but being the serious and responsible, and, of course, persistent girl that I was, he usually gave into my pleas. I enjoyed long, quiet drives along the old road that ran along the north shore, catching occasional glimpses of the river, surrounded by trees, interspersed with the last remaining farm fields of the island. Those brief escapades took me back to the peaceful tranquility of my early childhood.

Following in my grandfather's footsteps, I took up photography, a hobby that would bring me hours of pleasure and a wonderful sense of peace and quiet. It was the perfect hobby for me. Hidden behind the camera lens, I could look out onto an unsuspecting world without fear of being noticed. With savings from my summer job in a clothing store, I purchased my first SLR. The Pentax would become a permanent fixture around my neck for years to come.

My sewing skills had grown much over the years, and so, just before college began, my mom replaced the old Singer with a brand new Bernina, the Cadillac of sewing machines. I sewed some grown-up clothes for college, starting with a chic tweed suit, complete with French buttonholes on the jacket and down the front of the calf-length skirt. Always having had a sense of being old, I was very anxious to move away from childhood and be grown up. In my mind, college was grown-up time. When September rolled around, I was ready and very eager to enter McGill University.

Chapter 4

DARKNESS FALLS

Your goal was darkness, in which no ray of light could enter. And you sought a blackness so complete that you could hide from truth forever, in complete insanity. What you forgot was simply that God cannot destroy Himself. The light is *in* you. Darkness can cover it, but cannot put it out. (T-18.III.1:4–8)

*I*t was a perfect autumn day, not a cloud was in the sky, when I stepped up onto the train for the commute to the McGill campus downtown. It might have been a bit warm for my tweed suit, but I felt as fine as I looked. Preferring the train to the subway, I took it whenever possible. Its gentle rocking and rhythmic drumming reminded me of the long trips we had made from Lac Saint-Jean to Montreal when I was young. It also carried a more mature crowd, most appropriate now that I was grown up.

McGill was overwhelming. Hundred-year-old buildings interspersed with modern structures were spread high and low along the slope of Mount Royal. And so many students—thousands scurrying here and there, all appearing to know exactly where they were going. The moment I walked through the Roddick Gates onto the main campus, I realized that I was most definitely inappropriately dressed. The old high school uniform of jeans and T-shirt had graduated and moved on to college and university. It was the one and only time I wore my prized tweed suit.

In the biggest gymnasium I had ever seen, students lined up by the hundreds at long registration tables, competing for spots in the best classes. Unfamiliar with the routine, it took me a while to find my way around, and for my electives I ended up with a course in logic and the only other course with openings: The History of Latin America. For the rest, my program was already set.

During my last year of high school, I had come across an advertisement for a College of Metaphysics in California. Instantly, I knew I had found my calling. I would become a metaphysician. It was perfect. Eager to discover the mysteries of existence, I declared to my mother that I had decided to study metaphysics, making little of the fact that the school was clear across the continent and in another country. Her response had been as swift as it was succinct: "No." I had hit a very hard wall.

Having neither the financial resources nor the self-assurance required to break out on my own at the tender age of sixteen, I made what I thought was a very logical choice. Fascinated by Edgar Cayce's predictions about the future of the planet, in particular about the San Andreas Fault and other geological formations, I enrolled in the Pure and Applied Sciences program with a specialization in geology. I would channel my interests in the great beyond into the here and now. The sciences were highly valued in our family, my mother especially would be pleased with my choice and I would get a chance to pursue a subject that interested me. It was a win-win situation, or so I thought.

On that first day of college, I completed my registration, collected my class schedule, purchased my books and materials and scouted out the campus for the classrooms and auditoriums where my classes would be held. For the first time in a very long while, I felt so very small. I also felt very alone, not having seen one person from my high school. In the days that followed, I met up with a former classmate. We became fast friends, and would spend much time together between classes as well as on weekends during that year. She was in my logic class, and to alleviate the stress of our new environment, we joked about Boolean schemata. I think we just found the name comical.

I signed up for a photography course and joined a camera club on campus. My grandfather had given me his photography equipment, which I rounded out by purchasing an enlarger. My mom, bless her soul, allowed me to set up a darkroom in the laundry room downstairs. There I spent countless hours burning images onto photographic paper, watching them magically emerge in the developer solution. I spent days walking around the downtown core, framing the skyline and bits of intriguing architecture, making up the world as I wanted to see it. The Pentax became an extension of my body, and from my vantage point behind the lens, the world appeared less overwhelming. With the camera acting as a buffer, I could be in the world without being noticed. It occurred to me, though briefly, that I could pursue a career in photography—and looking back now, I think I might have done well—but I was simply too shy and insecure for a solo business venture.

My naive assumption that there existed a relationship between physics and metaphysics was very quickly quashed. Contemporary quantum physics would not come of age for some time yet. The popular New Age movie *What the Bleep!* was still decades away. Despite my best efforts to pass all the courses in the science program, it soon became clear that I was entirely ill-prepared for college. Not surprisingly, my best subjects were mathematics and logic. I aced calculus and differential equations and was able to memorize enough chemical formulas to ace mineralogy too, but in every other subject I just passed, or worse, failed miserably. Organic chemistry was the bane of my curriculum. Even by randomly selecting answers on the computer punch cards, I couldn't maintain a consistent failing grade. I went from twenty-eight percent to forty-nine and back down to thirty-five. Session after appallingly dismal session proved that academia was not for me. Feeling more lost than ever, I realized that I was entering adulthood, and there was no suitable spot for me in the world.

It was during my first winter at college that I had my first precognitive experience, or what I would later come to refer to as one of my *hunches*. If I had experienced any in the past, they had gone by unnoticed. Not that I ever considered myself to be psychic, actually, far from it, though occasionally, like everyone I do get *hunches*. This was not a sense that I could ever rely on with any degree of certainty, nor that I could command at will. It was just something that happened from time to time. It was early on a Sunday morning, and I was getting ready for a ski trip with a couple of friends from the neighbourhood. I had awakened with vague images of a dream in which I was warned against going on the trip. When it was time to leave, I couldn't find my Our Lady of Guadalupe medallion. It was a delicate gold medal on a fine chain I had received as a birthday gift on my trip to Mexico years earlier and was engraved *Pauline 14–8–65*. I wore it around my neck at all times, taking it off only to wash my hair. Although not superstitious by nature, leaving without my medallion that morning just didn't feel right. It even occurred to me that I should cancel my trip, but how could I explain why I wasn't going skiing without sounding like a total nut job? Misgivings notwithstanding, I left for the Orford slopes that morning without Our Lady of Guadalupe to protect me.

This turned out to be a bad idea. That afternoon I learned the hard way that I should listen to my hunches. Cold winds had left the hills hard-packed and icy. Although I was not a very experienced skier, I agreed to follow the others to an intermediate run higher up in the mountain where it was colder. I wore new boots in old bindings and the fit wasn't quite right. In the cold, the latch kept popping open and my ski would fall off. In order to make my way down the hill, I wrapped a lace around my boot through the binding to keep the ski in place. That was the second bad idea of the day.

My intention was to make it down the hill and call it a day. Feeling brave and quite clever for having fixed my boot problem, and wanting to stay with my friends, I agreed to go up for a second run downhill. Needless to say, I made it down all right, only not exactly on my own. I wiped out, broke a ski, twisted my knee and ankle and had to be carried down the rest of the slope on a gurney. It was by ambulance that I made it to a local hospital, where

I fought tooth and nail to convince the doctor to not give me a full leg cast. Finally I was allowed to leave with a pair of crutches, which I turned in for a cane a week later. Although my recovery was surprisingly quick, in the end, I decided to retire my skis for good. I was never really a big fan of this cold weather sport. However, what I did keep from that experience was a clear memory of the eerie accuracy of that hunch, something that would stay with me for a long while.

As it became more and more evident that academia was not for me, I drew inwards in search of guidance. I felt like a displaced spiritual seeker, a lost soul on a quest to find my Shangri-La in a world that was anything but ethereal. This was a time of budding consumerism, filled with hope and possibilities for those with worldly ambitions. I felt increasingly lonely and isolated, but, worst of all, dreadfully powerless.

During that first year of college, I developed a severe case of acne that would leave me scarred, not only physically, but also emotionally, for a very long time. Forget dating; I was a leper. There was one nice-looking young man who had helped me with a couple of math problems. I was attracted to him, but I saw how he looked at me, with a mixture of pity and disgust. I remember looking at my reflection in the darkened glass of the subway door as it sped through the unlit tunnel between stations. It was all I could do to hide my acne-ridden face from passengers boarding at each station—fifteen stations. Looking into the dark glass was the only time I didn't see the horrible pimples. The face that was reflected back appeared nearly flawless, the cheeks smooth, even planes tracing out high cheekbones. I might have been attractive from certain angles, I thought, shifting my head slightly from side to side.

But the darkness began to slowly swallow up any vestiges of light and hope in my soul. Gradually, I slipped into a profound state of depression. Sometimes, while waiting for the subway train, I would stand at the edge of the platform, just beyond the safety line and wonder what it would be like to fall in as a train arrived at full speed. What if someone pushed me in? Even accidentally? This became an increasingly appealing thought. The best part was that if it happened, it would not even be my fault. If it were to happen accidentally, then perhaps it might mean that it was my time to go. If that were the case, then I would willingly go. Sometimes, as I neared home, I would walk across streets without looking, again, taunting fate. "I dare you," I'd say to oncoming traffic.

> The world is not left by death but by truth, and truth can be known by all those for whom the Kingdom was created, and for whom it waits. (T-3.VII.6:11)

As much as the thought of death seemed appealing, I had no serious intention of committing suicide. It was not so much that I felt it would have been a sin—for Catholics, suicide was considered a mortal sin—or that it would have been wrong, but more that I was afraid I might miss out on something yet to come. It was like watching a movie to the end, or reading a book to the final page. No matter how bad the story, always hopeful for a satisfactory outcome, I have almost always read stories cover to cover. So, in spite of my deepening depression, I thought it preferable to stick around for a while, see what the future held in store for me. Something inside, barely perceptible, whispered to me that one day I would find what I was looking for.

When not in class, I spent most of my time at home alone in my room. Some days I would arrive for supper, head straight for bed and sleep right through until the next morning. Other times, I read and listened to music. I believe music was my saving grace. For hours I would lose myself to the sounds of Bach or Beethoven. The ordered strains of Telleman gave my soul a sense of structure. By then, my younger brother Michael had fully established himself as a musical genius, and since the piano was his instrument of choice, I was privy to recitals of Chopin and Rachmaninoff. Sometimes I would pick up a pencil and drawing pad and sketch out items from my room, knickknacks on my bookshelves or what I thought would be cool pieces of furniture. My room was my sanctuary. Away from the world, I found peace.

Severe daily migraines eventually drove me to the university clinic, where I was prescribed medication. At the same time, the doctor informed me that my acne symptoms could also be relieved with medication. Desperate for relief on all fronts, I gladly accepted the prescriptions. In a matter of weeks, my symptoms had disappeared, but then I was faced with a new dilemma: everything was fine as long as I consumed antibiotics and barbiturates. Given that regular use of antibiotics tends to weaken the body's natural immune system, I was told that it would be necessary for me to take breaks between prescriptions. While I took the medication, my skin was clear; when I went off it, the acne flared up. This battle, which persisted for the better part of the next four years, sent me on a brand new quest: I needed to find alternative ways of dealing with my health issues. The pharmacological route was not an acceptable long-term solution.

Although after my three years at McGill I would shy away from formal academia for the remainder of my life, I would always remain eager to learn something new. To heal myself of the headaches and acne, I researched, studied and experimented with alternative methods such as the flower remedies of Dr. Bach, reflexology, magnetism, herbology, raw foods, vegetarianism and various forms of cleansing and fasting.

I signed up for a vegetarian cooking class, which I thoroughly enjoyed. When the teacher asked me to assist in the class, I felt a surge of pride and delight. Here was something I knew I could do well. First off, I loved to cook and, secondly, I sensed that I might one day be a good teacher—one day, when I had overcome my paralyzing shyness. But because the idea that I should obtain a university degree was so deeply ingrained, I did not give it serious consideration.

A significant turning point came during my second year at college when I attended an information session for a new practice from India called Transcendental Meditation. On a yellow sheet taped to a wall in one of the buildings where I attended class, I read about a meeting scheduled the following Thursday evening. Although I had absolutely no idea of what Transcendental Meditation was, I had a *hunch* that this was where I needed to be.

The teachings of this school centred on the daily practice of meditation: twenty minutes in the morning and twenty minutes in the evening. Each person was given a unique mantra, specially chosen to suit his or her vibratory state. The mantra was assigned during a private initiation ceremony officiated by a trained instructor. It was never to be spoken aloud or shared with anybody else. The purpose of regular meditation practice was to facilitate the release of accumulated stress—referred to as *unstressing*—which, in turn, was to gradually foster an experience of profound bliss. Over time, this was to lead to the attainment of Cosmic Consciousness, the supreme state of human consciousness.

Needless to say, I took to TM like the falcon takes to the air. Meditation and the philosophy of this school instantly appealed to me, soothing my spirit and giving me a whole new purpose for living. This was a practical, non-religious system that did not challenge my deeply rooted Catholic conditioning. Eager to obtain my own personal mantra, I immediately signed up for my initiation, and yoga and meditation became an integral part of my daily routine.

I thoroughly enjoyed meditation and yoga practice, as they gave a sense of depth and purpose to my life. I had found an activity in which I could fully engage and which, over time, would lead me to a state of blissful peace. Eager to learn more, over the next couple of years I participated in numerous weekend retreats, many of which were held in nearby monasteries. One of my favourites was the beautiful Trappist monastery at Oka overlooking the lake and surrounded by trees. My life now had a significant spiritual component. The attainment of Cosmic Consciousness became my new goal.

One of my greatest joys during that period occurred when, after attending an information session, my parents agreed to be initiated.

For a while, I experienced a special closeness with my parents as we shared meditation experiences, lectures and workshops. For the first time in years, I felt a sense of belonging with my family.

TM opened up a brave new world of spirituality for us, leading to the discovery of philosophies and spiritualities that extended well beyond our Catholic boundaries. My dad, who had been educated by the Jesuits, sought to make a connection between Catholicism and Eastern philosophies. We discovered the works of Ramana Maharshi, Dr. Paul Bruntan and Allan Watts. Eastern and Western philosophies were being bridged, and the layperson was increasingly free to explore new avenues for establishing a relationship with God. This was the dawning of a new spiritual age.

Despite having failed miserably in the physical sciences, I continued to look for my place in academia. I tried my hand at psychology where I received a serving of Skinner's rats and Pavlov's dogs. When that didn't work for me, I tried commerce, for which I could not muster up the least bit of interest. Success eluded me in all subjects. After three desperate years at McGill, I accepted an offer to extend my summer job in the international economics department at the bank into a full-time research assistant position. My employers appreciated my work and made it clear that any time I wanted to return to school they would gladly pay for my tuition.

While the acne and migraines persisted, not surprisingly, romance continued to elude me. Weeks would go by when my skin was nearly clear and I felt I could comfortably face people; then, while off the meds, the condition would flare up again and all I wanted was to bury my head in the sand. At school, I had been able to hide anonymously in the back of darkened auditoriums, listen to my lectures, grab my books and then escape to my refuge at home. The situation was more difficult to manage at the bank, where I worked from nine to five, five days a week under the glare of neon lighting. Still feeling out of sorts with the world, my quest for health and inner peace continued.

In search of a Catholic perspective on Transcendental Meditation, my father had been introduced to Thomas Merton's *Contemplation*

in a World of Action by a monk who was also a TM practitioner. He
had been on my case to read Merton for some time, but Merton's
writings were too sophisticated for me, until I discovered his autobiography: *The Seven Storey Mountain*. This was the next most
important book I would read.

I was fascinated by, and perhaps in a way envied, the deep faith
and conviction that led Thomas Merton to convert to Catholicism
and join the order of Cistercian monks at Gethsemane. In January
of 1975, I picked up my pen and began to journal. I had started
a diary a couple of years earlier, but had disposed of my writings, because, in my words, "I could not stand to see such drippy
sentimentalism." But the urge to write withstood the assault of my
self-criticism, and the more I read, the more I wanted to write. In
the first entry of that new journal, I quoted a passage from Merton
that gave me a sense of peace such as I had not felt in a long while.

> [T]he life of the soul is not knowledge, it is love, since love is the
> act of the supreme faculty, the will, by which man is formally
> united to the final end of all his strivings—by which man be-
> comes one with God.[1]

In my journal, I described my state of mind over that Christmas
holiday as lonely and empty of God, tired and depressed, desperate
for more of what Merton described as *grace from God*. Although
that passage had brought me some measure of peace, I knew full
well that it would not last. As I wrote, I knew I would hit another
mountain and again I would struggle to make it to the top, over
and over again until I reached God, until I became an instrument
through which God manifests his eternal love and peace.

By grace I live. By grace I am released. (W-pI.169)

Perhaps due to his early lack of religious instruction, or maybe
it was because of his contrary Aquarian nature, Merton developed
a fascination with churches and prayer that bordered on obsession,
in particular, with Catholic Churches. Having enough with Sunday

---

1. *The Seven Storey Mountain*, Thomas Merton, page 191.

Mass, other than for special occasions, I had never attended Church on a weekday. Inspired by a growing need to be close to God, on my way to the train after work one day, I decided to enter St. Patrick's Basilica. I wanted to sit and pray for a few minutes before going home. To my surprise, the main doors were locked. I tried a side entrance, and it too was locked. It took three tries before I found an open door.

Once inside, I realized that a Mass was being held. Trying my best to remain invisible, I quietly took a spot on a pew at the back of the church. Only a handful of participants attended the daily five o'clock Mass. St. Patrick's was an incredibly beautiful Gothic revival church, and, as with all churches, I found temporary peace and closeness to God there. The following day, I read a passage in *Seven Storey* in which Merton described a similar experience in which he too found a church with locked doors. I saw this as a sign that I was being guided and, over the next several months, I attended many daily masses at St. Patrick's.

Occasionally on my lunch hour I would walk across the street from the bank where I worked to Notre-Dame Basilica, always careful to not be seen by anyone from the office. I had already encountered harsh criticism about my interest in Transcendental Meditation from a secretary who worked in the next office. The main front doors of Notre-Dame, also a Gothic revival church, were always open, and there were usually a few visitors, mostly tourists, sitting quietly inside. The interior of this church was truly exquisite, with its deep blue ceiling, rich colours and intricate wood carvings. I would sit at a pew at the back and breathe deeply of the peace and tranquility of this house of God. Where are You? I wondered. Can You hear me?

To my great chagrin, my parents eventually lost interest in TM. There was nothing there for them to learn, they said. But I persisted. For me, TM was a lifeline. If it hadn't been for Transcendental Meditation, I think I might have stood closer to the edge of the subway platform. In fact, I'm quite sure I would have. Given that it had saved me from an early demise, I was not ready to abandon it quite yet. In fact, believing that TM was my path, I applied for the teacher-training program.

In order to be accepted into the program, I was required to pass an interview before a committee comprised of TM instructors. During that interview, I openly shared my views and how eager I was to travel to Switzerland to study with Maharishi Mahesh Yogi. I told them of the issues I wanted to discuss with him, questions I wanted to ask. In my mind, I was an ideal candidate for TM instructor. I had been a regular practitioner for four years and had attended most of the weekend retreats offered by the centre.

At the end of the interview I listened in shock as I was told in no uncertain terms that I was not ready to become a TM instructor. It seemed that I had too many questions, which was interpreted as doubt and lack of preparedness. Holding my fury in check, I politely thanked my jurors and went out in search of the friend who had sponsored my candidacy for the program. I was furious with him for not having warned me of the inquisition-style interview. More than that, I could not understand how a spiritual school could discourage the intelligence of the questioning mind. Why else pursue a course of study if not to question and consider the answers?

This was a very disappointing turn of events, as my heart had been set on going away to study with the Maharishi. I had a very clear picture in my mind of myself as a TM instructor. It had felt so right. This event also marked the end of my practice of TM. Somehow, it had lost its appeal. The attainment of Cosmic Consciousness was no longer on my agenda.

Profoundly affected by the life of Thomas Merton, I began to yearn for the monastic life, imagining myself living in the Abbey of Gethsemani, enjoying the simple quiet life of a contemplative monk. I even spoke to the young priest who said the weekday evening mass at St. Patrick's. Unfortunately, I had been born of the wrong gender; women weren't allowed anywhere near the Abbey.

I joined a Catholic study group hosted by Sister Andrée, my younger brother's piano teacher. She recommended a book called

Le Christ est vivant[2] that gave me the courage to continue with my search for my place in the world. In my journal, I wrote:

> God had left me totally free to make my own decisions. If I ask Him to, He will watch over my actions and if they are good, or if they will lead to quicker growth, He will not intervene. Otherwise, it will be made known to me. He wants us to grow and find bliss through our work, not suffer and be miserable. I've got to pull up my socks and get moving … start getting busy and involved in something.

I think I attended these meetings just to see if I might get a sense of whether or not I was meant for the religious life. But convent life didn't resonate with me; it didn't seem as powerful as the life of the contemplative. Try as I might, I just couldn't see myself as a nun, whose role appeared to be based on service to church and community. I didn't see myself, as I wrote in my journal, *scrubbing floors and saying rosaries for hours and hours.* I saw myself more as a priest, a monk or a teacher. Somehow I had gathered that the more intellectual the role, the closer to God it must be. Had I taken the time to look further, I would have found similar paths for women contemplatives. That I did not do the research is indicative of the deep conflict that existed between my desire to live in the world and taste all of the things the world had yet to offer me, and my desire to flee the frightening complexities of that world. I wanted to live in the world and experience peace of a lasting kind, a peace I sensed was not to be found in the world.

My path must lie elsewhere, I concluded. For a while, I debated returning to school, my options being mathematics and computer science, or religious studies. But I really didn't have the stomach to face academia again. Anxious to find my place in the world and find at least a halfway interesting job, I looked for courses that might be interesting and stumbled on an ad for a tax preparation course. It was a three-month course and seemed just right for me. And it was. I worked one full tax season at H&R Block and,

---

2. By Michel Quoist (English title: *Christ Is Alive*).

not surprisingly, working with numbers, did very well. However, I couldn't see myself doing this full-time. There had to be something else, a course I could take, a trade I could practise.

Given my love of drawing and photography, I signed up for an architectural drafting course. I bought a drafting table and enthusiastically began to learn the trade. It was fun for a while, something else I could do very easily. But again, to my profound disappointment, I lost heart. There was always something missing, something else I needed to do. Weeks later, I found a job in an art gallery in the mall not far from home and learned to frame pictures. For a few weeks it was okay, but I was soon overcome by that same, now increasingly familiar, feeling of heading in the wrong direction.

Deep in my heart, I saw myself pursuing a spiritual path more than any other but I couldn't seem to find the right one. As much as a few years earlier, I had entertained the thought of becoming an astrologer, even very clearly seeing myself talking with clients at a wooden desk—in fact, exactly as I do now. However, I was well aware that I did not have the maturity to counsel others on how to live their lives. Still in search of answers, I decided to delve deeper into the religion of my upbringing and began to explore Catholic mysticism. I became a frequent visitor of the Diocesan Book Room, always hoping to find guidance and inspiration. Still convinced that the Catholic Church was the one and only church, I was careful to select only those books that had its stamp of approval, always looking for the *Imprimi potest*, *Nihil obstat* and *Imprimatur* on the first pages. If I read books that were approved by the Church, I reasoned, I stood a better chance of finding the truth. If I was ever to return home and be with God, this is what I needed.

I read *The Sign of Jonas* by Thomas Merton and *The Man in the Sycamore Tree: The Good Times and Hard Life of Thomas Merton* by his long-time friend Edward Rice. I read the lives of the saints: Augustine, Teresa of Avila, the Little Flower and Thérèse of Lisieux. I read the Bible, *The Imitation of Christ* and the Psalms, and then read *The Seven Storey Mountain* two more times. The saints possessed something that I clearly didn't have, something that eluded my grasp, a quality I admired greatly and, at the same time, something I knew I would need to develop if I was to make headway in my spiritual quest: they all had unshakable faith. I desperately longed for a way to connect with that faith but it invariably slipped from my grasp.

Bit by bit, I realized that Catholicism contained teachings that just did not sit well with me. How could one religion claim to be the one and only church, chosen by God? How could God choose one group of people over another? How could each different thought system claim to hold the truth? How many versions of the truth could there be? It seemed as though all the different churches and thought systems were vying for the top position on the ladder of spiritual specialness. If God was *all*-loving and *all*-encompassing, how could He love one group or even one person more than another? At what point did *all* become *some*?

As a Catholic, I had accepted that suffering was a normal part of the process of atoning for one's sins, a requirement for the return home to God. But what sins? I still was not sure what this meant. Suffering was a common theme in the lives of Catholic mystics. The greater the suffering, it seemed, the greater the saintliness, with Jesus being the champion of all suffering souls. I was honest enough to admit that since I wasn't really a big fan of suffering, I would never be a good candidate for sainthood, which was okay, since my aspirations were not that ambitious anyways. Nonetheless, I did think I deserved some measure of peace in my life, and this I was determined to find.

While much of what I read on Eastern philosophies made sense, I felt strongly that having been born in the West I should be able to find a spiritual path within my own culture, in my own world. Ramana Maharshi made that clear when he told his Western students that they should seek fulfillment in their Western lifestyle. The Eastern schools promoted detachment from the things of the world. Not having even begun to live in the world, I had nothing from which to detach. In fact, there were lots of things I hoped to obtain and experience, such as love, family and a home. I took

Ramana's words to heart, relieved to know that I didn't have to exile myself to a Himalayan hut in order to find peace.

I reconsidered my Catholic roots. This was the religion of Jesus; it must contain the truth. Oddly, it never occurred to me at the time that Jesus was a Jew, no more Catholic than Moses was. I was fascinated by the priesthood, but, in the Catholic Church, that function was open to men only. I thought I would have been a very good priest. Although I had no problems with celibacy as an individual choice, it didn't feel right as a strict requirement for the religious life. Why would it matter to God if you had someone with whom to share love? Wasn't the teaching of Jesus all about love?

Not only was the Church elitist and sexist, it was also hierarchical. There was a Pope, and there were bishops and archbishops, priests, monks and acolytes; in fact, there was little in the structure of the church that reflected the oneness of heaven. In the Catholic Church, there was a pecking order, and it seemed that only those at the top could be close to God. The rest of us mere mortals at the bottom of the ladder didn't seem to hold much importance in God's eyes, much less a chance of ever reaching heaven.

Despite my problems with the Church as the spiritual authority in my life, I continued to look to Jesus for hope and guidance. Somehow, I managed to separate the two. There was the Church, which in my mind was man-made and not infallible—as it claimed to be—and there was Jesus, a very special individual who had achieved what seemed like an impossible level of spiritual evolution. Even though I did not consider that I had committed any sin worthy of God's punishment, at least not in the world of form, my journal entries from that period typically ended with the Jesus Prayer: "Lord Jesus Christ, Son of God, have mercy on me, a sinner." If I was suffering, I must have done something wrong, somewhere. Every day, I prayed for guidance, I prayed for help, I prayed for support. Nearly thirty years would pass before I would learn that throughout this period of darkness and supplication, the book that would become the most important spiritual influence of my life—*A Course in Miracles*—was being written.

Chapter 5

A HELPING HAND

Put yourself not in charge of this, for you cannot distinguish between advance and retreat. Some of your greatest advances you have judged as failures, and some of your deepest retreats you have evaluated as success. (T-18.V.1:5–6)

*T*he day I met the palmist turned my life upside down, or perhaps, more accurately, it set me right on track for the true journey of my life. I had no idea of what to expect, only that I had been strongly urged by my neighbour to go for a reading. Marlene was in my life only briefly. Looking back now, it seems as though her parents had moved into my parents' upper duplex for the sole purpose of our fateful meeting. I made the hour-and-a-half bus trip to Victoria Avenue with my thirty-five dollars for the consultation fee in my pocket. I had never been to a palm reader before, and so I was filled with a mixture of apprehension and hopefulness. At twenty-two and still without a life purpose, I was desperate for answers.[1] True to her Scorpio birth sign, Marlene had sensed this and had insisted that I make an appointment.

Ghanshyam Birla's office was in an old commercial building in Westmount, a brick structure with darkened windows and hardly a sign of life. A stern-looking, heavy-set woman working in a diner on the ground floor served up the fast foods of the day: coffee, chicken noodle soup, fries and grilled cheese sandwiches. Smells from the grill, thick in the air, followed me as I rode the narrow

---

1. This was a number 9 Personal Year.

elevator to the third-floor offices of the National Research Institute for Self-Understanding.

There was a bit of irony in a visit to a palm reader. My hands were large; in fact, they were larger than those of most guys I knew, and I made sure that whatever coat or jacket I bought had sufficiently large pockets in which I could hide them. Adding to that the fact that I bit my nails to the bone, I generally kept them out of sight. The office door was barely a half dozen steps from the elevator; entering, I pressed my palms deep into my jacket pockets.

The Institute looked more like the chaotic offices of a research professor than a school for self-understanding. Shelves and filing cabinets piled high with books, papers and folders lined the walls to the right and to the left. There was a desk and small table next to the filing cabinets, and several wooden chairs along the book-cases. A pamphlet produced by the Institute bore the quote: "Man's greatest task is to know himself." This must be the place for me, I thought. Facing the entrance was a pair of doors, the one on the left, half open, led to what looked like a storage room—equally cluttered—and the other was closed. From behind that door, I could hear muffled voices.

A dark-haired woman about my age walked out of the storage room. Miranda smiled and greeted me with a surprisingly very firm, warm handshake, paying absolutely no mind to my super-sized clammy palm. Informing me that Ghanshyam would be with me shortly, she prepared a file with my birth information. Then she motioned for me to move to the small table next to the desk where she prepared my hands for printing. Still, she made no comments about my hands. Sometimes people would say "nice hands," but I knew they were just being kind. My guess was that Miranda had seen hands of all shapes and sizes, and mine did not shock her one bit. I felt reassured as she deftly rolled hand-printing ink onto my palms then systematically pressed my palms and fingers onto a legal-size sheet of white paper. The prints of my palms filled the page.

I cleaned the ink from my hands with a messy gel while Miranda drew up a quick astrology chart. I was wiping my hands onto a clean paper towel for the third time when a hearty laugh erupted and the office door opened. An older woman stepped out and closed the door behind her. My heart raced. Miranda collected the handprints and the file containing my personal information, and led me into the office. It seemed all very official and business-like. I held my breath as I followed her through the open door. In keeping with the decor of the outer office, the palmist's office was small and just as cluttered with books and papers. On the wall were framed photos of Paramahansa Yogananda and Sri Yukteshwar, teachers I recognized from my own readings. The familiar faces reassured me a bit.

Ghanshyam stood and shook my hand. His grasp was even firmer and warmer than Miranda's. He was a handsome man of medium stature, in his mid-thirties, with dark, shining eyes and a most welcoming smile. Motioning for me to sit, he took his place behind the large wooden desk and began to study my prints, drawing lines across the palms and circling clusters of patterns. He slid the prints aside, looked up and asked for my hands. I was so nervous that my hands were by now cold and very damp; stuffing them into my pockets was not an option. He smiled reassuringly, took my hands palm up in his warm, firm grasp and began to examine them, first together, then one at a time. With his pen, he made several markings on my palms, circling spots where lines intersected or ended, or took turns up or down my palm. I had never before paid attention to the lines on my hands and wondered how anything logical could be said about such a seemingly arbitrary mess of markings.

After what seemed like an eternity, he began. "My, oh my, oh my." My heart stopped. This was it. Things were as bad as I feared. I was doomed, I thought in panic, and my expression must have shown it. He clasped my hands reassuringly and smiled. There was nothing but gentleness and kindness in his expression. He took a deep breath, studied the prints once more, then, to my surprise, asked to see my feet.

Now this, I had not expected. Naturally, as related parts of my body had developed proportionally, my feet had grown to match my hands. In those days, the largest size carried by regular shoe stores was 10. I had grown accustomed to squeezing my 10½ feet into size 10 shoes, which was not too difficult to do given that the style at the time was for large rounded tips. But I also found that I could comfortably fit into certain men's size 8's if I laced them up tightly. It was summer, and while everyone wore sandals—everyone who had normal-sized feet, that is—I wore my usual shoes with thick cotton socks. Not only were my feet long, they were also now sweaty and snug in a pair of men's Wallabies. This was most embarrassing. As instructed, I hauled one foot up onto the desk, and then when asked for the other, I was very glad to be wearing jeans. Of course, I never wore skirts because I couldn't find comfortable dress shoes.

Minutes later, foot examination complete, Ghanshyam gave me the okay to put my shoes back on. He drew another long, thoughtful breath. I'd never before known anyone to breathe so fully and deeply. He must have had a very large set of lungs! While the palmist slid the handprints back to the middle of the desk, I braced myself for the bad news.

"My dear Pauline," he said.

My heart leaped to my throat; I didn't know if I could breathe. He smiled that broad, warm smile, and I felt safe for a moment, but only for a moment. Then he began. Without ceremony, without warning, he simply pried open the gates of the deepest recesses of my soul, touching on the yearnings, the hopes, the dreams as well as the pain, the darkness and the sorrow. This was my first reading of any kind; no one had ever before come this close to my soul. He expressed great pleasure at my choice of astrology as a course of study, and he encouraged me strongly to continue. Astrology, even palmistry was my path, he told me, and deep down I agreed, for this was something I could see myself doing.

The hour passed very quickly, and still he went on. Miranda knocked at the door and he sent an annoyed glance in her direction. Ghanshyam appeared to have so much more to say as he ignored the signal and continued. After the third warning knock, he finally stopped. Another client was waiting. Clearly disappointed that our time was up, he recommended that I return for another session. Much remained to be said, and I would benefit by an additional reading. Eager to learn more, I scheduled an appointment for the following week, and another the week after that.

The sessions with the palmist served to reinforce my inner yearning for the spiritual path, shedding light on why I had been unable to find my place in the world. He described me as *monkly*, and although this was not a word I could find in my dictionary, I got the gist of what he meant. Still very insecure and fearful of spending the rest of my life alone, I wasn't sure I liked the sound of that, but it certainly made a whole lot of sense. It's not that I was defective; I was simply not in the right environment.

To my surprise and great joy, Ghanshyam invited me to join the Institute. In exchange for my volunteer work, I would be allowed to attend classes and receive weekly private tutoring sessions in palmistry. It did not matter that I would not be paid for the work; all I saw was the opportunity of a lifetime. Feeling alive and with a whole new sense of purpose and direction, I eagerly took on my duties at the Institute. My functions were varied and included translation and note-taking for his French-speaking clients, drawing up astrology charts and preparing lunches. My quest for healing had led me to explore natural and vegetarian cooking, and I was very happy to share my passion and knowledge with the small staff at the Institute by making sure we had something healthy for lunch every day. I was elated; I had found my teacher, my guide. I had found my place, my home. Journal entries that followed were filled with prayers of thanks and gratitude for my good fortune. Carlos Castaneda had his Don Juan, Yogananda had his Yukteshwar and I had my Ghanshyam.

My tutoring sessions with Ghanshyam were the highlight of my week. Not only did we discuss my palmistry assignments, we also delved into various aspects of spirituality. His belief system seemed to work well for him, for he exuded profound trust, joy, peace and inner strength, qualities that my own religion had not given me. Ghanshyam's faith was as uncomplicated as it was unshakable, but, although I admired the simplicity of his spirituality, I could not completely embrace it. I was still very much a Catholic, and, from that perspective, he was a pagan; because of my appreciation for his knowledge and wisdom, I was conflicted.

Ghanshyam often talked about Mother Divine, pointing out many times—and rightly so—that I lacked faith. He said it with such a pained expression that I wished I could fix my lack of faith just to please him. Thinking back about why I couldn't relate to Mother Divine, the reasons are obvious. I simply didn't see the value of the feminine. Women were not the ones with the real power. Women were second-class. Men had the power. God was a man, Jesus was a man, Thomas Merton, Edgar Cayce, Lobsang Rampa... all my heroes were men. Mary didn't even have enough power to save her own son from crucifixion, nor was she even permitted to live out the full purpose of her female body, having instead to be spiritually inseminated. Then there was Eve, the sinful temptress ... How could I turn to a female figure for guidance?

I stayed on at the Institute for a year, volunteering my time, studying the ancient art of palmistry, even dabbling in a little Sanskrit. I had already read *Autobiography of a Yogi* and other works of Paramahansa Yogananda, and so the next logical step was to join the Self-Realization Fellowship, Ghanshyam's preferred spiritual path. Their meditation techniques were less structured than those of TM, and I felt a twinge of guilt for switching paths after four years, but I wanted to follow in my new mentor's footsteps. Although I followed the meditation method of this new school as recommended, I never fully connected with it. As the months passed, Ghanshyam grew increasingly busy with clients and my private palmistry lessons became less frequent. I missed them all the more because they were often more spiritual coaching than palmistry lessons. During those sessions, I felt connected to what mattered, I felt at home. Without them, I felt lost.

In one of the palmistry classes, there was a young man, Elliot, with whom I enjoyed chatting about palmistry and spiritually related matters. For months he had tried to talk me into visiting a new school he had discovered. There they were taught unusual forms of mental discipline, so unusual, in fact, that it was difficult for him to explain what it actually was. "They're called Mind Warriors," he said. He tried to show me one of the exercises, raising his arms up in an odd position, then, probably prompted by my frown of confusion, finally said, "You just have to come and see for yourself." Intrigued and eager to learn something new, I moved on down the buffet line to the next spiritual dish.

Chapter 6

IN SEARCH OF ANCIENT WISDOM

"Seek and do *not* find." This is the one promise the ego holds out to you, and the one promise it will keep. For the ego pursues its goal with fanatic insistence, and its judgment, though severely impaired, is completely consistent. (T-12.IV.1:4–6)

*A*fter a year of volunteer work at the Palmistry Institute, my funds had dried up. I considered my options. Given my less than glorious track record at McGill, academia was out of the question. The bottom line was I needed a job. I scoured the Help Wanted section of *The Gazette* and secured a job within a matter of weeks. Over the next year, I would work as the assistant to the contract manager of a two-man operation that bid on tenders for machine and engine parts for the Ministry of Defence. It wasn't what I really wanted, but I was happy to have found a small, safe corner in which I could safely blend in the big grown-up world.

At the same time, I accepted Elliot's invitation to attend an introductory session of the strange Mind Warrior school that had so captured his imagination. The meeting was held in a large, stately house, conveniently located near my new place of work. A bronze plaque on the wall next to the broad main doors read: Mount Royal School of Ancient Wisdom. The house was impeccably clean, the decor very Zen, with walls painted a neutral off-white, framed with simple mouldings, and oak floors that were buffed to a glowing sheen. Items of furniture were there only to serve a purpose. I was reminded of the monasteries where TM weekend retreats were held, and I felt right at home.

In the broad front hall there was a telephone on a small table; in a small office to the right of the entrance there was another desk, bookcases, filing cabinets and a few chairs, all unremarkable in design and very tidy. The second and third storeys were designated as residential quarters, where at any given time a dozen people lived, some locals, some from out of town.

The main entrance led to a double room that I imagined was long ago used as a formal living room, perhaps with a grand piano placed near the generous double doors that gave onto the terrace. This room was used for large classes, and other than a scattering of pillows on the floor, it was unfurnished. The room that caught my eye was the kitchen, complete with state-of-the-art appliances, ample workspace and all manner of food, supplies and kitchen tools organized with ship-shape precision.

The introductory meeting was held in the front office, where a row of chairs had been set up for the half dozen visitors. Glenda, a slender woman with short, sandy-coloured hair, who looked to be in her early thirties, and Sebastian, a younger man, tall and lanky with a mischievous air that I found to be both amusing and attractive, each took turns introducing the teachings of the school. This was the path of the mind, in which self-awareness and self-determination were taught. Progress was achieved with the help of a variety of meditation exercises, mantras and mental disciplines. The teachings reflected an eclectic blend of esoteric and metaphysical wisdom from Eastern and Western schools, including Christian mysticism, theosophy, Sufism, Buddhism and shamanism.

The school had been instituted by Walter Darnley, a man about whom little was known, at least by those outside the inner circle. From what Elliot told me, Walter had been approached by a mysterious man who one day simply appeared on his doorstep and informed him that he must start this school. Elliot knew nothing else about the man, nor did he seem to care how the school had been started. Walter referred to it as the School of the Mind, and its students were referred to as Mind Warriors. The structure and focus of the thought system I was introduced to that evening fascinated me, and I immediately signed up. I was intrigued by its broad, all-inclusive philosophy and particularly anxious to uncover the hidden powers of my mind.

Excited with my new job, earning a full-time salary, and enthralled by the discovery of a bold new spirituality, my time with Ghanshyam and my life at the Palmistry Institute quickly faded into the past.[1] In charge of introducing beginners to the teachings of the school, Sebastian became my new teacher. He was an eccentric Aquarian who took pleasure in freely expressing his opinions, while, at the same time, he encouraged us to express our own views. Sebastian was open-minded, highly intelligent and perceptive, quick-witted and friendly, and, above all, he didn't take himself too seriously. For a spiritual person, this was refreshing. I felt an instant attraction to him, something I hadn't felt in a long time, but while I waited for a spark of interest on his part, I learned that he was gay. Six years later, I would learn that he had died of an AIDS-related illness, news that I would have difficulty accepting, given his advanced level of self-awareness and spiritual learning. How could someone with so much spiritual knowledge allow himself to die at such a young age? In my naive idealism, I equated spirituality with good health and protection from the tragedies of life.

As Mind Warriors, we were encouraged to explore the teachings for ourselves, to question our perceptions and to look for the broader purpose of our existence through our experiences. In fact, at least in my experience as a beginning student, this school handed out very little metaphysics, and the little it did provide was then immediately redirected toward an experiential component. Our instructions were: Do the exercises and experience the results for yourself. At times, I found this to be a bit frustrating, always curi-

---

1. This was a number 1 Personal Year, typical of new beginnings and moving forward.

ous as to the how and why of what was being taught. But I did as instructed, without questioning.

There were three rules of behaviour that we were to apply whenever we interacted with others: smile; offer a handshake, a kiss or a friendly touch; and find a quality in the person within the first ten seconds. Love was acknowledged as the uniting and universal principle and service was the means of manifesting that love. We were taught the importance of paying attention to our thoughts and our intentions in all our actions and interactions, but, for the rest, there were no other specific requirements.

During one intensive weekend workshop, we were introduced to the Silva Mind Control method, a practical approach that I thoroughly enjoyed. At the end of the weekend, we were assigned an exercise, which at first I thought I could not complete. Having been instructed to bring with us three pieces of paper on which were written the names of three people we knew who were in need of healing, we were then told to split up into groups of three and exchange papers with each other. I was grouped with Elliot and another fellow whose name I no longer remember.

We were instructed to go to our special place in our minds that we used for healing, referred to as our *lab*. There, we were to focus on one of the names, allowing images to arise without resistance or interpretation, then we were to wait for guidance on the person's health or medical issue. We then shared what we had seen and experienced with our partners, who would in turn validate our perceptions.

Although I cannot recall which names I wrote on my papers, I do remember the experience I had with two of the cases I had been given. The first one stuck in my memory because he looked very much like the premier of our province at the time. My partner laughed when I gave my description, for apparently he did indeed look like Premier Bourassa. Although I do not recall this person's health issue, perhaps something to do with an injured leg, I do remember being surprised that I was most definitely in the right ballpark.

My next case was even more interesting. Sitting comfortably in my chair in the semi-darkened room, I closed my eyes and went to that place in my mind we had been taught to use for diagnosis and healing purposes. My lab consisted of nothing more than a narrow bed covered by a white fitted sheet. The room was painted white and the lighting, though diffuse, was bright and had an organic quality about it so that it was impossible to tell its source. Normally, I would imagine my "patient" lying on the bed, call on my healing guides—which, given my lack of any psychic ability, were little more than nondescript beings dressed in white—and together we would apply a healing technique, usually an energetic sweeping or magnetic therapy of sorts. Since all of this occurred in the privacy of my mind, I felt quite comfortable making up whatever needed to be made up at the time.

Back in my lab, I focused on the name of the woman from my slip of paper. Almost instantly, I found myself in another place, where I saw a surprisingly clear image of an elderly woman, petite of stature, apparently in the best of health, with clear eyes and a lively disposition. She was climbing a wooden staircase, heading toward a brightly lit upper floor, and seemed content, even joyful. Then I became aware of a commotion coming from the bottom of the stairs. The woman turned and smiled lovingly at a young man and a woman who were arguing heatedly on the landing below. Unperturbed, she turned and continued toward the brightly lit room upstairs.

At a loss to understand what I had seen, I described my vision to Elliot who had given me this case. He chuckled, but was clearly as surprised as I was. He explained that he had played a trick on me. Apparently my case study was not ill at all. In fact, he had given me the name of his aunt who had passed away just three days before. It appeared that her remaining survivors were quibbling over how to dispose of her belongings. Although no one in the group that day considered themselves to be particularly psychic, during that exercise, everyone fared remarkably well. Apparently, given the appropriate circumstances, we are far more capable of extra-sensory or psychic experiences than we might think.

My life started to come together during that first year as a Mind Warrior. My health issues cleared up, I enjoyed a regular paycheque and I felt that I had found a spiritual path that was giving me a sense of peace and inner strength. It was at the Mind Warriors that I met Mike, my husband-to-be, and although I cannot say that I was head-over-heels in love with Mike, a Capricorn, I liked him very much. We had great fun together, and we became the best of friends. Most importantly, he too was a spiritual seeker.

Mike and I shared a love of music, his pop and my traditional jazz intersecting where Ben Sidran and Mose Allison met. Through him, I discovered Michael Franks and Kenny Rankin, who would always remain among my favourites. In the fall of '77, I bought my dad's '68 Cutlass, and, the following summer, we travelled to the Magdalen Islands. We spent hours making cassettes of our favourite artists for the long drive, adding the element of music to the breathtaking beauty of the scenery. It was a wonderful trip during which I also had the opportunity to indulge my passion for photography. Things were looking up. There was light on the horizon; darkness was fading into memory. On our return to Montreal, Mike received word that he had been accepted into an MBA program at a university in southern Ontario. When he asked whether I would go with him, I agreed to do so. But needing the security of marriage, I said I would go as his wife. Less than two months later, we were married and on our way to London.

This was an exciting time, and I felt an optimism and a joy of living I had not felt for quite a while. We moved into a brand new unit in a housing complex for students. I played house—cooking, cleaning and decorating to my heart's content. I had finally left home and was starting a life of my own. London was a lovely small town, surrounded by a patchwork of orchards and farm fields, and it reminded me of my childhood in Lac Saint-Jean. It was a simple, peaceful existence. I felt profoundly satisfied with my new life. Though still insecure, shy and fearful, with Mike by my side,

I felt capable of dealing with grown-up life. When we went out, I never left his side for very long. In fact, most of the time, my arm was hooked tightly through his. People must have thought that I was the ultimate clinger—and I was. Not eager to attract attention, I was happy to remain in his shadow.

Barely a month after moving to London, I discovered that I was pregnant. This was a bit of a shocker, since I honestly and quite naively believed that following the rhythm method was a safe form of contraception. Though unexpected, this turn of events gave a whole new meaning and direction to my life, a change that I embraced with great glee. The birth of my daughter Natalie was my next big life-changing event. From the moment she was born, she became the central focus of my life. Mike was consumed with his studies, and I busied myself with my daughter. For a time, she was the sunshine that kept the shadows of my life at bay.

When not otherwise busy with cooking and cleaning, I participated in activities organized by the MBA Wives Club, where I learned to quilt and make all manner of crafts for the home. Wherever I went, Natalie came with me. She was a beautiful baby with a wonderful, friendly personality, always eager for the attention of strangers and passersby. I was very proud of my daughter and felt comfortable in my new life, thoroughly enjoying my function as mother and homemaker. After all, this had been my mother's chosen life path, and it had worked out quite well for her. So, why not for me?

Even though I very much enjoyed my two years of the simple, small-town family life, I sensed the call of unfinished business on the spiritual front. One of the first things I did upon our return to Montreal was to resume my studies with the Mind Warriors. Mike attended a few meetings, but soon expressed his disinterest. He didn't need it, he said. Unlike me, he was quite content to be who he was, how he was and where he was, and therefore saw no purpose in changing anything. He had a career, an enviable education, a wife and a daughter, and a great place to come home to after a long day at work. In a way, I might have envied his contentment and confidence, but I understood that we were different. At the same time, I was profoundly saddened to learn that I would continue my spiritual quest alone. It had been so important for me to share the journey with my life partner.

Upon my return to the Mount Royal School of Ancient Wisdom, I learned that Walter had stepped in to replace Sebastian as instructor. I never knew where he went or why he left, and I wished I could have spoken with him. I wanted to know how he could leave a school that offered such fascinating teachings. Walter's powerful personality was expressed in his strong Capricorn leadership style; he naturally commanded respect and, for some people, a certain awe. Although I never placed him on a pedestal, I sensed that he knew things, secret things about the meaning of life and its origins that I desperately wanted to know. So when we were assigned an initiation trial at the beginning of the season, I eagerly signed on. I would try anything if it would bring me closer to that knowing.

The initiation was held in the large room on a Saturday afternoon. There were at least a dozen in attendance that day. We were instructed to lie on the floor, on a mat or a blanket, and were allowed a pillow beneath our head and ankles and a blanket for warmth. Our instructions were simple and concise: we were to lie on our backs with eyes closed, without moving a single muscle, without even blinking and definitely without falling asleep. Simply, we were told to maintain this state of immobility for four hours. Despite the burst of burning pain that flooded my joints when we were told that the four hours were up and we could begin to move, all I could do was smile. I had done it. I felt as though I could do anything.

The next two years of Mind Warrior training were captivating. Compared to the relaxed style of Sebastian's class, Walter's was more rigorous and disciplined. We were taught some highly engaging meditation techniques that required Zen-like focus and discipline, couched in a metaphysics that centred on the smallness of our own identities in contrast with the vastness of the Infinite. While participation in exercises and activities was always optional, if we did choose to participate, we were expected to be impeccable in attitude and practice, one of the principal attributes of a Mind Warrior. We were taught to always be ready to serve and to maintain a *how can I be of help* attitude. Another requirement was that we remain vigilant for our thoughts and to become increasingly aware of our responsibility in creating the world of our experience. We were to do things and express ourselves through the filter of the highest expression, which was love. One of our mantras was simply the word "love" which we were encouraged to maintain in the back of our awareness at all times. We were *mind warriors*, always on the lookout for those thoughts that might interfere with our goal of love and service.

Mantras, or affirmations, as they are more commonly known today, were an integral part of our practice at the school. Typically, they expressed a desired positive attribute, such as "I am impeccable in all my actions and thoughts." We were required to repeat a mantra sixteen thousand times, a number whose esoteric significance I never learned. Most members carried counters around with them, like the ones used by ushers at large public events. My counter was always in my pocket. I actually wore one out and had to replace it.

It did not matter that I didn't understand the theory behind many of the exercises we were given nor the broader metaphysics of the school, although I suspected this information was available to the more privileged inner circle. What I understood was that the purpose of our training was to raise our level of consciousness, to bring us closer to that level attained by Jesus, the Christ Consciousness. As Gurdjieff taught, we were asleep, and if we were ever to rise to a higher level of consciousness, we needed to practise total focus, discipline and self-awareness. Without being told how or why, we were made aware of the fact that we were responsible for our state of unconsciousness and it was given to us to change it, if we so desired. Despite a lack of metaphysical foundation, I believed I got the gist of the teachings, sensing truth in the idea that I was asleep and needed to awaken and, although I did not understand much else, this was enough for me. I wanted to experience the Christ Consciousness.

Despite my limited understanding, I did enjoy the mentally and physically challenging disciplines. So when we were instructed to hold a particular Zen posture for thirty-minute segments for several hours at time without moving a muscle, I learned to put the physical discomfort aside. When we were guided to go back in time to revisit past lives, I set aside my doubts and clearly saw myself in other bodies, in other times. When we were instructed to visit a planet in another dimension of time and space, I went along for the ride and had an experience that was surprisingly similar to that of the others in the group. Later, when we were assigned a seven-hour immobility trial, despite the fact that I was eight months pregnant, I did as instructed.

After the first couple of months, we were divided into three smaller groups of nine or ten members. Each was assigned a different teacher. We were told that we would continue our studies with our new teacher for the remainder of the year. I belonged to Richard's group, a tall, quiet man in his early thirties I had not met before. Not long after our group had formed, we were assigned a special exercise, one that, it was claimed, Jesus had practised when he was a student of metaphysics. It was a challenging exercise requiring total focus and a certain amount of mental gymnastics. I felt so privileged to be given an exercise practised by my long-time hero Jesus, that, if asked, I think I would have tried to walk on water.

To begin with, we were given a mantra, a short prayer that we were to memorize and repeat seventy-five times a day while doing simple chores. Every other week or so, we were given another mental task to apply while we repeated the mantra, such as visualizing pure light around the cup or around ourselves. We added the thought of love, and then were instructed to join with the person who had made the cup. As we successfully integrated each new mental action into our daily exercise, new tasks were added. Over a period of nearly two years, one other member of the group and I had accumulated twenty-two of these mental tasks. All the while, during my daily practice periods, I felt privileged to be close to Jesus. One day, I will find my way home, I will be with Jesus, I told myself, believing that these exercises would lead me there.

During a weekend workshop, we were given specific information about ourselves, information that related to our personal level of spiritual development, past life influences and qualities that belonged to our higher selves. According to Walter Darnley, my planetary connection was with earth, making me an old soul of sorts, my unique ability was healing and I possessed seven bodies. The age of my soul and healing ability were not really news to me, but learning that I had seven bodies was.

According to the more esoteric teachings of this school, a person could have up to ten bodies. In this hierarchical structure, a person with four or five bodies was considered to be at an average level of evolution; six or seven bodies indicated above average spiritual development. The eighth and ninth bodies belonged to highly evolved beings who were on their way to enlightenment. The attainment of ten bodies was reserved for the fully enlightened such as Jesus.

Bodies, it seemed, were not easily acquired. In fact, we were told that it could take hundreds—even thousands of lifetimes to acquire a single body. This was distressing news, since it meant that I wasn't very far along the evolutionary path and the way I saw it, the journey home would be excruciatingly long. This bit of information about my seven bodies did not please me much, but I didn't let it hold me back. In fact, it made me even more determined to find a way of getting around this complicated evolutionary process.

Throughout this period, I continued to enjoy my role of mother and homemaker. I sewed cute dresses for Natalie, and continued with quilting and home crafts. As much as I would have liked to share my experiences with my life partner, in order to keep the peace, I kept my spiritual life to myself. As long as I didn't openly discuss subjects like astrology and reincarnation, subjects which I continued to read about, I was accepted by my in-laws. It was a small price to pay for having a normal life and for fitting in, and, for a few years, I experienced a certain sense of belonging.

One evening, we were having dinner at a restaurant with friends. After more than twenty-five years, I still remember that moment—that hunch—clearly. We were sitting at a booth by the window and had just ordered our smoked meat platters, when it occurred to me that I was pregnant. I was not late yet, but that didn't matter. I knew it with absolute certainty. The birth of Caroline the following spring was the next important joyous event of my life.

The one area of my life that was not so joyful was my marriage. In fact, it was becoming quite clear that, despite our solid foundation as friends and parents, we would never relate on that deeper level for which I yearned. Mike was a great person, reliable, intelligent and devoted to his family and friends, but we were just not on the same page spiritually, and it was becoming increasingly difficult for me to continue to pretend to be the happy wife.

As a last resort, in search of a solution to my marital problems, I sought guidance from my spiritual mentor. Although I would have preferred to resolve the problem on my own, I believed that Walter Darnley could help me find a way to live in harmony with my husband. We met in the small front office where I had first been introduced to the Mind Warriors. Walter listened with kindness and without judgment as I explained my situation. I told him about my unhappiness with my marriage and how I desperately wanted to find a solution to make it work. In my mind, divorce was most definitely not an option. Once I had finished telling my story, Walter surprised me by inquiring about the state of our sex life. Embarrassed, I murmured that it had become non-existent. He nodded, and acknowledged that he understood my situation very well and knew exactly what I was looking for. Instantly, I felt encouraged. Yes, I thought to myself, there *was* a solution.

Then Walter explained that what I was really seeking was *power*, and this was certainly something with which he could help. In order to accomplish this, however, I would need to unblock my sexual energy. Having worked with chakras before and understanding that the sex chakra was intimately tied to personal power as well as creativity, I saw nothing wrong with this line of reasoning.

To make his point, he offered to perform a test on my arm. At first, I thought it was a joke, the old schoolyard trick, only Walter wasn't joking. As instructed, I focused on his fingers while he made small rotations from my wrist up the inside of my fore-arm toward my elbow. Unlike the childhood experiment, this one had an entirely different impact. I was totally unprepared for the burst of fire that exploded from the base of my spine and shot up my back to the top of my head. I believe that, had I found him to be the slightest bit attractive, I would have jumped his bones right then and there.

Seeing that his experiment had worked, he then laid out his proposal. Very matter-of-factly, he told me that he would be happy to teach me how to access my true power if I was willing to work with him for a year, which, by necessity, would require the practice of certain sexual acts with him. "Call me if you decide that this is what you want to do," he said, as casually as though we had been discussing the weather on a slow day at work. On that note, our meeting ended.

When I left the School that evening, I was in shock, excited, energized yet, at the same time, incredibly bewildered. This was most definitely not what I had expected. I was profoundly disappointed that I was no further ahead in my quest for a way to mend my failing marriage. I couldn't hide from the truth that the idea of tapping into my power thrilled me, but then it was disturbing to learn that my power was to be found at the tip of this man's pecker. I did not believe that this is what Jesus would have told one of his followers in need of guidance.

For days after that encounter I continued to feel the intense aftershocks of that jolt to my lower chakra and as the days passed I began to allow myself to consider the possibility that Walter's proposal might be the solution to my problems. Still desperate to save my marriage, I even discussed this with Mike, presenting it as a sexual therapy of sorts. Although the thought of having sex with that man actually repulsed me, I felt I was ready to try anything, and so I decided to make the call.

Gathering up my courage, I dialed the number for the Mount Royal School of Ancient Wisdom. The woman who answered explained that Walter could not be reached at the moment, and then asked if I wanted to leave a message. As I was about to give my name and number, I felt a presence reach out over my right shoulder and arm, guiding me to lower the receiver. This was *not* the way, it seemed to say. "No thank you," I replied, and hung up the phone.

Instantly, I came to my senses. I felt shame for having even entertained those thoughts, but also relief and a sense of having been protected. Clearly, a bad outcome had been averted. The entire episode had been so surreal, that after a while, I had trouble believing that it had actually happened. Walter had been my spiritual mentor, filled with knowledge of things ancient and spiritual. I had been taught exercises that Jesus had practised. This was supposed to be the way home, the way to truth, the way to peace.

The devastation of this turn of events was profound, and would leave its mark for many years to come. As eager as I was to continue with the Mind Warrior program, something had changed for me that day, and it wasn't long before I decided that it was, once again, time to move on. The following session of Mind Warrior training began without me.

> It is quite possible to reach God. In fact it is very easy, because it is the most natural thing in the world. You might even say it is the only natural thing in the world. The way will open, if you believe that it is possible. (W-pI.41.8:1–4)

Chapter 7

FOR THE LOVE OF A SHAMAN

You are not special. If you think you are, and would defend your specialness against the truth of what you really are, how can you know the truth? (T-24.II.4:1–2)

*A*fter leaving the Mind Warriors, I settled back into my role as mother and homemaker. Between caring for the girls and sewing and cooking, there was little time for contemplating the meaning of life, a small blessing of sorts. For the next couple of years, I was relieved of the urge to turn everything upside down in search of the elusive truth. Instead, I became increasingly interested in the healing arts, and signed up for courses in herbology and reflexology, and read everything I could find on alternative health techniques.

I researched all manner of healthy living and eating options in order to give my daughters the best start possible. The "I can do it myself" theme of my personal symphony came into its full glory as I made my own tofu, sprouts, fermentations, herbal blends and cough syrups. My kitchen was a veritable laboratory. I fancied myself a healer of sorts and learned to work with magnetism and reflexology, techniques that allowed me to relieve the girls of most passing ailments without having to resort to conventional medicine. At that point, I had begun to consider returning to school to study medicine. To me, healing was the noblest of practices, and although I had no illusions about becoming a real healer, my small victories over illness gave me a sense of connection with the great healers like Jesus and Edgar Cayce.

When Caroline was around six months old, she came down with what I immediately recognized as the symptoms of the croup. As the hours passed, her breathing grew more laboured, and her cough became increasingly raspy. Having been through this with Natalie, I knew she would need to see a pediatrician for antibiotics. It was late, and Mike and Natalie were fast asleep. While inhaling cold air was one of the remedies for croup, that night it was far too cold to open a window. As Caroline struggled more and more with each breath, I knew I had to do something. One thing was certain: I really did not feel like spending the night in the hospital emergency ward, and, if I waited until morning, I would have to make arrangements for a sitter for Natalie.

With few appealing options, I decided to take matters in hand. Sitting in the bentwood rocker with Caroline pressed gently against my breast, I closed my eyes and connected with that place in my heart that I knew represented the deep love I felt for my daughter. Almost instantly, a warm energy began to flow from me into her tiny body, and I said to her, sweetly and lovingly, but with the utmost certainty: "We don't need this." I rocked her gently, adding, "We really don't." Bound by the simple warmth and wholeness of a mother's love for her child, we fell asleep in the rocker. The following morning, Caroline's symptoms had completely disappeared. It had been a simple, normal thing to do, I thought, something any loving parent could do, and I gave it no further thought.

When I wasn't in the kitchen, I was sewing clothes for the girls or designing quilts and all sorts of handicrafts for the house. I was surprised and received a much-needed boost of confidence when I sold two of my quilts at a fair at the downtown YMCA. Being able to do things on my own gave me a tremendous sense of satisfaction. Remaining constantly busy also served to cover the dark void that I knew too well lurked just beneath the surface of my worldly existence.

As my mother had done with us so many years earlier, I made books and music abundantly available to the girls. There was rarely a minute of the day when the house wasn't filled with the strains of a Chopin Sonata, a Beethoven Concerto or some light jazz or even occasional pop. For myself, I had discovered the healing power of music, and whenever I felt particularly down or anxious, I played the music of Kenny Rankin, whom I had affectionately named my personal Valium. I think had it not been for the soft, lyrical strains of his soothing voice and music, there were moments during those years when I might have exploded with frustration and desperation. Although I enjoyed my life with the girls, I was aware that I was suppressing a deeper yearning, my original quest for truth.

Caroline was a year old when I met Ghanshyam in the park. It was a summer fair, with tables and exhibits of all sorts scattered throughout the park. I was surprised to spot the Palmistry Institute's banner above one of these tables. Although this was the first time I'd seen him since leaving the Institute, Ghanshyam greeted me with the same broad smile and hearty hug I remembered so well. While one of his helpers made prints of Caroline's palms, I gave him a rundown of what I had been up to, mentioning that I had been accepted at university and that my intention was to complete an undergraduate degree, and then pursue studies in medicine. My passion for the healing arts had cleared away my fear of academia. He listened patiently, then, when I was done, he shook his head. With that knowing look that had so captivated me years earlier, he said simply, "I still think you would have made a great astrologer."

It seemed like an innocent comment, made in passing, but it resonated like a Tibetan gong, reverberating throughout my entire being. On my return home that day, I began to rethink the decisions I had made for my future, remembering well my true passion. I was older, more mature and now had some life experience under my belt, essential ingredients for the practice of astrology. The New Age was in full bloom. Whereas years earlier when I first began to study astrology there were very few books available, and what was available was very esoteric and occult in nature, now there was an explosion of new material on bookstore shelves. It was with a profound sense of relief that I abandoned the idea of pursuing medical studies, deciding to focus on astrology instead, no doubt a sound decision, given my bleak academic track record. My interests lay in alternative healing methods; traditional medical school would not have allowed me to develop or practise any of these approaches.

I scoured the local bookstores and journals for new astrology books and started to build a new collection of charts. Over the next couple of years, between family and household chores, I read voraciously. Still in search of the right course of study, I signed up with the Faculty of Astrological Studies in England and further immersed myself in my studies.

My profound unhappiness with my marriage eventually grew unbearable. Totally focused on my daughters and my family, there were no longer any spiritual connections in my life. I had no teachers, no guidance and no direction. At the end of my first Pinnacle[1] and in a number 9 Personal Year, I felt lost, confused and alone. In search of answers once more, I sought out the advice of Deena, a friend from the Astrological Society of Montreal. She recommended the astrologer's astrologer—Arthur Griffin. This was the man I needed to see, she affirmed in no uncertain terms.

With great trepidation, on September 12, 1985, I drove to my appointment with the astrologer's astrologer. I was excited and at the same time apprehensive. Would this experience be like my first meeting with the palmist? Would he reveal important things about my life, confirming my decision to become an astrologer? Would he be able to help with my marital problems? What would he see in my future?

I arrived exactly on time, as was my custom. Arthur's office was in a ground-floor apartment in a turn-of-the-century building in a newly chic part of town. He welcomed me with a boyishly shy but friendly smile, his manner quiet, yet very self-assured. The

---

1. See *The Power of Time*, "The Long-Term Cycles," page 173.

office was in the large front room, what would normally have been used as a living room. There was a huge bay window filled with an assortment of very healthy tropical plants facing the street. The office was simply decorated with floor to ceiling bookshelves made of planks supported by bricks. The large sheet of tempered glass that served as a desk was covered with books, pens, papers, an overflowing ashtray and a mug of hot coffee. The smell of books and stale cigarettes permeated the air and I felt instantly at home.

Arthur was a contemporary shaman of sorts, claiming to have been initiated by his grandmother into the secret mysteries of life. He laid out for me a fascinating metaphysics, dividing the major spiritual thought systems into broad categories that included those that were based on principles of oneness with a goal of merging with the source, and those that were based on individuation. He described the virtues of the path that he followed and taught, a path not unlike that of the Mind Warriors in its focus on self-aware-ness, but quite unlike the Mind Warriors and anything else I had ever studied in its total emphasis on creativity, self-determination, specialness, personal power and direct control over life and des-tiny. According to Arthur, the truly advanced person could have the power to create whatever they desired in life. In his system of knowledge, there was no hierarchy of evolution, and a person could develop as many spiritual bodies as they needed. My seven-body limitation was now a thing of the past. Naturally, this new thought system appealed to me without question.

That consultation with Arthur marked the start of my next sig-nificant stop along the spiritual buffet line. In fact, it was prob-ably the most captivating four hours I had ever spent with another person in my entire life. Unexpectedly, I fell head over heels for both this refreshing and liberating—and certainly very liberal—new philosophy of life, as well as for this fascinating and original Aquarian. A long-time student of all things esoteric and occult, there seemed to be no end to his knowledge about the subjects I had pursued all my life. He had answers for all my questions. During that meeting, a very deep bond emerged, where I felt as though we had known each other for a very long time. Throughout the evening, the air between us grew hot and electric. It was a struggle to tear myself away from him and return to my life as mother, wife and homemaker.

Over the following weeks, all I could think of was Arthur. Nearly two months later, we crossed paths at an astrology seminar. To my surprise, I could barely stand to be in the same room with him. We exchanged brief greetings, then, with knees shaking and heart racing, I scurried to the opposite end of the room, as far from him as possible. At the break, I avoided him entirely, something that was not difficult to accomplish since he seemed to constantly be surrounded by admirers, mostly female. At the end of the seminar, I snuck away unseen, and, upon returning home, blocked out as best I could the thought of this man. The battle between common sense and raging infatuation was fierce; it was a battle I feared I could not win.

It was a Friday morning in late January of the following year; I had just finished running errands with Caroline while Natalie was at preschool. As I was struggling with my keys to unlock the door to the apartment, I heard the telephone ring inside. Finally the lock gave way and the door opened. I hurried into the bedroom with one hand extended to grab the receiver, when these words came to mind: "All I need now is for Arthur Griffin to call and fuck up my life completely." Although the F-word was not at all a part of my vocabulary, it was a prominent part of Arthur's.

As it turned out, it was one of those hunches. Arthur didn't waste time with idle chit-chat.

"I'm calling to see if you'd like to get together for dinner sometime." He sounded calm and collected.

Meanwhile, I felt as though my stomach had fallen right through the floor. My response was cold, no doubt a desperate attempt at self-preservation, the only way I could prevent myself from going into the infatuation neurosis I felt I had successfully tamed.

"Regarding?" I said, surprised I could actually get one word out.

Evidently unperturbed by my icy response, he explained in his inimitable quiet voice that it would be nice to get together and chat.

In one single instant, self-preservation and everything I valued—home, family and marriage—went out the window.

"Okay," I replied.

The following Saturday I went to dinner with Arthur. He brought me to a wonderful Chinese restaurant on Saint-Denis, a trendy strip just off the downtown core. What little food I did manage to eat was delicious. Arthur was a wine connoisseur and had chosen a lovely Clos Saint-Odile to go with our meal. It was perfect. Tongue-tied, I asked questions, which he was only too eager and pleased to answer. Ten years my senior, extremely well-read and with a renaissance education, he knew so much more about life than I did. He had an extensive knowledge of mythology, history, alchemy, magic, spirituality and the world religions, subjects he spoke of with great authority and unusual insight. I was captivated. While he talked, I watched in amazement as images of faces that I understood to be faces from past lives in which we had previously met flowed between us like pictures from a film projector. Well, it was either past lives, I reasoned, or too much Clos. Try as I might, any resistance I may have felt dissipated and I fell totally and completely in love that night. To my surprise, the feeling was mutual.

Five excruciating months later, I packed up the girls and left my unhappy marriage to go live with the man with whom I was infatuated. Over the next couple of years, I deepened my knowledge and understanding of astrology in a way that I could never have done on my own or with any other school. According to Arthur, I had great potential both as a workshop facilitator and as an astrologer, and he was instrumental in pushing me forward with my career. To this day, I owe much of my accomplishments to his constant encouragement and support.

His broad psychological insights gave him a unique approach to astrology, enabling him to quickly tap into the core of a person's life journey. He was able to easily puzzle out the reasons behind a person's actions and the causes of inner blockages and conflict.

When he wasn't practising or teaching astrology, he gave workshops in which he taught his unique brand of metaphysics and spirituality of individuation, making extensive use of guided inner voyages and rituals. In a short time, he had taught me enough so that I was facilitating workshops of my own, as well as doing one-on-one work with individuals using these guided inner voyage techniques.

Contrary to all the other paths I had followed, in this new brand of spirituality, there was no hierarchy of advancement, no need for lengthy periods of prayer and devotion or meditation, no abstinence or sacrifice. There was no sin for which to atone, therefore no need for suffering or punishment. Unlike the more secretive nature of the teachings of the Mind Warriors, Arthur was very open and eager to share his impressive knowledge. He seemed to have read every book available on the occult, alchemy and spirituality, including texts in their original Greek and Latin versions. For the million-and-one questions I asked, he had answers, a refreshing experience, as my thirst for knowledge seemed unquenchable.

His philosophy was centred on individual will, desire, knowledge and the removal of blockages through creative inner journeys, mental focus and intention. This was not a spirituality of deprivation. On the contrary, the sky was the limit in terms of potential accomplishment, and life was to be lived to the fullest, guilt-free, pain-free and free of struggle. If anything, it was an easy and approachable thought system, if not brazenly hedonistic.

According to my new teacher, those religions and philosophies that taught the principles of oneness and unity with God were ancient history. Belonging to the Age of Pisces,[2] they were in fact in direct opposition to the more sophisticated and modern thought

---

2. The concept of Ages, or Eras, is found in ancient esoteric and astrological works and refers to periods determined by the precession of the equinoxes, the apparent backwards movement of the polar axis through the signs of the zodiac, a process that takes about 25,000 years to complete. An Age lasts about 2,000 years. Although experts differ on the exact start and end dates of each Age, it is generally accepted that we are presently leaving the Age of Pisces and entering Aquarius.

systems that were beginning to emerge, the new thought systems of the Age of Aquarius.

Arthur postulated that as one Age approaches its end, the next one gradually begins to emerge in an overlapping process that can take up to 300 or 400 years. Throughout a particular Age, the thought systems that best reflect the qualities and values of the sign, for good or for ill, usually a combination of both, become the predominating influences of that period. The Pisces Age, ruled by Neptune, was associated with universal truth, the collective unconscious, universal love, the search for an experience of oneness with the whole, and sacrifice of self for other. It embodied the myth of the sacrificial lamb, Jesus, sacrificed by his Father, sent to die on the Cross so we could all be saved from sin.

Given this context, it is clear why the Catholic Church became as popular as it did during this period, offering salvation for the masses in exchange for allegiance to the "one" church. Obey the Church, atone for your sins, repent and you will be saved. It promised salvation for all, including the sick, the poor, the oppressed masses and the powerless. Other than simple blind faith and obedience, little or no effort was required.

Arthur held very strong opinions about the Ages, and himself an Aquarian, he naturally favoured the attributes of that sign. According to him, Christianity was at the root of much of what had gone wrong in the world for the past 2,000 years. On the other hand, the Age of Aquarius, ruled by Uranus, reflects qualities that are essentially opposed to the universality and oneness of Pisces, ruled by Neptune, the dissolver of boundaries. While Aquarius is commonly defined as the sign of humanitarianism, it is individualistic at its core. It resonates with eccentricity, self-determination, uniqueness and specialness. In fact, the very idea of abandoning self for the *all* is fundamentally antithetical to the profoundly self-deterministic nature of Aquarius. Instead, it seeks to manifest its uniqueness and individuality on its own, with a community of people who share common interests, or within a group that supports uniqueness and individuality.

As a staunch individualist, Arthur positioned himself as a leader in this new Aquarian movement, dedicating his life to ensuring that the proper values would be well-established at the start of the New Age. In many ways, with a strong Aquarian influence of my own, I liked this approach, for it validated who I was in my own uniqueness and made me feel not only at home and accepted, but also very special.

> The special ones are all asleep, surrounded by a world of loveliness they do not see. Freedom and peace and joy stand there, beside the bier on which they sleep, and call them to come forth and waken from their dream of death. Yet they hear nothing. They are lost in dreams of specialness. (T-24.III.7:1–4)

Another unique aspect of this spirituality was the absence of a human-like God concept. There was a universal, essential energy, a power source that could be tapped into by anyone who knew how, but there was no distinct God who dictated the course of events in the world from on high. In a way, I was okay with this notion too, since I had been unable to reconcile the state of affairs in the world with the idea of an omniscient God who had power over the same world. If He truly had this power over the world, would He not have done something about its inequities long ago?

Arthur was a big proponent of manifesting what he called personal power, and as a tool for attracting and manifesting what he desired in life, he made extensive use of rituals. He adapted ancient esoteric practices combined with the symbols from various mythologies to form rituals that he felt were more appropriate for the needs of the day. A ritual typically consisted of the construction of a pentagram, usually skilfully illustrated with carefully selected colours, along with a text that clearly stated the goal and intention of the ritual.

That summer we celebrated our partnership with a beautiful joining ritual performed in the garden behind our house with family and friends. Although I found rituals fun to create and could appreciate the principles behind their design and purpose, my lingering Catholic conditioning prevented me from fully accepting the validity of a ritual outside the Catholic Mass. Though interesting, creative and even entertaining, they did not give me the sense of closeness to God that I had experienced while sitting in quiet contemplation on a church bench.

There was also the fact that I remained uncomfortable with the idea of manipulating my own fate. Even though I did not know what to make of God, I preferred to leave things at least partially in His hands, or in those of my guiding forces, not entirely convinced that I really knew what was best for me. In leaving the door at least partially open to higher guidance, I felt that even if I screwed up really badly, there was still hope that I might be rescued. For many years, *Into your hands oh Lord, I commend my spirit* had been one of my favourite prayers, and though long since abandoned, it is a prayer whose faint refrain would remain for a long time at the edge of my awareness. Holding on to a wisp of hope that there was in fact a force that was greater than me, a God who knew what I really needed, I resisted taking full control of the direction of my life.

It was a perfect August day; not a cloud was in the sky. Never before having performed a ritual in public, I felt more than a bit nervous. Before joining our guests in the garden, we rehearsed the text of our ritual one final time. That was when, to Arthur's surprise and, I would later learn, to his profound chagrin, I changed the last line of my vows, replacing "forever" with "for as long as this relationship serves us well." Because this was not something I had planned on doing, I was just as surprised as Arthur, perhaps even more so, since I believed I had met the love of my life—my true soulmate. Even though I did not fully believe in the power of rituals, I could not make a declaration that I knew deep down I could not honour. We performed our ritual, as planned in the garden, but with the alternate ending.

Misgivings notwithstanding, this was an exciting time. It was the mid-eighties, and astrology was experiencing a major revival. We were frequent visitors at the local New Age bookstores, where new titles appeared on shelves every month. As Arthur was a celebrity of sorts in the community, we were always greeted warmly. This made me feel special. On one of these visits, while Arthur was chatting with the bookstore owner, I wandered off in search of what new book might pique my interest. On the top shelf of a bookcase toward the back of the store a row of books attracted my attention. It was a course of some sort, and always in search of new learning, I reached for a copy. It had a beautifully bound navy blue cover with gold writing: *A Course in Miracles*. The course part intrigued me, but already struggling with rituals, I wasn't keen on more magic. Besides, I thought as I flipped through the pages, it had small print and lots of words and was written in an ancient, formal style of English that looked very difficult to read, so I replaced it on the shelf.

Arthur and I were inseparable. We merged our families—my two daughters and his son, we worked together, shared dreams for the future, attended events together. We even spoke at an astrology conference in New York together. He had total faith in me, supporting me in all my endeavours, and when I shared with him my old dream of writing, he had nothing but words of encouragement. Arthur was a doer. "Just do it," he said, without hesitation.

With his support, I picked up contracts for horoscope columns in local papers; seeing my ideas on paper gave me a great boost of validation. Arthur was a great fan of science-fiction, and, although not my genre, he introduced me to the writings of Marion Zimmer Bradley and Barbara Michaels. These authors further fuelled my desire to become a writer, and encouraged by Arthur, who seemed to think I could do anything I wanted, I thought seriously about writing a novel.

Arthur had a well-established reputation and his practice flourished. While he spent most of his days and evenings with clients, I had lots of time to pursue my own interests. The girls attended school nearby, which left me free to study, read and, as often as I could, enjoy long walks. I would put freshly charged batteries in my Walkman, load up Rachmaninoff, or if I was feeling a bit down, Kenny Rankin, then head out for a hike on the mountain. Those long walks were my way of claiming a sense of peace in my life, a way to calm the inner void that I knew very well was never far from the surface. Occasionally, I wondered what it would be like to enter the church I passed along the way up the mountain, but I never entered it. Even though I felt I had burned that bridge long ago, there remained a hint of longing.

Many years earlier, when I had first sensed that one day I would write, it had been with the understanding that it would be, as I wrote in my journal, "later in life, when I had something to say." Although now in my early thirties and still far from the age of "having something to say," I began to work on a novel. Like all budding authors, I imagined myself producing a bestseller and never having to worry about money again.

"Wings of the Soul" was the story of a healer, a story in which I incorporated everything about which I was passionate at the time: magic, love, romance, reincarnation, spirituality and, of course, healing. In just over a year, I proudly showed the first draft of my book to Arthur. Enthusiastic about my writing, he encouraged me to take the next step: to find a publisher. Naturally, my first batch of queries was met with rejections, and so I sent out a second batch, which encountered the same fate. Undaunted, I began to work on a second draft. I would reread that first draft years later and laugh at how naive I had been to think that a first draft written by an untrained writer could become an instant bestseller. In truth, it was simply appalling.

Other than work, Arthur and I had surprisingly little in common. We had very different parenting approaches, so to my great sorrow, my dream of a perfectly merged family never really materialized. For the rest, we had different tastes, from music to movies, I liked cooking, he liked eating in restaurants; I took up karate, a very linear form, while he took up aikido, a more subtle, circular martial art—choices that spoke much about our different natures. Living hand to mouth, I worried about money; he was very cavalier, making lots of money and spending at will. He was an isolator, perfectly content to do things alone; I had profound co-dependency issues and needed a partner to feel whole. On a metaphysical level, he was very much into making things happen through magic, while I remained more comfortable holding on to the idea of letting things happen. He sought power, I sought peace. He was an academic, I was a mechanic.

Financially, things were not going well at all. My practice was not picking up as quickly as I needed it to and I had bills to pay. Although Arthur strongly urged me to stick to astrology, I needed to find a way to supplement my income. Clients were not lining up at my door; they were lining up at his. Despite his encouragement, in his shadow, my own practice grew very slowly. When I was offered a small technical writing job by a friend of ours, I accepted. I understood and accepted that my practice would take a little longer to build.

My relationship with Arthur lasted six years. Since our life together was based almost entirely on our work in astrology and his brand of shamanism, there came a point when I sensed the need to branch out and become my own person. The material I was teaching in the workshops, although interesting, was his material, and I was beginning to have questions that he was not able to answer to my satisfaction. Doubts about the truth of his way of looking at the world began to surface. Some things did not make sense to me. We were employing rituals and practising visualization through inner journeys, but life was still difficult and I was not reaching my goals. He told me that I did not believe enough in myself. I believed that there was something missing in my knowledge about the nature of the world and my existence.

> Everything that is of God can be counted on, because everything of God is wholly real. (T-7.V.6:8)

There did not seem to be anything in this world I could reasonably count on, other than my ability to manipulate circumstances according to my desires, and that thought was not terribly reassuring. There had been more hope when I believed in Jesus and in God. Was this new Aquarian model really the way? If not, what was the way? Although I had accumulated more knowledge than ever, I was in effect, even more confused than ever. Life was complicated. Adding to this the fact that my infatuation for Arthur had long worn off, I began to sense the dark theme of the symphony of my life rise to a whole new crescendo.

Toward the end of that period, I began dating someone from my karate class, and, within months, I moved out into my own apartment. Surviving without anyone's help would be a big challenge, but I had picked up enough technical writing jobs to make ends meet. With a bit of child support as a base, I would be okay for a few years.

There was no spiritual foundation in the relationship with my karate friend; it was, in fact, refreshingly non-spiritual, non-magical and non-esoteric. Although it lasted barely two years, we did have fun and lots of laughs, something that had been sorely lacking in my relationship with Arthur. However, a passing conversation we once had on the subject of God does stand out in my memory. He stated flatly that he did not believe there was even a God. Although I had briefly toyed with the notion, hearing it expressed so unequivocally was disturbing. Deep down, I wanted to believe that there was a God, even though I was not sure what to make of Him.

> Now has the mind condemned itself to seek without finding; to be forever dissatisfied and discontented; to know not what it really wants to find. (M-13.3:3)

Chapter 8

A SPIRITUAL SABBATICAL

Forgive yourself your madness, and forget all senseless journeys and all goal-less aims. They have no meaning. You can not escape from what you are. For God is merciful, and did not let His Son abandon Him. For what He is be thankful, for in that is your escape from madness and from death. Nowhere but where He is can you be found. There *is* no path that does not lead to Him. (T-31.IV.11:1–7)

When I turned forty, I hit another turning point in my life. This was a number 9 Personal Year, with a new Pinnacle, a number 1, just around the corner. Suddenly, I found myself in a place where I once thought I could never survive: I was entirely alone. The number 1 Pinnacle foreshadowed a period during which I would be required to become completely self-reliant, independent, autonomous and willing to forge ahead on my life's journey with courage and boldness. Still reeling from the failure of my relationship with Arthur, the relationship in which I had felt the greatest sense of belonging and spiritual closeness, this was not a comforting thought.

To support the girls and myself I had accepted a full-time position as a technical writer for an R & D consulting firm. For the first time in my life, I was making some serious money. I had blended into the mainstream workforce, leaving behind my quest for all things spiritual, magical and metaphysical. One thing was very clear: I would never again have a guru, teacher, mentor or spiritual advisor of any kind. If I needed anything, I would figure it out on my own. Disillusioned, I set aside God and everything belonging to the realm of spirit and focused on being like everyone else, working and making a life for the girls and myself. All the while, I continued to build my astrological practice, seeing clients in the evenings and on weekends.

But, because I was basically making myself do something I was not really designed to do, after two years of mainstream living, I began to feel trapped. I lived in an apartment in the core of the city surrounded by cement and asphalt, and had started to crave a house with a garden and cedar hedge so badly it hurt inside. At some point, I would have to make the jump and focus all my efforts on my astrology practice, but I was dreadfully fearful of not being able to make it. The number 1 Pinnacle loomed ominously before me, and, although my client base was growing steadily, it was far from being large enough to replace my considerable salary and benefits. Try as I might to convince myself to stay on the job, my unhappiness deepened. Furthermore, management issues in the company where I worked were making the situation increasingly untenable. Clearly, I was clinging to a job that I disliked, desperately afraid of not being able to survive if I pursued my true life purpose. Not surprisingly, I fell ill.

In my exhausted state, not uncommon for a number 9 Personal Year, I contracted a virus that caused numbness from my waist down to my feet—a post-infectious polyneuritis, the doctors called it. The condition was not painful, nor did it prevent me from walking or moving my legs, it only caused a lack of sensation. The symbolism of my paralyzed legs and feet was not lost on me: clearly it was a reflection of my fear of walking on my true path. Months passed, and the condition did not improve.

When it became clear that traditional medicine could not help me, I decided to look for natural ways to heal my body. Although I was clueless as to what I should do, I understood that I needed to look deep inside and see what was driving my life. Adapting a technique I had learned from Arthur, I began a year-long process of visualization that led to the disappearance of my symptoms and to my making significant changes in my life.[1] Taking control of my life gave me a sense of empowerment.

The next step was to negotiate my way out of my full-time job into a contractual arrangement that allowed more time to work on building my astrology practice. Over the next several years, actually for the remainder of that nine-year cycle, I kept spirit and the inner quest at bay, focusing on tangible applications of mind. Placing practical matters first and foremost, I got down to the business of surviving in the world on my own. I gathered up my courage and immersed myself in business networking activities and lecturing. My profound fear of public speaking and painful shyness were set aside when I thought of the alternatives: it was either get over the fear or get a job. Since I thought that the latter would kill me, I decided to deal with the fear.

In order to reach a broader cross-section of the population and to better blend in with the networking crowd, I adopted a business-like persona and a philosophy of life that was unquestionably practical and down-to-earth. God and Jesus and most things spiritual were replaced by impersonal concepts such as the universe, the power of mind and energy. I maintained a comfortable distance from God and religion by snubbing anything that carried even a whiff of the New Age.

This approach suited my clients, who were more concerned with practical matters anyways. In fact, none of my clients ever questioned the meaning of life, more concerned with basic issues such as career, relationships and family. Over the next few years, as my astrology practice grew, I took on fewer and fewer technical-writing contracts. I had effectively given up the spiritual quest and become an entrepreneur, something with which I seemed to have some skill.

In a way, it was a relief to focus on the simple business of life. My years of searching had left me feeling more empty than full. At every turn, hope had been met with disappointment. Maybe

---

1. For a full account of this healing process and the techniques used, see *The Power of Time*, pages 140–141.

I had wasted my time. Perhaps my karate friend had been right, maybe there *was* no God. My spirituality had been reduced to a clean and neat notion of a neutral, universal energy source in a state of constant expansion as amply expressed by the rapid rate of progress in our world.

In my state of spiritual torpidity, the idea that the world was evolving toward its destined state of perfection was more or less acceptable. I concluded that there must be a sense of order and purpose in the universe. No longer engaged in an active search for truth, I was content to espouse the spiritual platitudes of the day. There was a reason for everything. What that reason was eluded me; but again, it didn't seem to matter. That an intelligence of sorts was behind all that happened in the universe seemed to suffice. These were convenient truths that were easy to plug in whenever a question of *why* arose either in my mind or in consultation. This neat and clean metaphysics suited my clients and it worked for me. Besides, the everyday affairs of life were keeping me sufficiently busy so that there was little time to ponder the imponderable.

In response to the needs of my clients and always eager to learn new skills, I took a certificate course in Bach Flower Remedies and integrated the remedies in my practice. On some level, I still fancied myself a healer of sorts, but although I had experienced some actual healings, I sensed it was not meant to be the main focus of this lifetime. I also studied an updated version of the Silva Method, a good review of the Mind Control workshop I had taken many years earlier. I felt comfortable working with tools that did not require faith in anything beyond that which I could experience directly.

The thought systems of the day extolled the virtues of the mind. We were encouraged to explore our untapped potential, while the mind was considered the ultimate power tool. We collectively harboured romanticized notions of a wonderful, abundant universe filled with mystery and endless possibilities, of a world in constant evolution, of bodies endowed with remarkable healing powers and of minds capable of extraordinary creation. Even though I understood that if I set my mind on something, I could make it happen, still uncertain of my own greater wisdom, I remained uncomfortable with asking for specifics. Just because I did not have the answers, it did not mean that there were none. Without making specific requests, I experienced the power of following my path. When I did what I believed I was meant to do, things fell into place; what I was not meant to do remained unsupported by the universe.

Despite the very tiny glimmer in the back of my mind that never completely disappeared—a spiritual pilot light of sorts—I deliberately avoided the name of God. I was, in a way, at war with God. By substituting the name of God with the more neutral *universe*, I enjoyed reading books like *The Science of Getting Rich*. These thought systems gave an acceptable meaning to the life I lived while validating the philosophy of life I chose to adopt at the time.

> The stuff from which all things are made is a substance which thinks, and the thought of form in the substance produces the form.... Every thought of form, held in thinking substance, causes the creation of the form ... The universe is a great living presence, always moving inherently toward more life and full of functioning. Nature is formed for the advancement of life, and its impelling motive is the increase of life.... There can be no lack unless God is to contradict himself and nullify his own works.[2]

These approaches seemed straightforward, easy and effective; the combination of thought and belief was indeed a very powerful force. Matter, it was said, like thought, is pure energy. I understood that concept and sensed it to be true, to a point, but there were still problems with this idea. If the world was the result of how we have used our minds, if it was the extension of our own pure energy, why had we not created a better world? Why did we create bodies that decay and die? Why could we not find cures for the horrible diseases of the world? If it were true that the power of mind is without limit, why was it that with so many people praying for

---

2. *The Science of Getting Rich*, Wallace D. Wattles, Certain Way Productions, Seattle, WA, USA, 2002, pages 10–11.

peace, abundance and health for everyone on the planet none of this had yet occurred?

Suppose I did attract a million dollars into my life. I would probably feel that the universe was indeed amazing and filled with possibilities and definitely on my side. I might also think that I must be doing something right. I would feel blessed, and no doubt overwhelmed with gratitude. Yet the world would still be as it was and always will be. How abundant would it be for those children who continue to die of sickness and malnutrition by the minute around the world, or for those who live in scarcity in my own neighbourhood? How amazing would it be for those whose countries were torn apart by war? For the victims of tsunamis and other natural disasters? How would my brand new BMW make the world a better place? Eventually, my million dollars would run out, my body would continue to age and, statistically, odds were that I would develop a serious illness and, with absolute certainty, I eventually would die. So, in effect, nothing would really change. My ability to attract abundance into my life, while making my life easier and more enjoyable and perhaps even enabling me to temporarily make the world a better place for some or even many people, would not have changed the fact that material abundance fades, we were born here in bodies and we will still die.

By the same token, if we affect our future with our thoughts of today, it follows logically that our present is a result of our past thoughts. Yet, I do not recall thinking myself into struggling for survival, experiencing loneliness, struggling with illness or aging, and I do not think anyone else would consciously attract those experiences into their life either. So why is there struggle in this world?

> Few appreciate the real power of the mind, and no one remains fully aware of it all the time.... The mind is very powerful, and never loses its creative force. It never sleeps. Every instance it is creating.... There *are* no idle thoughts. All thinking produces form at some level. (T-2.VI.9:3, 5–8, 13–14)

As much as I tried to get a grasp of the meaning of life from the perspective of these thought systems, too many questions remained unanswered. I couldn't completely accept the popular notions that we lived in an extraordinary time, with all sorts of amazing possibilities and opportunities and that we were on the cusp of a higher consciousness that would mend all the wrongs of the world. It was clear that as our opportunities for good developed, so would our opportunities for evil and harm. That was—and always will be—the way of this world. The years were passing by with increasing swiftness and I was no closer to finding the answers to the questions that had begun to resurface: Why was there sickness? Scarcity? Death? And the ultimate question: Why are we here at all? It troubled me that a perfect source or a loving God could have created this world. There was definitely something wrong with this picture.

These unanswerable questions were kept at bay when I plunged back into the mundane realities of what I knew of as my life. As uncertain as the world was, it was what I knew. Working, paying the bills and dealing with the day-to-day realities did not cause me to ponder much beyond the immediate. It was safe.

Still determined to become a published author, I reworked my novel. Feedback from agents and publishers had made it clear that if I was to become a successful writer, I would need to hone my skills. I took courses in fiction writing and joined a creative writing workshop. I read dozens of books on writing, editing and the publishing process. After completing another revision of "Wings of the Soul" and, confident that the story was much improved, I queried again. Since writing was starting to become an integral part of what I did, and perhaps also of who I was, when those queries were met with rejections, I didn't even flinch. In my gut, I knew that one day I would be a published author. However, when my psychic friend Ken told me that perhaps "Wings of the Soul" would not be my first published book, I panicked a bit. That was unpleasant news, since in my mind, I had only one book in me, and that was it. Undeterred, I rewrote "Wings" again, changed the title to "The Healer," queried again and collected more rejection letters.

It seemed that my friend Ken had seen correctly. Needing a break from fiction, I tried my hand at an astrology book. This was a reference work for students of astrology and had a more limited audience than my novel, which I continued to picture as a winning bestseller. To my surprise and great joy, a batch of queries was met with favourable responses, and I actually had a choice of publishers. In 2002, *Astrological Crosses in Relationships* was released. I was now a published author!

At the age of forty-seven, even though I had grown quite content with being single, I humoured my younger daughter and a friend by posting my profile on an online dating website. They had colluded to convince me that I should not spend the rest of my life alone. "You won't meet anyone if you spend all your time at home. You have to put yourself out there," they said adamantly. My years of business networking and public speaking had not only helped me overcome much of my shyness but had also allowed me to navigate comfortably in the world of normal, non-spiritual people. Ready for adventure, I completed a profile with a popular online dating service.

Over a period of several months I went on many dates with mostly nice guys, but with whom I had little in common. As a woman of advancing years, I found it mildly validating that I had "date appeal," but the experience was certainly not very fulfilling. It was clear that, despite having placed the quest on the back burner, spirituality remained an important criterion for a personal relationship. I did not find a soul connection online and, by the looks of it, I was not likely to find it in this lifetime.

Just as I was about to give up the search for a partner, I gave it one last try and joined a singles social group run by a woman I had met at a business networking cocktail. The concept made more sense than online dating. She would organize events to which members who shared common interests were invited. Bob and I met at a rollerblading outing. We were worlds apart, but I had come to accept that I would not likely meet anyone in my sphere of interests. Also, given my age, and my dismal online dating adventures, I began to think that my chances of meeting someone were slim to none. This was probably going to be my last opportunity.

Bob was bright, inquisitive, talkative, nice looking, very perceptive and, surprisingly, at least to me, he thought I was hot. Although on the outside he could appear gruff, deep down, he had a sweet and gentle disposition and was very attentive, probably the only man left on the planet that still opened the car door for a woman. Caring and thoughtful, always ready to be helpful, he was easily likeable.

After a few fun dates, we decided to give it a try. We pulled away from the singles group and dated exclusively. Meanwhile, we started spending much of our spare time together. We both enjoyed cooking, and spent many Saturday evenings whipping up gourmet meals in my kitchen. To my surprise, when I suggested that we take ballroom dance lessons, he accepted. We attended family dinners and went on outings as a couple, and our lives quickly became enmeshed. My folks took an immediate liking to him, in particular my brothers, with whom he shared a passion for motorcycles.

Although, on the surface we made a nice couple, Bob and I were as different as Saturn and the Sun. He liked noise and movement, while I preferred peace and quiet. He enjoyed fighting through city traffic and speeding down the highway; I preferred leisurely drives in the country. He liked winter and cold; I was more comfortable in the heat of summer. He liked AC/DC and classic rock radio; I listened to Diana Krall and smooth jazz. He liked clutter and chaos; I needed spaciousness and order. He ate hamburgers and fries, while I preferred salad and tofu. He was a dog person; I was a cat person. He was open and friendly; I was private and reserved.

Despite our differences, we managed to meet in the middle, so that, when in the car, we listened to jazz, and when we went for long rides, it was on the bike. I taught him to make healthier food choices to better manage his diabetes, and, on occasion, I would have a hot dog and *poutine* at a pit stop along the road. Aware of his innate impatience, I would get ready quickly so as not to make him wait, while he was understanding of my irregular work hours.

However, after barely a few weeks, issues began to surface, issues that were deal breakers for me. Bob and I came from very different backgrounds. While he dealt openly with conflict, allowing his anger to rise to the surface, my early family environment had been mostly peaceful, calm and free of drama, so I did not deal well with conflict, preferring to withdraw from situations rather than addressing them head on. We fell into a cycle of two to three weeks where things would go really well, we got along fine, laughed and did plenty of fun things together, then, we would meet an impasse, and conflict would set in. I blamed it on his mood swings, a result of his having been brought up in an environment that was fraught with violence and abuse. His dad had been a weekend alcoholic, a military man with a nasty temper that flared up when he drank. It had not been uncommon for Bob to suffer the brunt of his father's rage when he came home Friday nights.

I felt that these childhood experiences had been stamped deep into his psyche and, as much as Bob was unlike his father, the scars continued to affect his behaviour. I was quite certain that I was right, and had even consulted a psychologist on the matter. But Bob did not see things as I did. Equally convinced that he was right, he blamed our ups and downs on my menopause. Although I had never suffered from mood swings, I was aware that when things went well with Bob, I was comfortable with closeness, and when anger threatened to rear its ugly head, I withdrew. I saw my response as a natural self-preservation mechanism; I didn't see it as a mood swing.

It was just before our first Christmas together when my inner voice cried out: "End the relationship now, it's not going to work." It was a strong hunch, which I ignored, convincing myself that I should at least give it my best shot. If it didn't work out, then I would know I had done everything I could. But the issues did not go away. In search of a solution, I read dozens of books on relationships. Over the months that followed, I ended the relationship several times; following each breakup, I allowed myself to get talked back into it. Bob could be very convincing when he wanted something, and, when he was kind, he was very difficult to resist.

So I would return to the drawing board. Perhaps I was doing something wrong. Perhaps I could try a different approach. Perhaps I should be more tolerant. I would give it another chance. I continued like this until it occurred to me that perhaps I was not as defective as I thought I was. The issues were his, not mine, yet that knowledge alone did not give me the clarity I sought. Yet, I persisted. We were both getting on in years, and I believe what we had in common was a desire to have a relationship that worked. Neither of us wanted to spend the rest of our lives alone. Something was keeping us together and I was determined to find out what it was. What I would discover is not what I could ever have imagined.

> Seek not outside yourself. For it will fail, and you will weep each time an idol falls. Heaven cannot be found where it is not, and there can be no peace excepting there. (T-29.VII.1.1–3)

PART II: SEEK AND YOU *WILL* FIND

The Holy Spirit offers you another promise, and one that will lead to joy. For His promise is always, "Seek and you *will* find," and under His guidance you cannot be defeated. His is the journey to accomplishment, and the goal He sets before you He will give you. For He will never deceive God's Son whom He loves with the Love of the Father. (T-12.IV.4:4–7)

Chapter 9

GOD

Tolerance for pain may be high, but it is not without limit. Eventually everyone begins to recognize, however dimly, that there *must* be a better way. As this recognition becomes more firmly established, it becomes a turning point. (T-2.III.3:5–7)

*T*he year I turned fifty, a number 1 Personal Year, I began my fourth and final Pinnacle, a number 9. I had an uneasy feeling about what changes this new energy signature might bring into my life, as it was quite different from what I had experienced thus far. While a number 8 Pinnacle might have held the promise of worldly and material success, or a 6 might have brought a harmonious special relationship, the 9 Pinnacle, although holding as much success potential, was more intangible. The 9 is artistic, romantic, universal and even lofty and spiritual; it is the number of completion and endings.[1]

The spiritual quest that had haunted my youth had been on hold for a long time. I was living a normal and successful life. All in all, things were going relatively well in my business and in my life in general, except for my relationship with Bob, which continued its on-again off-again dance. Despite our ups and downs, one area in which we fared surprisingly well was with home renovation projects, something we discovered when he offered to help renovate my crumbling upstairs bathroom. Perhaps it was because he was the

---

1. It was only during the final revision of the manuscript that I noticed the numbering of this chapter.

authority in this department, but with construction work, conflict was a rare occurrence. He'd say "Get me a Robertson," and I'd fetch a number one, a two and a three, just to be sure I had all the sizes covered.

Home renovations were a great way for me to take a break from consultations; I believe he enjoyed it because it showcased his unlimited handyman skills. With my ability to visualize and his mechanical know-how, there was no project we couldn't tackle. Bob was highly intelligent, resourceful and multi-talented—a real problem solver. The man could fix anything and I mean *anything*: computers, sound systems, cars, motorcycles, plumbing and electricity. Unless a thing was broken beyond repair, Bob could fix it; he never gave up without having first made every possible effort. When it came to renovations, we were a great team and ultimately did a fabulous job with the upstairs bathroom. I was even forgiven for driving the electric drill into a live wire behind a wall!

However, cha-cha and foxtrot didn't fare quite as well as drywall and ceramics. Our cycle of conflict invariably rose to the surface on the dance floor, where, when things didn't work well, he would blame me for not following or not knowing my steps, and, of course, I would put the blame on his inability to lead or follow the music. We didn't hear the music the same way, nor did we learn the steps in the same manner. He was required to learn to lead; I was required to follow. Since we were both tense from the stress of learning new steps, he had difficulty leading and I couldn't follow. When I didn't follow, he got upset. Of course, he thought he was right, blaming the problems on my menopausal madness, and naturally I was certain that I was right. This was the foundation of our very special relationship.

Yet, for some unknown reason, we remained together. A book could be written about the incidents that occurred in our relationship—actually two books: one from my perspective and one from his, depending on who the hero was, and each would be equally true. But this is not about who was right and who was wrong; this is about uncovering the truth behind the conflict.

That summer, my daughter moved out. At the same time, Bob's lease was up, and despite the ups and downs in our relationship, guided by a bit of evidently skewed logic, we agreed that it would make sense for him to move in with me. He would save on rent, and I would have a little help to pay the bills. In theory, the idea made good practical sense; given our track record, this was really not one of our better ideas. A nasty shouting match between Bob and one of the movers the day he moved in was the first indicator that a terrible mistake had been made and that this partnership could never work.

As might be expected, sharing a roof did nothing to ease the stress of our relationship; it actually increased it. Bob continued to manifest his anger openly while, unaccustomed to coping with open hostility, I withdrew further. In my mind, I preferred peace, and, by withdrawing and building a wall around myself, I had peace, or at least a semblance of peace. I did not yet understand that, on a very deep level, we all live with conflict; some of us simply live it out in the open, while others work hard at keeping it either deeply buried, or, when that approach becomes intolerable, cleverly projected onto unsuspecting hosts.

As the first year of that new cycle came to a close, having spent more and more time turning inward seeking refuge from the daily tension and far too frequent manifestations of conflict with Bob, I began to sense a need to get to the bottom of all things that might come to disturb my peace. This need led to a profound and over-whelming urge to make peace with God. I don't recall a unique event attached to the awakening of that urge, only that one day—there it was. All I knew is that we had been on opposite sides of the universal divide for far too long.

However, the idea of God posed more questions and problems than solutions. The God of my childhood had not heard my prayers, so either I was too insignificant to merit His attention, or He just did not care. I didn't think that I was that insignificant, nor did I like the idea that God didn't care. Yet it certainly did seem as though he did care more for some people than others, otherwise why would some live in ease, enjoying harmonious relationships and abundance, while others were given to live in scarcity, illness and hardship?

> Seek not another signpost in the world that seems to point to still another road. No longer look for hope where there is none. Make fast your learning now, and understand you but waste time unless you go beyond what you have learned to what is yet to learn. (T-31.IV.4:5–7)

There must be answers somewhere. The concept of a dispassionate universal principle no longer worked for me; it seemed cold and indifferent. The universe would provide; the universe would show me the way; the universe existed in all things. And if it didn't show me the way, if it didn't fix things, it must be because I was doing something wrong. But the universe wasn't doing a very good job of ridding the world of suffering and struggle, was it? Surely, there must be some *thing* or some *being* endowed with an intelligence that was superior to ours.

Back at square one on the spiritual board game, I considered the popular self-help approaches; these felt stale, even naive and infantile, leaving me longing for more. The idea that *everything was unfolding according to plan* caused me to bristle with annoyance. What kind of idiotic plan was that? Who would make up a world that included starving children, war, disease and all the other horrible facts of life that people conveniently overlook when they declare that "God doesn't give us more than we can handle"?

In my renewed quest for truth, I sensed that there had to be an intelligent form—a *God*—who was more sane than the punishing, vengeful, demanding God of the religions of man. But then who was I, an ordinary gist learner, to ponder questions that had preoccupied the great thinkers of history? Who was I to question the Divine Intelligence? Well, there I was, questioning It. Strike me down and condemn my soul to eternal damnation, but what the hell kind of Divine Intelligence was behind this creation anyways?

Clearly I needed a more substantial spirituality and, not knowing where to turn for guidance, I decided to go back to the beginning. It was time to revisit God. Perhaps He would have the answers. If the concept of God was good enough for the likes of Deepak Chopra and Wayne Dyer, it certainly should be good enough for me. Surprisingly, it felt natural to set aside the impersonal universal principle and once again think of the Almighty as God. So again, the name of God took its place in my vocabulary—or at least in the ongoing dialogue of my mind.

Nothing can prevail against the Son of God who commands his spirit into the Hands of his Father. (T-3.II.5:1)

I attributed this renewed acceptance of God in my life as an indicator of my recent shift into the number 9 Pinnacle. With a renewed glimmer of hope, it occurred to me that this 9 energy might be a good thing after all. *Let go and let God*, I thought. This became my new mantra and from the dark recesses of my mind an ancient prayer echoed—*Into Your hands O Lord I commend my spirit*. A tiny spark was ignited and, for a moment, I felt that things would one day be right, that I would find comfort for my ailing soul. After a lifetime of patient waiting, the seeds of the silent, unanswering God of my childhood were about to burgeon.

My Name, O Father, still is known to You. I have forgotten It, and do not know where I am going, who I am, or what it is I do. Remind me, Father, now, for I am weary of the world I see. Reveal what You would have me see instead. (W-pII.224.2.1–4)

Throughout my life, whenever troubled or in need of guidance, I would turn to my vast library in search of a book—any book—that might provide the insight I needed to understand or resolve my dilemma. I would pull out a book, open it at random, and begin to read. Many times I found the inspiration I needed; other times, the momentary distraction was all it took to relieve the troubling stress. Occasionally, I had been urged to reach for a book with a navy blue cover and gold lettering. Each time I pulled it out, only to realize that it was not the one I needed. This book was navy blue, with silver lettering, a book on healing. The one I was urged to read had gold lettering and was apparently not in my vast collection. Puzzled, I would replace the book and continue my search for help in other works. Until, one day, I came across a reference to *A Course in Miracles.*

It might have been while reading Wayne Dyer or Marianne Williamson, I don't recall now, but instantly I knew that this was the navy blue book toward which I was being guided. Although I did not exactly relish the thought of tackling the big book with the small print I had glanced at many years earlier, I understood that it was time to read it. *A Course in Miracles* was added to my Christmas wish list. When I finally did get my copy, I eagerly opened it to the introduction and began to read.

1. *This is a course in miracles. It is a required course. Only the time you take it is voluntary. Free will does not mean that you can establish the curriculum. It means only that you can elect what you want to take at a given time. The course does not aim at teaching the meaning of love, for that is beyond what can be taught. It does aim, however, at removing the blocks to the awareness of love's presence, which is your natural inheritance. The opposite of love is fear, but what is all-encompassing can have no opposite.*

2. *This course can therefore be summed up very simply in this way:*
   Nothing real can be threatened.
   Nothing unreal exists.
   Herein lies the peace of God. (I.1–4)

Although I wasn't any more interested in making miracles than I had been when I first came across the book, I liked the idea of taking a course, especially one that I could do on my own time at my own pace, but especially on my own, without the need for a teacher. This aspect really appealed to me. I also sensed truth in the words I read, and decided that I would read the book and just skip over the miracle-making parts.

Eager to experience the peace of God, I read on, but my enthusiasm was short-lived. Within the first few pages of the first chapter, "Principles of Miracles," I was stumped. In search of something I might actually begin to understand, I skipped ahead to the next section, "Revelation, Time and Miracles." But I got nothing, not even the gist of what I was reading. I didn't understand the meaning of *revelation* and was clueless as to the significance of *miracles* in the context of this book, a book that was a course in *miracles*. This was more than a bit disappointing. Why had I been guided to this book when it was clear that I was not going to get very far with its convoluted language? It was written in a highly sophisticated, and, from what I could tell, far too complicated style for my rudimentary academic or literary skills. It might as well have been written in Icelandic kilometre, the iambic pentameter being entirely lost on me. I wanted answers. I needed to know how to deal with the situations in my life that were disturbing my peace. In particular, I wanted to know what to do with my relationship with Bob.

Disappointed, I set the book aside and returned to my bookcases, pulling out title after title in search of inspiration. Wayne Dyer and Deepak Chopra had been nice to read, but I needed more. I tried reading Thomas Merton again, but I had already long ago turned the page on my Catholic roots. So I rethought my decision to make peace with God. Maybe there was no God after all. Maybe this world was no more than an accident of nature, and maybe that was simply all there was. Maybe it was foolish, even childish to think that there was a Divine Presence that actually cared, that our lives—*my* life—actually mattered. It had long ago comforted me to think that there was a loving God out there somewhere and that, one day, there would be peace for all, if only we could get rid of our collective bad karma. But He had not and, by the looks of it, did not seem likely to make Himself known, at least not to me.

> He wanders on, aware of the futility he sees about him everywhere, perceiving how his little lot but dwindles, as he goes ahead to nowhere. Still he wanders on in misery and poverty, alone though God is with him, and a treasure his so great that everything the world contains is valueless before its magnitude. (W-pI.166.5:4–5)

But I could not let the matter go. Perhaps it was a natural consequence of advancing years, facing the inevitability of my mortality, maybe it was menopausal madness, as Bob liked to point out, the truth was that I just couldn't shake the need to turn my attention inward. The embers of the old familiar quest had been stirred back to life with a renewed fury that could not be ignored.

Although I did not consider myself to be a pessimist, when I looked at the world, I could not see the wonderful place many of the popular spiritual teachers saw. As a pragmatist, I simply could not adopt the it's-all-good philosophy of life. One didn't have to look far to see that it *wasn't* all good. Neither had I ever believed in an imminent Golden Age that would one day descend upon mankind at the appointed time. There was no logic in this type of magical thinking. Unless things changed radically in the mind of man, there could never be a Golden Age, and it certainly wasn't *all good*. Man had murdered for the sake of survival from day one. The same old wars that had been waged for millennia continued, or were taken across the border to the next country. The true definition of love between people was "you give me what I want so I'll keep you around." While cures for long-standing diseases were discovered, new diseases emerged just as quickly. Children continued to be born into horrible conditions, and man's inhumanity to man progressed. The rich continued to get rich, while the poor continued to be poor. Sure, advancements were being made and technology was moving forward at an incredibly rapid pace, but this only meant that mankind had fancier tools to do what mankind has always done, only with more speed, power and effectiveness.

For myself, I did not seek hoards of money or fame or power. I wanted peace, not just any peace, but peace of a lasting kind, and I felt that this peace could come with the certainty of knowing. Knowing what—now *that* was the question. If I could find this peace and share it with my clients and the people I would meet during my remaining years, then perhaps I would be doing my tiny share, no matter how miniscule, toward making the world a better place.

The feel-good New Age teachings of the day held no appeal for me. Trying to hold on to fleeting moments of peace was like trying to grab the flow of water from a faucet. It simply could not be done. There was something missing. What was it all about? It just couldn't be that we were born to live, procreate, celebrate gains, mourn losses, age and die. It just didn't make sense. This couldn't be all there was. There had to be something better! There had to be more! Was I being unreasonable? Was I reaching for the impossible? Would I ever find the elusive peace I longed for, or had I simply joined the ranks of the perennially discontent?

> You do not ask too much of life, but far too little. When you let your mind be drawn to bodily concerns, to things you buy, to eminence as valued by the world, you ask for sorrow, not for happiness. (W-pI.133.2:1–2)

Disappointed with my fruitless close encounter with *A Course in Miracles*, I returned my spiritual pursuit to the back burner and focused once more on the business of day-to-day living. One day, I told myself. One day, there will be answers.

And answers came—far sooner than I expected. Barely a couple of weeks later, Bob and I drove out to pick up his sons for dinner. It was his birthday, and every year it was their custom to go out for BBQ chicken. Bob had enjoyed a book on anger management recommended by his therapist, so for his birthday, I had bought him a set of CDs: *The Art of Mindful Living*, a series of talks by the Buddhist monk Thich Nhat Hanh. Since he did not have much time to read, I thought the CDs would be perfect. He could listen to them on his way to work or while on the road between business meetings. Not having read the book, it never occurred to me that this might be something that I would find helpful.

Bob slipped the first CD into the car's player and we listened in silence as Thich Nhat Hanh began his lecture. It didn't take long for it to strike me, maybe five minutes, maybe less. These teachings were not new to me; I had heard most of them before in various formats. But somehow this time, it felt different. Or perhaps I was different or more receptive to a message of peace. Before I knew it, something deep inside was unleashed, like a geyser awakened after lying dormant for what seemed like lifetimes. Tears welled up fiercely as I listened in silence. Thich Nhat Hanh's soothing voice filled the empty spaces of the car… *Breathing in, you see yourself as still water… breathing out, you see that in that state of calm and stillness you reflect things as they are…*

Not wanting to sit in the restaurant facing the boys with red eyes and mascara-streaked cheeks, I fought the tears for as long as I could. Alone, there is no doubt that I would have allowed myself to savour them. These were not tears of sadness. No. These were tears of a peaceful relief so profound that I knew I had tasted truth. I took a deep breath, in fact, I took several deep breaths before feeling calm enough to speak; then I asked Bob to turn off the CD. "I just need a break," I answered when he wanted to know why.

Over the weeks that followed, I listened to several of Thich Nhat Hanh's lectures. In fact, during the two days I spent repainting my office, instead of engulfing myself in my favourite music, as was my custom while doing any kind of work around the house, I listened to the same set of CDs, over and over and over. There *was* a way to peace. I began to think that perhaps Buddhism should be my new path. It did not matter that there was no talk of God in what I was listening to; I just thought that this might be the way I could make peace with God. It was a first step. Buddhism. Yes, I thought, there I might find peace.

A couple of days later, I received a newsletter from the Wayne Dyer website promoting a new book called *The Disappearance of the Universe* by someone I had never heard of, Gary R. Renard. It was subtitled *Straight Talk about Illusions, Past Lives, Religion, Sex, Politics, and the Miracles of Forgiveness.* After reading the description, my immediate reaction was "Oh no, not another channelled work." But there was a reference to *A Course in Miracles* and, despite my initial misgivings, I felt strongly urged to order a copy, and so I did.

For some reason, at the time of my budding love affair with Buddhism, I felt compelled to take a Reiki course. It wasn't that I thought I really needed it, since simple magnetism and other natural healing approaches had worked quite well in the past. Besides, with the girls grown up now, I had no real need for healing. Healing was not something I promoted as a service in my business, in fact, I very rarely ever brought up the subject. On occasion, I would use magnetism to remove pain from Bob's ankle, a recurring pain from an old sports injury that would act up after dance class. Other than that, healing was a thing of the past for me.

A couple of years earlier, my dad had been diagnosed with a rare blood cancer; to add to his discomfort, in the last year, he had also contracted shingles. Once strong as a bull—a real Taurus—he was now considerably weakened, bit-by-bit shrinking in on himself, a sign of the extreme pain he suffered. Despite his condition, he had a remarkably positive attitude, even joking about his symptoms, showing off the bruised flesh on his side. Surprisingly, at least in our company, he managed to maintain that certain peacefulness that had in my youth both irritated and intrigued me. While I seemed to be on a perpetual quest to find peace, my father had always appeared immune to those idiotic things that would invariably usurp my peace.

Although my mom and I had for many years experimented with alternative health practices, my dad steadfastly placed his faith in the traditional medical system. Respecting his choice, I never interfered. Despite wishing there was something I could do, deep down, I had no illusions about my skills as a healer. Colds, tonsillitis, earaches and bruises were simple ailments to heal; my father's condition was clearly far beyond my humble capabilities. Nonetheless, I had grown curious about Reiki; wanting to know what all the fuss was about, I thought I might take a closer look.

On a hunch, I invited my mom to take the course with me. To my surprise, with very little coaxing, she accepted. Perhaps we both harboured a secret wish to relieve some of my dad's discomfort. We never did speak about why we signed up for Reiki, but I think it did us both good. Other than those few occasions when I had worked on Bob's ankle pain, it had been a long time since I had practised any form of healing. Once in the class, I enjoyed having the healing energy flow through me once again.

The day following our first Reiki class, my cat Bubby, not yet two years old, fell ill. Over the previous few weeks, he had been growing increasingly listless and lethargic and had lost his appetite. I tried giving him Bach Flower Remedies, but his condition worsened. That morning, I found him lying on the floor soaked in his urine; he was unable to make it down the stairs to his litter box. Realizing that I could not handle this situation with the means at my disposal, I brought him to the vet, where he was diagnosed with a common bladder infection. Treatment was straightforward; an overnight stay at the clinic for a bladder flush and antibiotics, and he should be fine. I was relieved.

Over the days following his visit to the vet, Bubby's condition worsened. I returned to the clinic, where he was then diagnosed with a congenital degenerative bone disease for which the only remedy, the vet explained, was surgery. The plan was to cut him open, cut off the top layer of his leg bones and then reattach the muscles. Never mind that I could not afford the procedure, the thought of putting him through that amount of pain was simply out of the question. Thanks, I said, then picked him up and took him home. I'll take care of him myself. I would use Reiki, magnetic therapy or whatever I had; I was determined to heal my cat.

Temporarily setting Bubby, Reiki and the meaning-of-life aside, I turned my attention to my business. It was already mid-March and I had not yet completed my annual ritual of planning and goal-setting for the year. I reviewed and updated my goals, and also completed a new exercise: *The 101 Things I Want to Accomplish in the Next 10 Years.* Having no interest in climbing the highest mountain or being rich and famous, I had to really force myself to come up with even fifty things. My list included the books I hoped to write, the publication of my novel, home renovations, an occasional vacation, time spent in the garden—simple things. The most important items dealt with more immediate concerns and were placed at the top of my list: heal my cat Bubby, generate more business by attracting a regular number of clients each week, become a Reiki master and, the fourth item on my list, learn to *see* clearly into people and circumstances.

Needless to say, Bubby loved his daily Reiki treatments, and it was a matter of days before he was walking on his own again, and a few short weeks before he was running around the house. Either he had been misdiagnosed or I had managed to heal my cat. Either way, I had achieved the result I wanted. Item one was quickly crossed off my list.

To generate more business, I made use of affirmations, a practice that had worked well in the past, and which I was confident would serve me well again. Whenever I needed more clients, I would write how many I needed and, within days, my agenda would fill up. This goal was straightforward, as was the third item on my list, to become a Reiki master. All I needed was to complete the course.

The fourth item on my list of 101 things I wanted to accomplish, to *see* clearly, was an odd wish that stemmed from a feeling that there was something out there that I was missing. For some time, I occasionally had a strange sense that there was something that I needed to see, that there was something calling out to me, as though on some level I was blind. There was no apparent reason for this condition; it simply was. Occasionally I would even look over my shoulder, wait and listen, sensing that someone was present in the room with me. Although the feeling was very real, it never occurred to me that I should be frightened. This goal would not be as easily accomplished since I had no idea where to look or, for that matter, *what* to look for.

Chapter 10

A COURSE IN MIRACLES

If this were the real world, God *would* be cruel. For no Father could subject His children to this as the price of salvation and *be* loving. (T-13.in.3:1–2)

*T*he month of March 2005 was a number 5 Personal Month for me and, naturally, I was eager and ready for more new experiences. As soon as I received my copy of *The Disappearance of the Universe* (DU), I dove into it as though it were my last meal. What I found was a very readable collection of conversations between the author, Gary Renard, and a couple of *ascended masters*, a lovely lady and a dashing gentleman, who one day simply appeared on his living room couch. Admittedly, channelled material had generally caused me to be cautious, never having seen any reason to believe that a disembodied spirit would carry any more of the truth than someone who was still alive. I was also skeptical of claims of ascendance, given that many who claimed enlightenment seemed to forget to manifest that enlightenment in their behaviour. But because I felt I had been guided to the book, I did what I had done so many times in the past: I jumped right in with an open mind. If DU didn't cut it, there was always Buddhism; it certainly had given me moments of intense peace, which in itself was worthy of my attention.

The author, Gary Renard, was a regular, down-to-earth guy, a former musician who had dabbled in a variety of spiritualities, much as I had. Although he did not have much formal academic or religious education, he had maintained a sense of closeness with Jesus throughout his life, something with which I related. His smart-ass manner transpired here and there as a way of underlining that he had a personality just as the rest of us do. It also served to bring a measure of levity to a subject that was not at all light or easy reading. With a minimum of preamble, conversations began to flow and generous helpings of information, which I soon began to sense as bearing some serious degree of truth, were dished out. The style of the book may have been conversational, but there certainly was not much time wasted on small talk. In fact, although I did not see it the first time I read the book, the very first words expressed by Pursah summed up the essence of the teachings that would follow:

> We are appearing to you as symbols whose words will help facilitate the disappearance of the universe. I say we are symbols because *anything* that appears to take on a form is symbolic. The only true reality is God or pure spirit, which in Heaven are synonymous, and God and pure spirit have no form.[1]

At first, I found what I was reading to be provocatively interesting, but as I advanced through the long second chapter, I was shocked by what was being proposed. A comment made regarding the fact that Buddhism would not quite take me to the full experience of God I sought caused me to take a closer look at the source of these radical new ideas—*A Course in Miracles.*

The miracle minimizes the need for time. (T-1.II.6:1)

Resigning myself to my spiritual destiny, I pulled out the navy blue book with the gold lettering and began its study. *A Course in Miracles* is a progressive contemporary spiritual document that uses a highly sophisticated psychological approach to lead the student through a rigorous and systematic process of perceptual and mental re-education or "correction of perception," as it is referred to in the text. It is designed to awaken the student to the truth and to

---

1. *The Disappearance of the Universe*, Gary Renard, page 5.

an experience of a deeply buried level of mind. It states that it is a simple course; however, given the enormous power we have given to incorrect perception, to most of its students, at least initially, it appears difficult, and some would say even impossible. Although it uses Judeo-Christian language and symbolism as a convenient and familiar vehicle for conveying its message, its teaching is universal.

This voluminous work is written in a dauntingly formal Shakespearean style, and is comprised of a text that is nearly 700 pages long, a workbook containing 365 lessons and a ninety-two page Manual for Teachers. It came to be following a cry for help made by Helen Schucman and William Thetford, Professors of Medical Psychology at Columbia University's College of Physicians and Surgeons in New York City. Having struggled for some time with very difficult relationships and constant conflict in the workplace, William Thetford one day declared "there must be another way." That moment would mark an important turning point in their lives, not long after which Helen began to hear the Voice that would dictate the contents of *A Course in Miracles*.[2]

Despite my initial difficulties with the language of this book, having also reached the conclusion that there must be a better way, I made the firm commitment to do whatever it took to get through it. The first order of business was to process the fact that it claimed that Jesus was the Voice behind its dictation. Again, another channelled work, or so it seemed. But I kept an open mind. In fact, if it had been any more open I would have been mindless, which in retrospect would probably have been a far better thing than I might have imagined at the time since I would have experienced far less resistance to its message.

Having for most of my life held a fascination for the historical Jesus, I was more than a little intrigued by this contemporary work. The dating of the original scribing of the Course corresponded with the darkest hours of my life, something that I considered to be an

---

2. For the definitive and engaging story of Helen Schucman and her scribing of *A Course in Miracles* see *Absence from Felicity*, by Kenneth Wapnick, Ph.D.

answer of sorts to my own supplications for guidance. However, I would soon learn that the Biblical Jesus and the Jesus of the Course were not at all the same person. The first had been made up to suit the purposes of Christianity, while the second was the Voice of that part of the collective mind that had awakened to Truth. The two were fundamentally different.

In no uncertain terms, the Course boldly and unceremoniously addressed those issues for which I had in the past not found satisfactory answers. Although much more accessible, at least for a non-academic such as myself, DU was just as direct in its presentation of the truth, never once sparing my misguided, ego-driven sensibilities. DU was in fact the ACIM for Dummies that I needed to unlock and begin to understand the incredible teachings of the Course.

For the first time in my life, I was finally getting substantial, though admittedly shocking, answers to those important and unanswerable questions such as: Why did God make this world? How could he play favourites? How could He choose sides in a battle? How could He even *incite* battle? Why was an experience of lasting peace so elusive? Why did He not hear our cries? How could God sacrifice His only Son? If God and Heaven were expressions of eternal love and peace, why did they end at the edge of our universe? Why was eternity not eternal?

The unique thought system proposed by the Course might have been easier to grasp had I not already consumed so many contradictory ontological notions. By the looks of it, I had quite a task of mental unravelling ahead of me. My belief systems were not only deeply rooted, they were also tangled and confused. Probably the single most challenging concept I needed to process was that *God has nothing to do with this world*, in fact, *He does not even know anything about this world* and, more importantly, probably the toughest morsel to swallow was that *God does not even know I exist!*

This notion stirred up mixed feelings, even anger and outrage, and for a while caused me to be more confused than ever. If this were true, then it meant that all those years spent praying to God and going to church had been a waste of time, since He was not even around to hear me. I had to admit that I felt a bit foolish but also kind of pissed off. All of a sudden, God could not be counted on, or even expected to fix my life or the world, ever. But this also meant that He could not be blamed for what was going on in the world. I had been taught that God was All Knowing. If that were true, He would have had to know about this world. If it were true that He did not know about this world, then what was this world?

Though baffled, at the same time I felt a wave of profound relief as I toyed with this revolutionary new idea. This was indeed a radical concept and quite frightening too, but it made very good sense. I had considered that maybe there was no God, but not that there was a God who didn't know we existed. This gave me pause for serious consideration. Maybe it was a good thing—perhaps even a really good thing that He had nothing to do with this world. In some mysterious and twisted way, I understood that, if God had nothing to do with this world, then there might very well be hope.

I didn't quite understand how yet, but I sensed that this idea must be true. If there was a God who had nothing to do with this world, this would mean that there was something better than this world, that there was in fact what I began to think of as *not this*. While this was a most interesting thought, it also carried some serious ramifications. If God had nothing to do with this world, then *who* did?

> Oneness is simply the idea God is. And in His Being, He encompasses all things. No mind holds anything but Him. We say "God is," and then we cease to speak, for in that knowledge words are meaningless. There are no lips to speak them, and no part of mind sufficiently distinct to feel that it is now aware of something not itself. It has united with its Source. And like its Source Itself, it merely is. (W-pI.169.5:1–7)

A Course in Miracles was radically different from all the other spiritualities I had encountered in my life in that it proposed a thought system that was absolutely non-dualistic. It was, to my knowledge, the only teaching that did not have God interacting with the world in any way. Essentially it teaches that God is perfect oneness, whole and undivided. Consequently, the simple Truth is that only God is. This means that anything that is not God cannot be true. If only perfect oneness exists, nothing can be distinct and separate from God, so anything that is not God cannot be real.

The Course explains that from that place in eternity where all is One, there occurred a thought—a kind of what-if—nothing more than a passing notion, an idle thought that disappeared as soon as it seemed to appear. It was as though the one mind could momentarily entertain the idea: *What if I separated myself from my source?* Or, *What if I could be separate from total abundance?* Or, *What if I could be something other than perfect oneness?* Or, *What if I could be something other than selfless love?* It was nothing more than a fleeting thought, a reflection on something that could never occur anyways, since how could anyone or anything actually *be* separate from perfect oneness? How could anyone or anything *be* what it is not?

At first glance, it all sounded very logical, and I desperately wanted to understand, except for one problem—one gargantuan problem: for all intents and purposes, I *was* here; I *did* exist as a unique being, with a body, a mind and sensory apparatus, separate and distinct from everyone else and especially from God. From what I was now learning, it appeared that my entire existence was based on an impossibility—that anything *could* be separate from God, which implied that what I believed to be *me* could not *really* be. What I believed to be me was actually false!

At this point, I really did not know what to think, or *who* I was or *what* I was or whether or not I actually *was.* If anything, I was growing more bewildered than before. But I couldn't let these ideas go. Deep down, something made sense. The notion that there must exist an attainable and, above all, sustainable perfect peace was most appealing. There *had* to be; otherwise, why bother? What was the purpose of life if not to attain our perfection? Although far from comprehending exactly what that perfection was, I was certain that it had nothing to do with anything that was either in or of this world.

So, if God did not put us here, if God did not even make this world, if this world was not unfolding according to a divine plan—a thought for which I must admit I did feel a certain perverse delight—then what *did* happen? How could the seemingly impossible have happened?

> Into eternity, where all is one, there crept a tiny, mad idea, at which the Son of God remembered not to laugh. In his forgetting did the thought become a serious idea, and possible of both accomplishment and real effects. (T-27.VIII.6:2–4)

The truth of the matter, the Course says, is that nothing happened. *Nothing.* No more, no less. There is one quality about the Course that stands out above all others and that is that it is truly *absolute.* It doesn't waffle in its statements, offering half-truths for one person or occasion, other half-truths elsewhere. It is clear, concise, unconditional and refreshingly absolute. It is probably this very quality, no doubt combined with my dogged persistence that would enable me to navigate through the entangling and confusing objections that my ego would place on my path as I struggled to remove the barriers to my understanding of the truth. It is the absolute, uncompromising nature of this work that held the attention of my linear-thinking mind.

The Course uses the dream as a metaphor for what we consider to be our life in the world. As sleep blankets our awareness, we slip into a dream world in which we completely forget that we are really lying safe and snug at home in our bed. Fully believing that we are actually in the dream, we face any number of situations, some pleasant and enjoyable, others tragic and frightful. No matter the dream, for the most part, we truly believe we are here, even though the dream is nothing more than a made-up story projected by the unconscious levels of mind.

> Dreams show you that you have the power to make a world as you would have it be, and that because you want it you see it. And while you see it you do not doubt that it is real. (T-18. II.5:1–2)

In answer to the age-old question "What is the origin of life?," the Course proposes an alternate to the Judeo-Christian myth of Creation. By using the what-if scenario that says that filled with creative potential and, at the same time, without ever really leaving his Source, the Son of God momentarily entertains the possibility that there might actually *be* life outside of the Mind of God, a life outside of wholeness, complete abundance and perfect love. If this were actually possible, then perfect oneness would no longer be perfect, so, in truth, nothing really happens and the Son of God remains at home in God. In other words, this remains *a tiny mad idea*.

> You are the dreamer of the world of dreams. No other cause it has, nor ever will. Nothing more fearful than an idle dream has terrified God's Son, and made him think that he has lost his innocence, denied his Father, and made war upon himself. (T-27. VII.13:1–3)

However the Son of God chooses to toy with the idea of being an individual. The thought of being distinct, unique and separate from God seems appealing, at least on the surface. But the Son could not ever *be* separate from God, since God is perfect oneness and he is one with God. It is only an idea and how can an idea ever leave its Source—the Mind? As long as there is God and perfect oneness, there cannot *be* separateness. The ability to make a choice between perfect oneness and separateness reflects a dualistic principle and can only be illusory.

Nonetheless enchanted with the thought, the Son chooses separateness. Since power resides in the mind, the choice has an impact on the outcome of the dream. Being in a state of *choosing*, the mind of the Son, thinking there is actually a choice to be made—perfect oneness or "not perfect oneness"—now becomes split. This engenders, on the one hand, what the Course refers to as the ego's wrong-minded system of individuality and separateness, and, on the other hand, the right-minded thought system of the Holy Spirit in which resides the memory of oneness. Where there is choice, there is duality; where there is duality, there no longer is oneness. Having chosen separateness, the memory of oneness fades from awareness.

Excited about an experience of separateness, the Son indulges in his dreamland fantasy. This experience is similar to that of a young child playing a pretend game with her dolls in her playroom. Imagining that her dolls are real and nothing else exists, she blocks out everything that does not fit into her fantasy world, even obliterating the sound of her mother's voice when she is called for dinner.

The ego knows that at any time the Son can look inside and recall that he has the power to make a different choice—with the right mind—and simply return to his real life in perfect oneness, what the Course refers to as the principle of the Atonement. In order to survive, the ego must make certain that the Son never makes that choice so he makes up a very convincing story. He tells the Son that he has indeed accomplished the impossible: he has separated from his Source. Since there cannot be anything outside of perfect oneness, in order to have life, the Son had to steal it from God. Given that the nature of perfect oneness is essentially non-dualistic, it's him, or God, but not both. By all appearances, in order to exist as a separate being, the Son had to kill off God!

Believing he is guilty of a terrible crime, the Son has a really big problem. God won't be happy; in fact, He is no doubt going to come after him to exact the punishment that is his due. Having by now lost touch with the memory of his innocence, the Son believes he has sinned, a natural consequence of which is a serious case of guilt. Even worst, as he certainly deserves to be punished, he now fears for his life.

This line of thought is all too horrible to sustain. Fearful, the Son struggles to bury this monstrous guilt in his unconscious mind, guilt that is going to have to come out somewhere, for that which is repressed must eventually be projected. Having forgotten that he has a mind with the ability to make a different choice and no longer able to hear the voice of the Holy Spirit, the Son now turns to the ego, who is only too eager to help. He has a solution. Since the ego owes his existence to the Son's choice for separation, he has a vested interest in keeping the Son in the dark, away from his mind, where he could make that different choice. So he grabs his attention with an incredible plan, a plan that remains just as unreal as the ongoing dream.

I'll make up a world, the ego says, a special place in which you can hide from God. In desperate need of a solution to his problem, the Son thinks this over. That part of his mind that can make the choice between the real world and a world of illusion having now been buried deep in the unconscious, he is unaware that his problem is really non-existent and that he has another choice. All he wants now is to be rid of the dreadful sin, guilt and fear that hang over him like a menacing cloud and the ego's solution seems to make sense.

To save the Son from further agony, the ego makes up a world, with millions upon millions of people and things, a very clever construction, for now the Son has a world in which to hide from the wrath of God. And just to make certain that the Son never takes a serious look inside, the ego, again looking after his own best interests, gives the Son a very fascinating device: a human body with a brain and sensory apparatus. He makes the Son a perceiver. This body, with all its special needs—air, water, food, emotional comfort, material comfort—will keep the Son so busy that he will never stop to wonder if there is anything else.

> The body is the central figure in the dreaming of the world. There is no dream without it, nor does it exist without the dream in which it acts as if it were a person to be seen and be believed. (T-27.VII.1:1–3)

This body and this world, at times threatening, at times pleasing, keep him so busy that he in fact doesn't even have the time to ponder his real origins. It's a full-time job just staying alive! For one, he has to breathe, then he has to eat, then he has to find shelter. This bodily experience is a never-ending proposition! Then there are all the emotional and psychological needs: companionship, love, acceptance, belonging, approval ... the list is endless. Now believing himself to be a separate individual, the Son constantly struggles with feelings of emptiness, a symbol of the original separation from his Source. He works hard to fill this emptiness with love, affection, food, alcohol, friendship and worldly possessions.

Having thought of everything, the ego points out to the Son that this fascinating world of multiplicity is the ideal place for projecting his guilt. That way, the ego plots, you'll be innocent, and God won't come after you. He'll go after all those other guilty people, and you'll be safe. The Son, now thinking with the ego, likes very much being a separate individual. So what if there is hunger, pain or suffering, as long as he gets to be special. Besides, when he suffers, it's really not his fault, it's the body that is hungry or his enemy inflicting pain. He didn't ask to be born; his parents brought him into the world. It's never his fault. This proves that he didn't really do anything wrong. What a trip!

> Although you are one Self, you experience yourself as two; as both good and evil, loving and hating, mind and body. This sense of being split into opposites induces feelings of acute and constant conflict, and leads to frantic attempts to reconcile the contradictory aspects of this self-perception. (W-pI.96.1:1–2)

In order to keep the whole separation system spinning, the Son needs to maintain all these other bodies distinct from himself. The ultimate experience of separateness is expressed in special relationships, which include parents, siblings, children, spouses, bosses, friends and enemies. In fact, special relationships provide a great two-for-one bonus. By cleverly manipulating the special people in his life, the now seemingly separated Son gets to have some of his many needs met. At the same time, he has handy targets onto which he can project his anger, frustration, resentment—all manifestations of the deeply repressed original thought of sin, guilt and fear that must inevitably rise to the surface.

Of course, the special people in his life will never entirely meet with his needs since his true need is to awaken from the dream and return home, the memory of which remains buried. As a final stroke of genius, the Son invents thought systems and religions that make God the cause of this world. Now it's *really* not his fault. By the same token, now there really is no hope of returning home.

> Of one thing you were sure: Of all the many causes you perceived as bringing pain and suffering to you, your guilt was not among them. (T-27.VII.7:4)

After having been introduced to the basic metaphysics of the Course—actually, after having been hit over the head with this outrageous new teaching—it occurred to me that I had about as much use for this myth in my life as I'd had with the myth of Adam and Eve fifty years earlier. Clearly, I was a separate individual, in a body, dealing with mundane issues, issues that were very real to me and needed to be addressed. That was the truth I knew. Although intrigued by these ideas, I couldn't see how to make them fit into my life. For as long as I could remember, I had sought answers about the meaning of existence, and here they were, but as a hands-on, practical person, I was at a loss as to what to do with this radical ontology.

Chapter 11

A PROMISE OF PEACE

Stop for a moment now and think of this: Is conflict what you want, or is God's peace the better choice? Which gives you more? A tranquil mind is not a little gift. (M-20.4:6–8)

*I*t took barely a couple of weeks to get through a first reading of DU. Feeling as though I'd had the rug pulled out from under me, and not quite knowing what to do with this new and unusual knowledge, I began to read it again. One idea that captivated my attention was the promise of an experience of ever-lasting peace—the peace of God. Despite that I had as yet no clue as to how to integrate this revolutionary teaching into my life, it resonated with something deep inside, and there was no question that this would become my chosen path.

While the unequivocal statement that God had nothing to do with this world was disturbing and left me feeling more alone than ever, it did carry the hope of something better. That the separation never occurred was a most difficult concept to comprehend since, according to the information derived from my sensory apparatus, I was clearly here in a body—hunger, thirst and hot flashes being regular reminders of that fact. I had spent a large part of my life in the pursuit of uniqueness and individuality, both for myself and for my clients, and the trusting of one's perceptions had long been one of my working tools. To learn now that this authentic, perceiving self was little more than a mistaken notion at best was disturbing, if not frightening.

The miracle establishes you dream a dream, and that its content is not true. (T-28.II.7:1)

That I was responsible for the making of this body *and* this world would take a little clarification. Why would I cause myself to suffer scarcity, illness or emotional pain? Why would I put conflict in my life, when I was certain that I really wanted peace? If I was the creator of my life, why would I not give myself a life of abundance, love and peace?

Then there was the whole other matter of sin, guilt and fear, the star trio of the Catholic Church, on which the Course had an entirely different take. According to this new teaching, there never was a sin, just a silly idea, therefore no guilt and no need to fear retribution. This would definitely take time to understand, and in fact would require some serious undoing at the level of my deepest belief systems. Although I was aware of my various fears, I did not relate with the guilt that was referred to with such insistence. Given my childhood pact with God, I believed I had lived a relatively sinless life. I certainly did not *feel* this guilt, nor did I think I was projecting guilt onto the people in my life. I was generally a nice person, not one to openly attack others or engage in conflict. At first glance, I sincerely thought that despite my lack of understanding, given my relative sinlessness, therefore relative guiltlessness, I should probably fare quite well with this Course. This much was encouraging.

Overflowing with these fascinating new concepts, I immediately wanted to share my findings with everyone close to me, the first person being Bob. Deep down, I still wished to be sharing the spiritual journey with a special partner and I hoped Bob would be the one; otherwise, given how conflict seemed to be woven into the very fabric of our relationship, it was clear, at least to me, that it would sooner or later have to come to an end. We had been living together for just over six months and, although we had a lot of great times together, our recurring cycle of conflict was wearing me down. It was not something I saw myself living with for the rest of my life.

Not wanting to be left behind and eager to share in something that I evidently felt passionate about, especially if there was a chance that it might bring us closer, Bob began to read DU. I was thrilled and, for the first time in a long while, I felt hopeful. We would ponder the meaning of life together, discover the knowledge we needed to resolve our relationship issues, all our problems would disappear and then we would share a peaceful journey and live happily ever after. Well, that was the general idea.

Excited by this new direction in my life, I also spoke about DU to my two closest friends. However, the concepts were so multi-layered and difficult to explain that I probably didn't make much sense. The glazed looks and heated arguments were certainly fair indicators of not only my inability to convey its message in a coherent manner, but also of my thorough lack of understanding of its essential message and purpose. To this day, I am not sure if my new-found philosophy of life was the cause, but those friends with whom I was so eager to share my metaphysical discoveries are no longer in my life.

Although I was clueless as to how far this path would take me, I knew I must follow it. The Workbook lessons, though very odd at first, seemed straightforward enough, the reader being simply instructed to "not undertake to do more than one set of exercises a day."[1] As usual, I was quite eager to tackle a new course of study, especially one that involved mind training, something with which I felt I already had a good base.

> The purpose of the workbook is to train your mind in a systematic way to a different perception of everyone and everything in the world. (W-in.4:1)

Having spent a fair portion of my life in some form of spiritual pursuit, I considered myself to be in touch with myself. I could easily pinpoint the psychological and emotional patterns and motivations that influenced my behaviour and choices, and if ever I sensed I was losing my way, I could always count on the astrology and

---

1. W-in.2:6.

numerology charts to put me right back on track. Although I had no illusions about attaining spiritual enlightenment in this lifetime, I liked to think that I was on my way to eventual awakening, despite my seven-body handicap. And I may very well have been except that, from what I was now learning, given the tools at my disposal, awakening would likely have taken thousands of lifetimes. It was that one, single, clear and very frightening thought that made me sit up and pay very close attention to what the Course had to say. Although I wasn't sure what I understood anymore, one thing was perfectly clear: I most definitely did not want to experience a thousand more incarnations.

As I applied myself to the daily practice of the lessons, I sensed that, even though I did not understand everything I was reading, I should simply continue to practise as best I could. More and more frequently, as I progressed through the lessons, I would get the gist of what I was reading. Sometimes it was only a whiff of an understanding, but those moments further fuelled my perseverance. In fact, on some level, I understood that it was probably normal to *not* understand everything, at least at the beginning, since there seemed to be a lot of uncovering that needed to be done before the truth could finally be fully experienced. I would turn to the following paragraphs several times while doing the Workbook lessons as a way of sustaining my courage to continue.

> Some of the ideas the workbook presents you will find hard to believe, and others may seem to be quite startling. This does not matter. You are merely asked to apply the ideas as you are directed to do. You are not asked to judge them at all. You are asked only to use them. It is their use that will give them meaning to you, and will show you that they are true.
>
> Remember only this; you need not believe the ideas, you need not accept them, and you need not even welcome them. Some of them you may actively resist. None of this will matter, or decrease their efficacy. But do not allow yourself to make exceptions in applying the ideas the workbook contains, and whatever your reactions to the ideas may be, use them. Nothing more than that is required. (W-in.8:1–6; 9:1–5)

As much as I managed to get through the Workbook lessons without too much difficulty, reading the Text was a whole other matter. It was certainly intellectually challenging. True, academia had not been my forte; nonetheless, I knew that I wasn't a complete moron. Except when it came to *A Course in Miracles*. Reading this document was like climbing blindfolded up a mudslide in the rain. Sometimes I would read a paragraph five, six or seven times and absolutely nothing would sink in, not even a glimmer of under-standing. On occasion I had wondered if, in my youth, given my difficulties with reading schoolbooks, I might have been slightly dyslexic. Now I was beginning to feel decidedly dyslexic.

In desperate need of help, I searched the Internet for learning aids and came across a series of CDs by Kenneth Wapnick called *Classes on the Text of A Course in Miracles*. At the same time, curious about the origins of the Course, I ordered a copy of *Absence from Felicity: The Story of Helen Schucman and Her Scribing of A Course in Miracles*. Despite my resolve to never again follow a spiritual teacher, considering that there was a mention in DU about Ken Wapnick being the greatest teacher of the Course, I thought I was probably making a good choice.[2]

While awaiting my learning aids, I continued to read DU. This work was much more accessible than the Course and I would read it a third time that year. Despite still not knowing how to integrate this new learning into everyday living, I felt for the first time in a long while that life was taking on a very profound meaning. While I had enjoyed being a businessperson and tackling the challenges of establishing my astrology practice in the practical, mainstream world, I was now ready to reignite the spiritual quest of my youth. It was not so much the memory of the darkness that appealed to me as the yearning for hope. If anything, this new thought system gave me hope.

I am determined to see. (W-pI.20)

---

2. *The Disappearance of the Universe*, page 95.

When I reached Lesson 20 of the Course, the first in a series on *seeing*, I immediately recalled the fourth item on my list of *101 Things I Want to Accomplish in the Next Ten Years*: "To see clearly into people and circumstances." Instantly, I took this as a sign, the first of many, that would help keep me focused on this path. Maybe I didn't understand everything that the Course was teaching, but at least I was on the right track! One day, there would be no more floundering in the dark. No more doubt. No more questions about the truth about the world and about life. I was finally going to *see*.

When Bob and I first began to explore DU together, things were looking up. He had been making progress with his therapy and I started to think that we might be able to make a go of our relationship. But things weren't going so well with my dad. Barely a couple of weeks after my mom and I completed our Reiki course, he suffered a stroke that left him blind, unable to speak and paralyzed over much of his body. I will always recall standing at the foot of his hospital bed letting the Reiki flow through my hands into his feet while he lay there unconscious. I never knew if he actually felt anything, but I liked to think he may have felt some comfort. Forty-eight hours later, he passed away.

Many times in the years that followed, I would wonder if my dad might have enjoyed reading DU just as he had enjoyed Thomas Merton. It is something I regretted not having been able to share with him. My dad's passing marked a difficult transition period for us; struggling with our grief, over the following months we all mainly kept to ourselves. My reading of DU had given me a sense of the relative meaninglessness of life in a body, in fact, of the entire world of form, but I was too acutely aware of having suffered a loss to derive more than a little comfort from this knowledge. The Course was not something I could share with my brothers, but I did order a copy of DU for my mom, thinking she might find it enlightening.

This was a quiet period during which I pondered not only the impermanence of life, but also its meaning. With the radical framework of the Course beginning to trickle into my understanding, life was starting to take on a whole new significance, one that left me with very mixed emotions. At times, I felt profoundly hopeful that there was another truth and that one day I would fully know it; at other times, I was confused and uncomfortably doubtful as to the veracity of this challenging book I was reading.

The first set of Ken Wapnick CDs arrived none too soon, for I was growing increasingly discouraged with the dullness of my brain so far as reading the text of ACIM was concerned. I borrowed my dad's portable CD player and dug out an old headset from my Rachmaninoff days. From the very first lecture on the Introduction to the Course, I knew that I had been led to a very fine teacher, although Ken's Elmer Fudd accent did cause me a few chuckles until I became accustomed to it. I established a habit of going for long walks in the afternoon with my portable player and a spare set of batteries. There was nothing more frustrating than having to walk home for fifteen minutes with a dead Walkman. I called it power multitasking; I got my exercise, ran errands along the way and learned the Course. It was a winning proposition all around.

With the help of these classes, a faint glimmer of light began to shine in the dark corners of my brain. I also made a habit of reading the text at night before going to bed, and, while many times all I could manage was a page or a paragraph before falling asleep, on good days I was able to get through two or three full pages. Although at first I interpreted my painfully slow progress with the Course as an intellectual defect of sorts, after a while I understood that my slowness was simply an indicator of my resistance to learning its message. Out of a sense of twisted logic, I took this to be a good sign. Resistance was good. If the goal of the Course was to uncover the truth that lay purposefully hidden from my awareness, then my intense resistance seemed to indicate that I was knocking on the right doors.

In the series of Classes on the Text by Ken Wapnick, there were two CDs per chapter. As a way of motivating myself to read through the Text, I established that listening to the corresponding CDs would be my reward. The rule was: No new CD until the chapter had been read to the last word! Sometimes it would take me two to three weeks to get through one chapter. Over and over, I would listen to the same CDs. Sometimes, I would go back a chapter, but never forward. As long as I had not reached the last line of the chapter, I would not listen to a new CD.

As can be imagined, over the year and a half it took to read the text and complete the lessons, I listened to some of the same CDs many, many times over! It was a childish game, but it worked for me. Eventually, I ordered all of the Lessons, without which I doubt very much that I would have gotten very far with the text. Actually, I'm quite certain that I wouldn't have gotten beyond the first chapter.

The face of Christ has to be seen before the memory of God can return. (C-3.4:1)

Eager to apply what I was learning in the Course, I decided to practise this new thought system at a breakfast meeting. The Women's Business Network met once a month at a Swiss restaurant nearby and catered to the needs of businesswomen from all walks of life and ages. Meetings were always upbeat, friendly and lots of fun. It seemed like the ideal place to practise seeing the face of Christ in everyone and to look for that experience of oneness the Course talked so much about.

As was the custom in networking meetings, each member was given the opportunity to stand up and introduce herself. Not everyone was comfortable with this part of the meeting, those who were just starting out in business being the most nervous. Mostly I sympathized with the rookies, recalling quite well the terror I felt the first few hundred times I introduced myself in front of a group. But that morning, I was anything but compassionate. To my surprise and utter horror, as I listened politely while the women presented themselves, one after the other, my mind began to churn out all manner of criticism and negative comment. This one was a bitch, that one had no style, the fat blond was an idiot and didn't know what she was talking about... and on and on it went. I was horrified! The bashings just kept on coming, each one more colourful than the last. The face of Jesus was nowhere to be seen.

Although, like everyone, I was guilty of making judgments, I considered that I was generally open-minded and accepting of people's choices. In all my years of networking, I had never experienced anything like this. Sitting there in my chair, calmly, perhaps even blushing a bit, but completely astonished, I watched as this runaway train of critical thinking mowed down woman after woman. And all for absolutely no reason. I hate to imagine what might have surfaced had I actually had a reason to be upset with someone that day! Thankfully, no one could actually *see* what was on my mind, but I was ashamed of what my mind had manifested that day.

Given that I was already into my second reading of DU, I had a sense of *what* was going on, though not quite *why* it was or what to do with it. From what I could see, it had not taken long for the resistance generated by my unconscious mind to kick in. Clearly, the ego was boss and it wasn't about to give up its throne any time soon! It wouldn't be rushed into experiencing shared interests and seeing the Christ—or anything good for that matter—in another person. On my return home, I loaded a fresh set of batteries into the CD player and went for a very long walk with Ken Wapnick.

Although disappointed, I was not surprised when my plunging into the Course eventually became a source of conflict for Bob and me. He blamed me for not practising forgiveness with him, and I argued back that he didn't understand what forgiveness meant. More and more, he accused me of being impossible to live with, and, more and more, I became convinced that living alone would be better than living with constant conflict. He pointed out that I couldn't survive financially on my own and that I needed a man around the house to fix things; on which point, I had to at least partially agree with him. My practice allowed me to barely pay the bills, and I wasn't able to put money aside for the much-needed renovations around the house. While in the past I had been able to call on my dad for help with home repairs, without Bob, I would have no one. Bottom line was that the prospect of living alone did cause me some concern, and I hesitated to make the final break. Why Bob persisted in staying in the relationship was still not clear to me.

I scoured the Course for clues as to what to do with our strained relationship, but found no clear answers. The sections on special relationships were particularly difficult to understand and I was nowhere near even beginning to grasp what it was teaching. I desperately wanted ours to become a "holy relationship" in which all would be forgiven and healed, but I was clueless as to how to make that happen. One thing I did understand was that suffering was not a requirement for awakening from the dream; the Course did not call for martyrs. That summer, Bob moved out of my house.[3]

That separation from Bob made our inability to resolve our differences very real to me, and I felt disappointed at not having been able to heal the relationship. After a time, I wondered if the reason for Bob's moving in with me in the first place had been to reassure my father that I would be all right, that I would have someone to take care of me after he was gone. In the end, I was glad he wasn't there to witness our breakup. He had liked Bob very much and it would no doubt have saddened him.

For the first time in my life, I was alone on all levels. My children were grown up and living downtown, I had no partner with whom to share the journey, no one with whom to discuss business issues and no one to share the spiritual quest. My mom and I had occasional conversations about DU and ACIM. I was glad when she said it had helped pull her through this most difficult of times, but although sharing my experience of the Course with at least one family member had seemed important, we both had many questions and much to learn, and struggling with my own occasional doubts, I had no answers for her need for guarantees. "If only there was proof," she said once, needing certainty that what the Course

---

3. Note that this was a number 2 Personal Year. See Chapter 5 of *The Power of Time* for more details of events of that year.

was teaching was the truth. Sadly, I recognized this doubt as my own.

My brothers made it clear that they had no interest in the subject. One even made it his duty to prove that Gary Renard was a fraud and *A Course in Miracles* was a cult by digging up stories on the Internet to make his case. He was passionate about conspiracies and there was plenty of cyber fodder to support his claim. Although brought up at one or two family dinners, for the sake of peace, the subject of DU and ACIM was dropped from our family discussions.

That summer, looking for ways to expand my business, I invited a few of my clients to receive free sessions while I established a Reiki practice. My cat Bubby was a regular and popular participant, stretching himself on the Reiki table alongside my clients. Sometimes I wondered if it was simply the joy he brought that made them feel better. While I provided Reiki energy, Bubby contributed zootherapy.

But for me, Reiki was about much more than healing the body. As I delved further into the teachings of the Course, I couldn't help but think about Jesus during Reiki sessions. In fact, Reiki became a way for me to reconnect with Jesus, who will always remain for me the greatest healer of all time. Although this was not part of Reiki practice, I took to visualizing him standing to the right and slightly in front of me, while the Holy Spirit stood at my right shoulder, slightly in back. I wondered a lot about what approach Jesus might have used in healing.

From what little I was beginning to understand through the Course, healing was not so much about the transfer of energy or the removal of an illness, but more about the mind of the healer and the patient. It was in fact about the joining of minds on a level where there was only wholeness. Over the next few months, I began to recognize that Jesus did not even see illness, at least not the way we perceive it. He saw only the wholeness of spirit. On a few occasions, I caught glimpses of the loving kindness that had the power to cause illness to dissipate. Given that his mind was free of the shackles of wrong-minded thinking, that he was not bound by judgment, by not acknowledging illness, only wholeness remained. Recognizing wholeness, a person could not help but be healed in the presence of Jesus.

I also began to see that healing was not about any particular practice, whether natural or allopathic; it was about the mind. When a person was ready to heal, the right technique or medicine came along and the healing began. This is why not all techniques worked all of the time, a point with which I had taken issue. In the end, this meant that Reiki—or any medicine, for that matter—was not the essential ingredient for healing. Healing was in the mind of the healer and the patient, who was in effect his own healer. There was also the important point that healing of the body was not always the desired or even necessary outcome. It was possible to live in a body that was not healed, but to have a mind that was healed: to be in the body, and not of the body. Ultimately, healing was of the mind.

That fall, not ready to give up on us completely, Bob succeeded in convincing me to remain as his dance partner. Now that we were no longer living together, and having spent some time apart from each other over the summer months, things were considerably easier between us. There was also the fact that I enjoyed dance and looked forward to moving up to the fourth-year class. Occasionally, Bob would drop hints, letting me know that he believed that one day we would get back together, but as much as I would have liked to be in a relationship, I did not share his vision. The old conflicts began to resurface not long after the new session began and I questioned the wisdom of my decision. But I had made a commitment and I would see the session to the end.

Gradually, I came to terms with the reality of living alone. I had a business to build and plenty of clients to see, a family and, of course, my Course studies. A relationship was the furthest thing from my mind. Approaching a number 3 personal year, I began to feel a surge of creative energy and, still determined to become a writer, I took a long hard look at "The Healer." Although my mom and Bob had really enjoyed my latest revision, my publisher wasn't as enthusiastic. Once again, my query was rejected. But with my new perspective on healing and the meaning of life, this work had lost its appeal. In fact, its themes now seemed naive and outdated, and instead of giving it another rewrite, I accepted the fact that as a learning tool, it had served its purpose. "The Healer" was laid to rest. Undaunted, I began work on a new novel with *A Course in Miracles* flavour, which I called "Forgiving Kate." By now, I was mature enough to not have expectations of becoming a best-selling author, so I wrote for the pleasure of writing. It was a relaxing, quiet and enjoyable activity, a nice break from consultation work.

Still feeling somewhat disoriented and not sure how to fit the Course into my life, I did my best to practise my daily lessons, all the while focusing on the practical matters of day-to-day living. One way in which I did work these teachings into my life was to ask the Holy Spirit for guidance on a daily basis. Upon rising in the morning, my first thought of the day would be a variation of: How can I be helpful today? Or, Where do I need to be? Or, What needs to be done? This practice produced a state of receptivity that often led to clear knowledge of what needed to be done during the day. It didn't have to be anything big or complicated, but I was usually inspired to do what turned out to be what actually needed to be done that day, from simple things like calling my mom, producing my newsletter or following up with a client. This was the beginning of learning to trust my new teacher.

One morning, as though in answer to my concerns about how to augment my business practice, I awoke with the very clear thought that I should gather up my numerology notes and articles and write a book that I could use to promote myself and my workshops. Still clinging to the dream of becoming a fiction writer, my initial reaction was to reject the thought outright. But, being that this was one of those early morning "out of the blue" kind of thoughts, I regarded it as a nudge of sorts from the Holy Spirit to whose guidance I had been opening myself more and more.

At first, I hesitated, thinking I would have preferred inspiration for my novel, but, in the end, I realized that it might be a good idea after all. Almost immediately, in my spare time, between consults and networking activities, I got busy producing this little book that would help take my business to the next level. It was a neat, clever and especially quick solution. Sensing that I had been guided in that direction, I affectionately referred to it as "The Holy Spirit's Book." Almost as an afterthought, I sent a query letter to my publisher, never for one minute thinking they would be interested. It was neither their usual genre, nor target market, but there was a first options clause in my previous contract that I felt should be respected. The plan was to publish the book quickly myself and then return my attention to fiction writing and my studies of the Course. That was the plan.

Chapter 12

A PERIOD OF LEARNING

Be still an instant and go home with Him,
and be at peace a while. (W-pI.182.12:9)

*I*t didn't take long for me to feel the positive effects of the new year, a social and buoyant number 3 Personal Year. Filled with exciting ideas for my new book and looking forward to expanding my network of contacts, I updated my goals for the year, replacing the publication of "The Healer" with the completion and publication of my numerology book, which I called "Living Numbers," a title with which I was quite pleased. Since this was going to be a quick book project, I also planned to draft the outline for the novel I had just started. The other item at the top of my list of intended accomplishments for the year was to finish reading the Course. It was going to be a busy year, and I was more than ready for it.

There was much about the Course's metaphysics that was yet beyond my comprehension, but I was pleased with my slowly growing understanding. I continued to enjoy the daily lessons, for they were more accessible and easy to grasp than the text, even though there were busy days when I could barely remember to read my lesson in the morning and at night. Before going to sleep at night, I dutifully pushed myself to read through the text. Some of what I was reading was beginning to make sense, thanks mostly to Ken Wapnick's Classes and a fourth reading of DU. But it remained a challenging read. Some nights it seemed as though I was just reading words on a page, words made up of letters that appeared to represent concepts in the English language. Holding on to the profound belief that this Course would take me to the Truth, the thought of quitting never once entered my mind. I continued with my childish reward system of listening to a new CD when I had completed a chapter. Sometimes I would count the remaining pages in the chapter I was reading, just to see how soon I would be listening to a new CD. When there were just a couple of pages left, I would make every effort to read to the last line of the chapter.

> You are still convinced that your understanding is a powerful contribution to the truth, and makes it what it is. Yet we have emphasized that you need understand nothing. Salvation is easy just *because* it asks nothing you cannot give right now. (T-18. IV.7:5–7)

Despite my struggles, the Course took a very important place in my life. I treated my copy of the book with reverence, never stacking other objects over it, underlining important parts in pencil with a ruler instead of with a highlighter, as was my custom with other works. To my mind, *A Course in Miracles* held the key to peace; it was the way home, it was the answer to the prayers of my youth and I desperately wished I could share its message with the people in my life. Unable to bring up the subject with family or friends without stirring up arguments and debates, I looked for other ways to express my thoughts and experiences.

Fired up with more creative juices than I could channel into my work, I decided to start a blog. That I was clueless about the mechanics of blogging did not for a moment deter me. I longed for someone with whom to talk about the Course; writing filled that need. It took some research and experimentation, but within a few days, *My ACIM Journey* was birthed into cyberspace. Although as far as I am aware, only a few people ever read my blog, it helped me integrate what I was learning. My first blog entry[1] sums up my general impressions of my experience of the Course.

---

1. Original blog entries have been edited and condensed for readability.

I Am as God Created Me

It has become very clear to me, now halfway through the Course lessons and at Chapter 14 in my readings, that this leg of my lifelong spiritual journey is the most important, most significant and also most difficult in that it challenges the foundation of all my belief systems, from my beliefs about the nature of reality to my beliefs about God and spirituality and to my beliefs about myself.

Now and then, as I read the lessons and the Course, I get the tiniest flash of insight, so tiny—but so significant that it keeps me moving forward in my studies. Yet, at the same time, I know that no matter how difficult to understand or how insignificant the progress may appear, this was meant to be and it came at the right time in my life.

Curious about how other people lived with the Course, I did an Internet search. From what I found, the experiences of other students were quite different from mine. Their accounts were filled with praise and awe; many saw great beauty in the writing and some reported experiences of light and spiritual awakening. After nearly a year of study, reading the Course continued to be a chore and I cannot say that I even remotely appreciated its poetic beauty. Perhaps one day I would welcome the finer aspects of the work; perhaps never. I did not believe this to be a requirement, since I was reading it for content, not form. The text had been transmitted to Helen Schucman, a highly intelligent and educated woman, an admirer of Shakespeare; understandably it was coloured by her personal style. For a gist learner like me, it would simply take a little more time. My goal was to learn how to live with the Course in my daily life. This was the real challenge.

The niggling doubts that arose from time to time when I allowed myself to question the truth of what I was learning were quickly laid aside when I reminded myself that the Course had found *me*, and not the other way around. I took this to be a sign that I was being guided by a higher intelligence; given the limitations I felt on my own intelligence, this was enough to sustain my resolve to persist with this path.

It is literally impossible for you to do this on your own. You are certainly welcome to try. If you will let yourself be helped, then much time can be saved for you.[2]

While it was one thing to open my mind to the guidance of the Holy Spirit early in the morning when things were calm and quiet, it was a whole other matter when the day kicked into its normal frenetic pace. At the ripe old age of fifty, I believed that I could do just about anything that needed to be done all on my own. Even though *A Course in Miracles* was presented as a self-study course, it made it clear that not only was it okay to ask for help, it was actually necessary. From my place in darkness, I needed a guiding hand if I was to reach my goal of returning home. A second blog entry illustrates this struggle:

On Asking for Help

Naturally, having for so many years relied on myself, done things on my own and basically shunned help and support of any kind, one of the many challenges of the Course was to accept that I was in fact not alone and, moreover, that I could not return home on my own, that I needed the help of the Holy Spirit to undo any blockages along the way. I let the idea hang around, without rejecting it, but without fully understanding it. Why should I bother God or the Holy Spirit with my insignificant problems?

Then one day, I understood. I'm not sure what exactly triggered my understanding, no doubt a combination of readings from the Lessons, the Text, listening to the Ken Wapnick CDs or reading DU, but it struck me. Significant or not, my issues were real to me, and since there is no order of difficulty in miracles, it didn't matter if I thought the matter too trivial or too great to be presented to the Holy Spirit; if it prevented me from experiencing peace, it should be brought before the light. In that moment, I understood that it was okay to ask for help, I understood that I needed help and I also knew that I welcomed help.

---

2. *The Disappearance of the Universe*, page 85.

So I set aside my pride, one of the many devices used by my ego-mind to hold me prisoner of the dark, and accepted with humble gratitude the help I was being offered, the help that had always been there. I knew then that all those times I had prayed to Jesus in my youth, when I thought he couldn't hear me or that I wasn't important enough to be helped, that he had indeed heard my prayers, that he had no doubt known of my pain and that he had voiced an answer to my plea. But from my place of profound darkness, I had not heard his gentle voice or seen his loving hand reach out to me.

Now I know that I am heard, that I have all the help I need. I will gladly bring my problems to the altar of God so that His light may shine on them, not so that God will fix things on the level of form, for this is not His domain, but so that I may see them for what they really are, broken fragments from my dream of illusions that simply disappear when brought to the Light.

As a way of getting closer to God, I decided to incorporate meditation into my daily routine. Though sincere in my efforts, given my hectic lifestyle, my sessions were sporadic and brief. The best time I found was just before going to sleep, if my reading of the Text had not already knocked me out. At first, I wasn't sure what approach to use in my meditations; mantras and mind control didn't seem to fit the need. Several times I had wondered what it would be like to simply jump over the threshold between this world and what the Course refers to as the Real World, where in my true waking state I belong. Would I one day return home? When a person was ready, was it that simple?

Then I recalled my childhood nocturnal journeys, where alone in my room, late at night I wandered to that place where the universe ends and God begins. Why not, I thought. It didn't matter that they had been childish imaginings; I didn't think God would be concerned much with technique. So I sat cross-legged on the couch, closed my eyes and took a few deep breaths. Like I had done as a child, I simply imagined myself wandering to the edge of the universe, where I lay down my burdens and worries of the day. I knew better than to ask for specific help with my worldly concerns, since doing so would only reinforce my belief in the world. Since my goal was to awaken from the dream and return home, the last thing I needed was to strengthen the dream world's hold on me. Without holding onto any expectations, I simply emptied my mind and surrendered. Although no great revelations occurred during these simple meditations, I did experience a tremendous sense of relief and peacefulness. During the few minutes I could muster here and there, I began to yearn more and more for that total release that would one day come.

Between meditations, readings and lessons, there was a life to be lived. To my great astonishment, a couple of days after having written the blog post on asking for help, I received a phone call from my publisher. It seemed they were very interested in my new book idea and they wanted to know when I could submit a first draft of "Living Numbers." This was not the response I had anticipated. In fact, I was a bit disappointed, since it meant that, if they published my book, it would take much longer to see the finished product than if I published it myself. I felt strongly about getting it done quickly so that I could use it to promote my business and move on to fiction writing.

While as a writer I was well aware of how difficult it is to get published, and in a way I was grateful to have a publisher interested in my work, a part of me looked forward to doing it on my own. As they had not yet seen the complete manuscript, chances were that it might be rejected. I jotted down the acquisitions editor's suggestions for content and direction of the book, and we agreed on a submission date for the first draft.

Still unable to talk about the Course comfortably, it remained a private part of my life. Throughout most of my years of practice, very few of my clients ever brought up questions about God or spirituality. Most people wanted to know about the mundane aspects of their lives, issues that concerned relationships, family, job and career. Since beginning my Course studies, though, I began to notice a new trend. The New Age/Self-Help movement was in full bloom, and clients were starting to seriously question the meaning of life. Usually, these questions would arise at the end of a consultation, and they were often tentative, "What about the spiritual aspect of my life?" one businessman asked.

Having embraced a whole new way of looking at the world, I felt uncomfortable recommending the popular books of the day. Sometimes a client would ask if I was familiar with Wayne Dyer or Deepak Chopra, authors for whom I had tremendous respect, and I would say "yes." But when they asked for my thoughts on the subject, having understood that one could actually go all the way home instead of hanging around making a nice life for oneself, it was a different matter. A few times, I tried to explain that I had found a path that was designed to help us awaken from the dream, or a path that went further than those to which they were referring, but invariably the words didn't seem to come together in a coherent manner. Instead of engaging in complex discussions, I took to recommending DU. At first, I would give an overview of the book, then, seeing that most of what I said was met with dazed stares, I simply made the recommendation and moved on to more mundane matters. It was frustrating to know that there was a better way of looking at the world, and to not be able to adequately convey this message.

It took over a month before I produced another blog entry. This one shows a growing optimism about my progress as I struggled to apply the Course's teachings in my life.

A Challenging Thought System

It's been nearly a year now since I first read DU and began the Lessons in the Course. For much of that year, I couldn't see how I could apply the seemingly complicated ideas of this new and certainly provocative thought system. But lately, even though I thought that nothing was going into that thick head of mine, I feel as though a heavy veil has begun to lift from my awareness. Even though I can't fully explain the metaphysics of the Course, it is beginning to make sense, and I'm starting to apply some of what I have learned to my everyday life.

When I find myself upset with something or someone, I remind myself that there is nobody out there, that whatever I perceive is a projection of my ego-mind—something evil or mean or ugly that I don't want to acknowledge as my own. I remind myself that I am not really here in this body, but only mistakenly think I'm here, that I'm really still with God, but have forgotten that I'm safe, with Him.

Even though I don't always immediately feel better, I've noticed that even though the hurt or anger or resentment or frustration does not instantly go away, it doesn't seem to last as long and it's not as intense. I'm not left brewing up some kind of justification for my bad feelings, or some kind of revenge, a revenge I would never really exact, yet a revenge that would make my ego-mind feel better.

Using this thought system doesn't make the world a different place or a better place, at least not from where I stand looking at it. I don't think the world can be other than it is, since it is made up by our collective unconscious ego, which means it will always have its ugliness and hatred and violence, at least until we collectively choose to think with our right minds and choose against the ego. That thought alone, the thought that the world will never be the peaceful place I seek, makes me want to continue to practise the Course's thought system. I understand that this Course doesn't make everything and everyone look nice. It's not about changing the world; it's about changing how I look at the world and remembering why the world was made in the first place and what it represents.

I thought I lacked in academic sophistication, that I could never get through the metaphysics, never understand the Course's meaning, but then it was given to us by Jesus, a most brilliant and compassionate teacher, and so who am I to question his methods?

While I was beginning to learn how to apply these new teachings in certain areas of my life, it was a whole other matter in my relationship with Bob, which continued as it had in the previous year, balancing between fun moments and stressful confrontations. Though he professed his continued interest in the Course, it did not evolve much beyond listening to the audio version of DU in his car, and so our conversations on the topic became rare. Whenever conflict arose between us, I tried to look at the situation as being part of the dream, as being *not real* but the pain I felt was all too real. Each time the storm would blow over and things would be fine until the next tempest. What compounded the situation now was that Bob had additional weapons with which to push my buttons. "It's just an illusion," he'd snap, or one of my hottest button pushers: "Forgiveness—you need to practise forgiveness!" Unable to avert the feelings of annoyance, I'd withdraw into myself until the irritation passed and I once again found a semblance of peace. Since we no longer lived together, I had plenty of time to calm down between clashes.

In contrast to my bumpy relationship with Bob, more and more, I found peace in the concepts I was learning in the Course. On occasion, while going for my daily walk and listening to a Ken Wapnick lesson, I would experience an instant of such intense love and joy that I thought I could explode. If someone happened to be walking by, it was all I could do to stop myself from hugging them. Sometimes, I would smile; most of the time, my smile was returned. During those moments, the universe could have disappeared, right then and there, and I would have welcomed it. Though infrequent and fleeting, those experiences—so powerful and so unlike anything I had ever before experienced—strengthened my conviction that I was on the right path. It was during this period that I was inspired to write the poem found in the opening pages of this book, *Only in a Dream*, a couple of days after which I wrote the following blog entry:

What Relief I Find in God

For so many years, I have struggled for the survival of this body, strived to perform, worked hard to grow and develop myself and my abilities. All these years I have struggled to maintain the reality of an error, sustaining a never-ending battle against imagined foes, against diverse adversities. All my life I have worked hard to make myself as unique and as special as possible, keeping others at bay, further reinforcing the separation that keeps me from my true self, from my true home. All this effort and energy I have applied in a world that is but a mirage, for goals that are but illusory.

What relief I find now in knowing that I do not need to continue to hold this false world intact, this world that is the making of my projections, this world that exists only because I choose to perceive rather than to know.

What a relief it is to know that in truth, there is no need for this or any struggle.

What a relief it is to know that I need do nothing.

What a relief it is to know that there is only God.

Over a period of a couple of months, I experienced what can only be described as episodes of extended learning, usually relating to the part of the text I was struggling with at the time. These occurred during the night while asleep and in the dream state. Someone, an unfamiliar voice, would talk to me in a language I could easily relate to, explaining the finer aspects of the themes I was trying to understand in my daily readings. I would wake up in the morning with a clear recollection of the dream lesson, but try as I might to hold on, the memory would fade the moment I stepped out of bed. This was no doubt an indicator of my lack of readiness to consciously integrate what I was learning.

The Course talks to us where we believe ourselves to be, that is, asleep, in a body in a dream world of form and matter. Its message is designed to awaken us to a reality that is deeply buried. The goal is to take us from one level to another deeper and completely distinct level. One of the difficulties of this process of moving from one level to the other is that both cannot be experienced at the same time, so that the more I delved into the teachings of the Course, the more I felt split, like I was living in two worlds. One was quite hectic, and the other occasionally brought intense glimmers of peace, as the following blog entry shows.

I Have Two Minds!

It occurred to me yesterday that my mind is indeed split. I do have two minds! There is the mind with which I look upon the world every day, in fact, every minute of the day, the mind that has kept me in darkness for far too long now. While looking upon the world with this wrong mind, I continuously make judgments: this is good, that is bad, I like this person, I dislike that person, this makes me happy, that makes me angry. Each time I make a judgment, each time I focus on the attributes of that which I perceive, I make it real. Each time I use my wrong mind and make the world real, no matter the nature of my perception, I reinforce my belief in it.

But I am being reminded now that I have another mind, this one seeming so quiet and so distant for having so long been ignored. Also, long drowned out by the noise and clatter of my wrong mind is a tiny place where one of my greatest powers lies, my ability to choose. For as far as I can remember, I have been choosing with the wrong mind. Now, I am learning to choose with the right mind.

As I learn to choose with the right mind, each new perception becomes an opportunity to re-educate my mind. Instead of passing judgment and making a thing real, I am learning to look beyond it, with my right mind. Instead of becoming angry at a situation, I remember that there is nothing real out there but the projection of my ego. When I find it difficult to see things this way, I ask my greatest ally for help, the Holy Spirit. Eventually, I come to release my wrong-minded way of seeing a situation. Sometimes it can take days, but eventually I release the error.

I am choosing with my right mind when I experience peace. Sometimes, I am reminded that I am as God created me, and there is only peace. Thinking with my wrong mind doesn't bring peace, and when it brings pleasure, that pleasure is soon taken away, for it is not eternal as is the peace of God.

It will take a lifetime to learn this new way of thinking. My ego struggles for survival when I choose to not think with its servant, the wrong mind. But I have tasted droplets of peace, and once tasted, nothing else can take its place. So I will learn to think with my right mind. No matter how long it takes, I will do it.

One of the most challenging teachings of the Course is that it clearly places the responsibility of our experience of the world, in fact, of the existence of the entire universe, squarely on our shoulders. *We* are the cause, not God or any other external or divine force. This was a difficult concept to accept, since I preferred to think of myself as being innocent of any wrong-doing, even if it meant that I must see myself as a victim of something or someone that is outside of me. In this way of looking at things, the pain or the trouble or the difficulty is not my fault.

> Projection makes perception. The world you see is what you gave it, nothing more than that. But though it is no more than that, it is not less. Therefore, to you it is important. It is the witness to your state of mind, the outside picture of an inward condition. As a man thinketh, so does he perceive. Therefore, seek not to change the world, but choose to change your mind about the world. (T-21.in.1:1–7)

The Course teaches that at any time, we can make a different choice, but since we value our separateness, we choose that which reinforces and maintains it. Since it all begins with a thought in the mind, it always boils down to a matter of choice. Choice ultimately is determined by purpose. I make a certain choice because I value its outcome. The Course asks: Do I want to experience oneness and the peace of God, or do I want to continue to experience separation? The following blog entry shows that at least on an intellectual level, I was beginning to get the gist of the metaphysics of this Course.

I Have What I Value

If I experience scarcity in my life, it is because I value it. Scarcity is the ego's proof that I am guilty, that I have sinned and have been banished from my true home, a place of infinite abundance. Scarcity is a symbol of the fact that I have chosen with the wrong mind. According to the ego's way of looking at things, I have sinned, and for that sin, the abundance of my Father should be withheld as punishment. In choosing with the ego, I choose to believe this fate and its accompanying reality, because this is what the ego wants, this is what the ego values.

If I choose with my right mind, I will know only abundance, for in God, how could there be anything but absolute abundance? But the ego doesn't want me to choose with my right mind, for in so doing, I will certainly realize that I have no need for the ego. I may in fact abandon it altogether, for, who would choose with a master that serves up scarcity and suffering over a Master who knows only love, peace and abundance?

Out of a justifiable fear of its own demise, my ego continues to devise ways that will keep me from seeing what I truly am—as God created me. And it is a clever ego, for it manages to keep me quite busy. Now, whenever I perceive scarcity, I try to remember that it is not who I truly am. Almost instantly, I feel relief and most of the time, this brings peace of mind, and is this not the purpose of this journey? In these moments, I know that I value peace more than I value the ego's options.

While I was beginning to appreciate the benefits of choosing with the right mind, I was also starting to see that this choice would not be easily made. As I continued to push myself to read the Course and understand its metaphysics, my nocturnal learning sessions were replaced with nightmares generally centring on loss— the loss of my home, explosions, fires. Several times I awoke with laboured breath and paralyzing fear, symptoms of severe anxiety. There was a period of several weeks during which I began to fear leaving the house, staying indoors as much as possible, even turning down invitations to networking events. I took these dreams as symbols of my ego's resistance to the work I was doing with the Course, my fear of letting go of the things of the world that clearly were growing less and less valuable, my fear of awakening from the dream.

I Am a Prisoner of My Own Choice

If I am created in the mind of God and in fact have never left my source—God—then I must be under the mistaken belief that I am elsewhere, not in God. This world to which I attribute great value, this world that I believe to be real, cannot be the world God created for me, for what God creates must be eternal, peaceful, loving and constant, qualities not reflected in this world I choose to make real.

When I look for God's world, I am blinded by all things made by the ego. When I try to hear the Voice for God, I am deafened by the noise made by the ego. I see bodies where I should see spirit, I see differences where I should see sameness, I see danger where I should see safety, I see competition where I should see compassion, I hear words of anger, threat and hatred where I should hear expressions of love, comfort and kindness. When I look inside, I see want, struggle and turmoil where there should be peace and abundance.

As I try to awaken, I feel more and more trapped. The senses that have until now been my instruments of navigation in this world I have for too long called my home act as the bars to a jail made by my ego. They are the blinders that keep me in darkness, the chains that bind me, the drugs that keep me asleep in the dream I call life. The more I understand the nature of the world I have chosen to believe in and the reasons for my choosing it, the more clearly I see the barriers my ego sets before my true vision. With each step forward on this journey, the tighter grows the ego's grip. As I grow more determined to return home, the ego grows fiercer in its dedication to its own survival; it would not want me to know that *I am forever an Effect of God.*[3]

The night terrors and the anxiety eventually passed, and, as I approached the final chapters and lessons of the Course, I began to grow increasingly eager to experience more of that profound peace I had glimpsed. The promise of a return home had become my beacon in the oftentimes overwhelmingly agitated sea of my life. During one of my meditations, I decided to try to accelerate the process a bit, wanting very much to see if I could simply go home. I recalled a line from DU where Arten makes a suggestion for meditation. Clearly, Gary had found peace in God, and I very much wanted the same experience.

Each day for at least a few minutes, think about God and how much you love Him.[4]

---

3. W-pII.326.
4. *The Disappearance of the Universe*, page 86.

Settled comfortably on the couch, I prepared for meditation. In that place where the universe ends and God begins, that quiet place where I have waited for God, there is a threshold, with darkness on one side, the side in which I appear to exist in the world, and pure light on the other side, where my true Self resides in waiting for me. After taking several deep breaths and with quiet mind, I visualized myself stepping across the threshold, into the light which was for me a symbol of perfect oneness, my sense of joining with God. Looking deep in my heart, I repeated the words—*Tell God how much you love Him... Tell God how much you love Him...*

To my surprise, from where there should have been only peace, a black rage exploded. It came from deep within my gut, and released a horrifying beastly awareness. My hatred for God was palpable; my terror nauseating. Snapping back to the side of darkness, I knew I had experienced the viciousness of the ego with which I continued to identify.

> The ego is therefore capable of suspiciousness at best and viciousness at worst. That is its range. (T-9.VII.3:7–8)

As much as I should have been rattled by this experience, the instant the image disappeared I recovered my sense of peace. In fact, looking at it with Jesus, I had to smile a little; knowing that He would not judge me, I should not judge myself either. I knew exactly where and what the enemy was and I knew it was not ready to give up its stranglehold any time soon. This would be a long journey of undoing, but I was up for the challenge. Besides, this was a battle that I knew deep down, I had already won.

A few of my clients returned after having read DU, expressing a need to talk about it. Since there was no ACIM study group in our area, that summer I decided to start one. Although I knew this was a self-study program that involved the student and the Holy Spirit and Jesus, I felt guided to start this group. Seeing myself as a student—like them—struggling to integrate these new teachings into my life, I saw no problem with a role of facilitator. Besides, with my extensive collection of CDs, we had enough learning aids to last us a hundred years.

When the city approved my request for the free use of a community hall, I took this to be a sign that I was doing the right thing. Meetings were set for the first and third Thursday of the month, and I was excited when I saw that eleven people had signed up for our group meetings. Not long after having started the group, I received an e-mail from one of our members. Sandra is the gentlest of souls, a healer and a deeply spiritual person. I had recommended DU to her over a year earlier. Occasionally we would bump into each other at networking breakfast meetings. Eagerly, we would engage in lively discussions about the book, its bold new perspective and its deep insights. In her e-mail, she apologized for having missed a few meetings, saying that she had been focusing on shamanism and energetic healing. She added that she found ACIM very insightful but a bit confining in what to do and what not to do.

Clearly, she was struggling with the application of the Course in her life, and admittedly, I was a bit disappointed, because of all the people I knew, Sandra was probably the most in tune with its teachings. I watched as my ego stepped right onto centre stage and made me and all of the people I knew who were struggling with these teachings victims of this impossible book. Why did the Course have to be so difficult? They didn't really want us to get it. It was for that special group of intellectuals only; not for the rest of us ordinary mortals. They could have made it easier.

> In every difficulty, all distress, and each perplexity Christ calls to you and gently says, "My brother, choose again." (T-31.VIII.3:2)

Trying hard to remember to *choose again*, I caught myself just in time, so that my loss of peace was brief. I immediately looked at the situation in light of my new learning, applying what was now becoming a familiar thought process. Since there really wasn't anybody out there and we all share one mind, and one mistaken choice, my friend's comment must be a symbol of my own resistance to the teachings of the Course. As the Course says, the world

I see is an outward picture of an inward condition. My condition was not only one of resistance, but also one of victimization. Sure, Jesus had given us this wonderful Course, but he made it in such a way that, unless you were a brilliant academic like Ken Wapnick or had private coaching from a pair of ascended masters, it seemed almost impossible to learn—much less apply. It wasn't our fault if we couldn't get it or couldn't bring it into our lives. They should have given us a course we could actually understand.

This little victim song could have gone on and on with a wide range of variations, if I allowed it. But it would only have reinforced the thought system of the ego, which I had already determined was not leading to my awakening. In fact, by choosing with the wrong mind, I was reinforcing the thought system of an insane world. The price I would pay would be a loss of peace, an increasingly high price to pay to play the ego's game. This was a small event, insignificant in the grand scheme of things, but I needed to begin my practice somewhere, and easy was a good place to start.

> Each small step will clear a little of the darkness away, and understanding will finally come to lighten every corner of the mind that has been cleared of the debris that darkens it. (W-pI.9.2:5)

It was clear from the beginning of my studies that *A Course in Miracles* makes very careful and often unique use of language. For example, this was not a course in miracles such as "raising the dead" or "turning water into wine." The miracle, as defined in the Course, is what the ego is not. The ego embodies the thought of separation and its resulting experience of darkness; the miracle reflects the light and peace of our true Self. Both remain in the realm of the dream, but while one maintains the illusion of the dream, the other leads to eventual release from the dream. While the ego's world is diverse and complex, the principle of the miracle is clear and simple: everything in the world is all the same, it is all part of the dream, and therefore is not real. Make a different choice, and experience peace.

The Course is also unequivocal in its teachings: in any and all circumstances, either choose with the ego or choose with the Holy Spirit. It's one or the other, but not both. As long as I continue to see things from the perspective of the ego's thought system, I'm not going home, I'm staying right here, in this dream, an outcome that is clearly opposite to what I desire. The choice I make in my mind will determine in the long run to which thought system I adhere. It's the *choice* that's important, not the event. The more often I choose with the right mind, the more is the wrong-minded thinking weakened and its hold lessened.

Given my ultimate goal, I wanted to apply right-minded thinking as often as possible, but the more I tried, the more difficult it seemed to become. Although I do not recall the specific events that prompted the following blog entries, it is most likely that they were the result of conflict situations with Bob. They show the inherent difficulty in working with a mind that is specifically designed to keep the truth hidden from awareness. Each step forward seems to be met with an equal step backwards.

True Power of Mind Unveiled

I saw my mind at work this morning. It was an awesome experience. I struggled to capture it in writing so that I could remember it and repeat it, and searched deeply for the proper words to adequately describe the experience, but words are but a pale version of the actual experience. Hopefully they will be sufficiently clear to remind me of the importance of minding my mind.

I had been thinking about a situation that occurred yesterday, and how my immediate response had been to find blame in the other person who I thought had let me down. He could have, and should have acted differently, I concluded, as I had wanted him to. However, in an attempt to integrate the teachings of the Course and to not fall into the trap of attack and judgment, I thought instead of how that person might be feeling. There is only one mind, after all, and we are all one. Before I say or do anything, I should consider the other person.

So it occurred to me that it was possible that he was feeling guilty for what had happened, maybe wondering if he could have done things differently. Then I reasoned that if I acted on my thoughts of blame and expressed my displeasure, I would be engaging in attack. Given his feelings of guilt, he might have responded with defensiveness, and very possibly anger.

What would happen if I made a different choice? What if I chose not to pursue my judgment-blame-attack line of thought? The other person probably wouldn't feel compelled to engage in defensiveness and anger. He wouldn't be able to project his guilt onto me and respond to me as though I was the cause of his discomfort.

That's when I saw it. I pulled back and observed my mind at work. It was like a giant energy-filled-bubble-wave at the level of perception, rolling out before me, just ahead of my experience. It was electric and organic, alive with potential power. At that level of mind, I saw clearly that I always have two choices. I could choose thoughts of love, and promote healing and a hasty return home, or I could choose judgmental thoughts of hatred, attack and blame and perpetuate the insane idea of a world of separate bodies and form.

I saw my life roll itself out before me. I saw that, with each experience encountered, I have the opportunity to make a better choice, no matter the circumstances. I can use the experiences of this life to learn to choose with the right mind, or I can continue to choose with the wrong mind and stay forever trapped in the dream. The choice I make from within the mind-bubble has the awesome power to either heal or to imprison. For the briefest moment today, I witnessed my mind, saw its power and hopefully understood the importance of being vigilant for each choice I make.

I Lost My Mind

As excited as I was about having recently caught a glimpse of the power of my mind, last night, when it came right down to it, I couldn't even find it. A situation occurred, a minor one at that, a situation at which I should simply have laughed. Instead, I fell for the lure of the ego's thought system and chose to dwell on the idea that things had not gone the way I had wanted them to go. Of course, I was not alone. When we lose our sense of peace, does it not all too often involve another person? I struggled to hold on to my sense of peace as I watched it dissipate, burned up by the fire of my specialness. Had my sense of peace too been illusory? Perhaps at least in part. The ego is so clever; I know it can fool me into thinking that I am actually making progress with my studies. Had my peace been complete and true, it would not have left me.

As the evening wore on I became increasingly mired in the ego's thought system. Trapped in this wrong-minded way of thinking, I became consumed in a colourful and most childish display of responses of displeasure, disappointment, impatience and frustration. My ego revelled in this activity; it was now in attack mode. It did what it does best, it found fault. Clearly, I was choosing this line of thought because I wanted it. This reinforced the idea that my interests are separate from those of another person.

Stepping back from the battle in my mind, I saw the ugliness and the power of my ego. I saw how it seeks to attack, how it lives to divide, how it is strengthened by separation. Being born as a thought of separateness, this is what it does best. This is what validates its existence. The choice for wrong-minded thinking reinforces my belief that I am here, in a body, with someone else, whose interests are separate from mine.

As I grappled to hold onto the thin thread of peacefulness that was rapidly slipping from my grasp, I called out to the Holy Spirit to take me out of the wrong mind, to help me remember that to attack or to manifest defensiveness is foolish and not necessary, to help me remember to think in terms of shared interests, that no matter what is going on in the world outside, that inside, we are one, and we all share one goal, to return to Him who loves us as His Son.

It took a whole night's sleep for me to recover my state of peace. Again, this wasn't a significant event, but I suspect that it is these seemingly tiny, insignificant occurrences that most severely test our ability to remember to choose with the right mind. Hopefully with the next incident—and I know there will be more—I will choose with the Holy Spirit sooner.

That fall, I signed a contract with my publisher. Needing to focus on completing the final draft of "Living Numbers," I retired my ACIM blog. Besides, I think I had been writing more for myself—for my own healing—than for my readers. When my editor informed me that the title of my new book would be *The Power of Time*, I was taken aback, not only because I thought that "Living Numbers" was a great title, but more because the Course makes a clear point about the illusory nature of time. In the end, I actually saw humour in the situation, seeing it as the Holy Spirit's little joke, a lesson in not taking the things of the world so seriously.

Excessive hours spent at the computer working on my manuscript over and above my normal work of writing up client notes, responding to e-mails, writing my newsletters and maintaining my website were taking their toll on my body. Tightness in my shoulders and upper arms was causing pain and limiting my range of motion. I scheduled appointments with a massage therapist and an osteopath, asking them to keep me going just long enough to submit my manuscript on time. I would rest afterwards.

Pleased and relieved to have completed the entire Course, I was a bit at a loss as to what my next step on this new spiritual journey would be. I continued to listen to the Classes on the Text during my daily walks and anytime I did chores around the house or spent time in the kitchen. In fact, except in the car, Course lessons had completely replaced music in my life. At night, having finished reading of the Text, I sat cross-legged on the bed and played rounds of solitaire, while I listened again to the Ken Wapnick classes.

Alone, without a guide or teacher and not having the courage to tackle a second reading of the Course, I sought out additional learning aids. Looking for material that might help me better integrate the Course's teachings in my life, I ordered Ken Wapnick's *Climbing the Ladder Home* and *The Lifting of the Veil*, and in the hope of healing my relationship with Bob—with whom I continued to dance—I ordered a series of lectures on Special Relationships. I had a strong hunch that, on a deeper level, our relationship had a purpose, which ultimately would have to be looked at if it were to be healed.

Well aware that my appreciation for the Course was intellectual, I would need plenty of additional help and lots of practice to reach a level of sufficient proficiency, one that would allow me to choose with the right mind more often than with the wrong mind, hopefully every instant of my remaining time in this body.

> Would you not want to make a holy instant of every situation? For such is the gift of faith, freely given wherever faithlessness is laid aside, unused. (T-17.VIII.3:1–2)

After submitting my completed manuscript, instead of taking a break from computer work and giving my shoulders a much needed rest, still fired by the creative energy of the number 3 Personal Year, I decided to design a website for our family recipes. Web design was the worst thing I could have done for my aching shoulders, for it required a lot of mouse manipulations, the main source of my tendonitis. Once the website was uploaded, I looked for another writing project. It felt odd not having a book in the works, so I considered my options. "The Healer" was definitely dead in the water, and "Forgiving Kate" didn't really inspire me. One morning, as though in answer to my question, I awoke with the very clear idea that it was time to dust off my old journals and begin to work on "My Story," as I called it. Writing would become a part of my healing process.

Chapter 13

A LESSON IN TRUST

There is no challenge to a teacher of God. Challenge implies doubt, and the trust on which God's teachers rest secure makes doubt impossible. (M-4.II.2:5–6)

*T*he number 4 Personal Year is typically a year of hard work, the need to pay attention to details, home, health, family and foundation issues, all of which would surface over the course of 2007.[1] In early January, I revised my life goals, but found it difficult to be motivated by anything material. The study of *A Course in Miracles* had made its way up my priority list, and the *101 Things I Want to Accomplish in the Next 10 Years* was whittled down to one goal: awaken from the dream and return home. Nothing else could come close to this objective in terms of importance.

Our ACIM study group had settled down to five regular members, so I decided to move the meetings to my home. That way, we could make use of the DVD player. Since most members had still not graduated from DU to ACIM, we watched the DVD of Gary Renard's *The Art of Advanced Forgiveness* workshop and listened to his *Secrets of the Immortal* CDs. We were all very much looking forward to Gary's Montreal visit in April, and had even arranged with his local publisher to take him out for supper. The plan was to knock his socks off with an authentic Moroccan dinner complete with belly dancing show, something that was not too difficult to arrange in a cosmopolitan city like Montreal.

---

1. 2007 was a 22/4 Personal Year for me.

The first session of dance was wrapping up at the end of January, and, again, I hesitated to sign up for the second. Little had changed in my relationship with Bob, but it was difficult for me to quit and leave him without a partner in the middle of the year. There was also the fact that, although I was no Ginger Rogers, I did enjoy dance. Admittedly, this was the oddest relationship I had ever had, while, on the one hand, we were the best of friends, on the other hand, we invariably landed in the same old pit of conflict. Conflict had never been a problem for him, but, for me, with each new clash, one more nail was added to the coffin of our relationship, and after four years, the coffin was just about nailed shut. But something kept us together; I wanted to know what it was.

I believe it was after one of our dance floor disputes that my hunch about the deeper significance of our relationship was at least partially confirmed. I had been pondering the reason for our fated friendship when, one night, I had a very vivid dream—so vivid, in fact, that I woke up, certain that what I had seen had been very real, far more like a memory than a dream.

It was nighttime in fourteenth- or fifteenth-century Europe. I was running gaily down a wet and muddy road, the hem of my long skirt heavy with grime, my feet caked with dirt. I had no care in the world as I hurried to the local pub; in particular, I felt no concern for the young son I was leaving behind. He was accustomed to fending for himself—he had to be, since it was just the two of us. I don't think I even knew who his father was; there had been so many. Besides, I would always be there in the morning. As I ran down the road, I looked forward to spending the evening drinking and laughing with my friends; in fact, I lived for my nightly revelries. In that past life, my only concern had been for the satisfaction of my abundant sensory appetites. I lived a carefree but brief life, leaving a child to suffer the pain of abandonment.

Although I had long accepted the concept of reincarnation, I never made a big deal about past lives, not only for having heard too many people use this knowledge to make excuses for present day circumstances, but also because they were impossible to verify.

If minds are joined, as the Course and other thought systems suggest, then it is possible to capture images and memories from the collective memory. If this be true, then there is really no way of knowing for sure if the memory is actually your own.

But when I awoke in the dark of my room that night I knew with absolute certainty that the little boy in my dream was a previous incarnation of Bob. Suddenly, it all made sense. Each time I had pushed him away or tried to end the relationship, he managed to talk me back into it. Although our present-day situation was entirely different, I saw that in a way we were re-enacting an old pattern of abandonment. With this new understanding, I saw that this relationship was indeed an important healing opportunity for both of us, and it did bring a measure of peace, at least for a while. Although we joked about it, I think Bob was less amused than I was with his newly designated status of "son."

When I wasn't busy seeing clients, I worked on my new writing project, which, inspired by one of my blog entries, I had tentatively titled "Waiting for God." Looking back over my life with the new perspective of the Course proved to be not only enlightening but also liberating. Instead of seeing specific events of varying degrees of significance, I saw symbols that told a story with far deeper meaning. The strong themes of separateness and specialness woven into the background of the symphony of my life stood out clearly, as did the themes of duality.

For example, Isle-Maligne, my birth town, perched on a jagged rocky island surrounded by rapid currents and difficult to access,[2] was an excellent symbol of where I have stood much of my life. To the west of the town lies the lake, a symbol of peace and wholeness for which I have always held a profound fondness, and, to the east, the gushing waters of the Saguenay River flowing away from the peacefulness of the lake, toward the busy St. Lawrence River. Sometimes when attempting to apply the principles of the Course in my life, I felt as though I were swimming upstream against

2. Hence its name, Isle-Maligne, roughly translated as "difficult or mean island."

an impossible current that was pulling me from my Source. Isle-Maligne was a great metaphor for my feelings of being trapped in the flow of my busy life, an existence entirely made up in my mind, a world designed especially to keep me from my true Self. There I stood, pulled between my desire for the peace of God and the allure of my life as a separate and quite distinct individual.

While gathering up material for the chapters on the early years, I searched the Internet for information on the churches of my youth and was pleasantly surprised to find that all of them had websites. I was flooded with clear memories of our family visits to Saint Joseph's Oratory, and later my lunchtime meditations at Notre Dame Cathedral and evening masses at St. Patrick's. Of my youth, these are some of the memories that stood out with the most force.

Needing a break from work one February afternoon, I went for a walk, stretching it out longer than usual, enjoying the clear sky and crisp minus five temperature. I was listening to a Ken Wapnick lecture, and although I had not been trying to understand anything specific, in a slightly veiled flash I understood that the more often I applied the teachings of the Course, the more my ego's thought system would loosen up and eventually crumble away. It was an intensely peaceful and reassuring moment in which I saw how the Course was working, how my wrong-minded thought system was slowly becoming undone, even though I did not have any conscious control over the process.

While on another walk a couple of days later, it occurred to me that it was one thing to apply the teachings of the Course when one was healthy and things were going along smoothly, but it must be a whole other matter when a person was ill or suffering in some way. While I thanked my lucky stars for having my health, little did I know that I had just experienced a hunch. It wasn't long after I projected that thought into the universe that it became manifest.

Years spent accumulating tension in my shoulders from spending far too many hours at the computer combined with a lack of exercise finally took its toll. It had become increasingly difficult for me to hold up my arms at dance, and I had long given up attaching my bra fasteners around the back. Once while trying on a camisole in a store, I nearly had to call for help to remove the top, unable to raise my arms because of the pain. Bob would phone me during the day and remind me to do my arm and shoulder stretches, which I would do sporadically and half-heartedly throughout the day, preferring to return as quickly as possible to whatever I was doing at the computer.

I mixed up some Bach Flower Remedies and added homeopathy and Reiki to my daily regimen, but when nothing in my repertoire seemed to help, I scheduled an appointment with an osteopath. Of course, it never occurred to me to stop doing the things that caused the pain in the first place; working at the computer was at the core of my business and writing.

When I arrived at the sports clinic for my appointment, the pain in my shoulders had grown so intense that I had trouble getting out of my car. My left shoulder was so jammed up that I had to reach across with my other arm to open the door. If it had been the right arm, I wouldn't have been able to handle the gear shift. Fortunately, the wait in the clinic was brief; not much longer than it took to fill out the patient questionnaire, which took a while, given the pain and numbness that extended down my right arm and fingers.

Within minutes, John introduced himself and then led the way to a small exam room behind the reception area. He took detailed notes as I explained my situation, the ergonomics of my work environment and my overall health history. I was instructed to stand in various positions while he observed and took more notes. The next step was a series of manipulations and movements while I sat and then lay back on the exam table. As he worked on my left arm, pushing it up into the tension, tears came to my eyes until I could take it no more. I cursed loudly and immediately apologized for my rude language. John seemed immune to such outcries.

To my relief, the treatment was brief. I waited eagerly while John scribbled more notes on his pad, thinking that with a proper diagnosis, we would get to work, and after a couple of sessions I would be as good as new. He finally put down his pencil and began to explain. I had rotator cuff impingement in both shoulders aggravated by stress at the top of my spine. It was imperative that I get the arms moving he said or else within a few months capsulitis would set in, at which point my shoulders would become frozen in place, a condition that might go so far as requiring surgery.

Okay, we can work with that, I told myself, even though I was clueless as to what he had just said. The way I saw it, there was nothing that couldn't be fixed. Eager to proceed, I asked what I should do to speed up my recovery. He recommended that I bring down from the shelves anything that I would need on a daily basis. I was not to raise my arms above shoulder level, nor carry any heavy weight. He gave me a couple of exercises to do several times a day and recommended that I sleep on my back to alleviate the stress on my shoulders. Icing the shoulders several times a day would help reduce the inflammation.

Not particularly fond of illness or pain, I promised to do exactly as recommended, and then asked how long he thought it might take for my shoulders to heal. In my mind, a couple of weeks should do it. I had a book to write, websites to maintain, a business to run, a new book to launch—a million things to do. Summer was just around the corner, which meant gardening—I needed to be able to use my arms. Noncommittal as most medical professionals are, he hemmed and hawed, shrugged and grimaced until I pushed for a time frame.

"A few days? Weeks? Months?" I said.

It would depend on how well and how frequently I did my exercises, he said finally, adding that, realistically, a condition such as mine was likely to take a few months.

Overlooking the "few months" part of the diagnosis, I returned home, hopeful and determined to fix the problem without further delay. As instructed, I modified my living space, lowering the things I used on a daily basis onto the counter: a set of dishes, a mug, coffee and filters, salt and pepper—the basics. I studied the ergonomics checklist to see whether there was anything I could do to improve my workspace, but found that I had already done everything I could, except perhaps lower my desk a couple of inches. I searched the Internet for a more ergonomic keyboard and mouse. No problem; I asked Bob to trim the legs of my desk and order new hardware for my workspace.

Over the next few days, I diligently exercised my rotator cuffs, setting a timer by the computer to remind me to take breaks every hour. I sewed together a wrist weight, which I filled with two pounds of rice for the hanging arm exercise. I avoided carrying anything heavy, using my knapsack when going out for errands. With throbbing pain shooting down the backs of both arms, it was difficult to find a comfortable position in which to sleep at night. I tucked cushions around myself, but that didn't work. As recommended, I tried sleeping on my back, but this was really not my preferred position. I'd had lower back issues for years, and was more comfortable on my side.

As the days passed, contrary to my expectations, my condition worsened. At dance class, I joked about the pain, barely able to hold my left arm up in dance position. We were practising the Viennese waltz, a dance that requires a great deal of arm and shoulder extensions. I'm not sure whether it was the stress from dance, the strain of the rotator cuff exercises, having slept on my back or a combination of factors, but when I awoke the morning after dance class, my back hurt like hell. I took ibuprofen, Bach Flowers and homeopathic remedies hoping that something would dull the pain so I could get some work done. Rather than wait for my usual late afternoon time slot, I put a CD into the walkman and went for my walk, which I had fully expected would be beneficial. To my surprise, as I walked, I found it increasingly difficult to keep my back straight. By the time I arrived home, the only way I could manage the pain was with my head bent forward, looking down at my feet.

I had arranged to meet a group of students from my numerology workshop that evening to see the movie *The Number 23*, but now I was beginning to think that I wouldn't make it. Afternoon came and the pain worsened. I was not going to be able to sit for two hours in a theatre. Stooped over my keyboard, I fired off a quick e-mail to the group advising that I was too ill to attend, at the same time hoping that everyone would receive the message in time.

While the pain continued to intensify, I considered a visit to the clinic, but only as a last resort. I called my acupuncturist to see what she suggested, but we both agreed that a medical consult might be best. Then it occurred to me that not only could I not walk or drive my car, but sitting in the back of a taxi cab wouldn't be much easier. Facing a situation I couldn't fix myself, I was beginning to feel increasingly uncomfortable. However, the pain being far worse than the helplessness, I called a friend with whom I had spoken earlier in the day. She lived near the clinic and often had occasion to come out my way to pick up her daughter.

Although she had no plans to pick up her daughter that day, without hesitation, Veronica offered to drive me to the clinic. I dreaded the thought of sitting in a hard chair for two to three hours waiting to see a doctor, but at that point, I saw no alternatives. If I had to, I'd lie down on the floor. I really didn't care. All I wanted was relief.

By the time we reached the check-in desk at the clinic, it was all I could do to hold myself upright. With both hands on the counter for support I looked up and was surprised to be greeted by a friendly face.

"Hi Pauline!"

It didn't matter that I looked like a wreck, I welcomed the familiar face. Helen and I briefly exchanged small talk; then I explained my situation. Seeing the extent of my discomfort, she promised to accelerate my check-in and, within minutes, I was sitting with the triage nurse. It pays to know people, I thought, as she took my vitals, noting my high blood pressure. Once I was processed, Helen took me aside and suggested that since the wait would be long, I would probably be more comfortable at home. Although not a normal practice, they would call me just before my turn to see the doctor. I was relieved to not have to sit in the crowded waiting room; all I wanted was to lie down, and the floor didn't look appealing.

Since Veronica lived around the corner, this is where we waited. Three very long hours passed before the clinic called; when I arrived, I was immediately led to a waiting area in the back. Within minutes I was in an examination room with a doctor being diagnosed with tendonitis of the rotator cuffs and given the standard menu of prescription drugs: an anti-inflammatory, a muscle relaxant and a painkiller. Despite my aversion to prescription medication, I looked forward to getting some relief.

Although it might have been only a couple of minutes, it felt like forever before the pharmacist filled my prescriptions. As soon as she put the painkillers on the counter, I took my first tablet. The recommended dose was one or two tablets every four to six hours with a maximum of eight per day. Not accustomed to taking prescription medication, I was certain that the minimum dose would suffice. By the time I arrived home, I felt no effect from the painkiller. I took an anti-inflammatory and waited a little while longer before taking the second painkiller. I paced the house, trying to find a comfortable position to sit while waiting for the hour at which I could take my second dose. It was another very long wait before eleven o'clock, at which point I eagerly took a full dose.

I prayed to Jesus and the Holy Spirit to help me see that on a deeper level, this was not my real self. I searched the teachings of the Course for relief.

I am not a body.
I am as God created me.
I am not a body.
I am spirit.
This world is only an illusion.

But the pain was so intense that there was no doubt in my mind that I could be anything other than a body. If I *was not* my body, at the very least I believed that I *had* one and it was making its presence very clear. No amount of prayer or metaphysics could convince me otherwise. With pillows piled around me, I tried to get some sleep, but by four in the morning, the drugs had still not taken effect; in fact, the pain had worsened. Exhausted from lack of sleep and constant pain, and unable to find a comfortable position, I grew seriously concerned. I delayed my next dose for as long as I could, but by five o'clock, the pain was stabbing through my back on the left side, my fingers had grown numb and I was having trouble breathing. Something was definitely wrong. I began to panic. What if I was having a heart attack?

I considered calling 911 but, unable to lie down comfortably, I didn't see how I could handle being strapped to a gurney. Since I knew he was an early riser, I took a chance that Bob might be awake, but when he picked up the phone, I knew he had been asleep. I struggled to keep the tears in check as I explained that I could no longer stand the pain, that I needed to get to a hospital and that I thought there might be something terribly wrong.

By the time Bob picked me up, I was trembling from head to foot. Putting on shoes, getting into the car, sitting—whatever I did, I was engulfed in pain. The emergency room nurse was not the friendliest of caregivers. She asked on a scale of one to ten how I would rate the intensity of the pain. I was exhausted and having trouble breathing, but, at the same time, I realized that the painkillers were beginning to take effect. My mouth was dry and I had trouble focusing. Compared with the night before, my blood pressure was back down to normal. Showing signs of impatience, she repeated her question. I thought about the pain, and realized that, although when I left the house I would have rated the pain at eleven, it seemed that it might now be a nine. She must have taken my symptoms seriously enough, for it wasn't long before she gave me an ECG. I was relieved to find that there was no problem with my heart, but the nurse, clearly annoyed that I had wasted her time, left in a flash, leaving me to fend with fasteners and clothing for a good ten minutes. She must have wondered what drugs were floating my boat. Since I wasn't having a heart attack and the pain killer seemed to be kicking in, I decided not to wait the four to five hours it would take to see a doctor. Besides, if we left right away, Bob could get to work on time.

The next few days were pure hell. The meds were barely effective, they made my mouth pasty and put my bowels on hold. Unable to work, confined to the house, not able to find a comfortable place to sit and read, or lie down and rest, or even to go for a walk or sit in a hot bath, I felt like a prisoner in my own home. I was a prisoner of my own body. The sight of my office, which I had associated with the cause of my pain, made me nauseous. I would sleep for a couple of hours, then, awakened by pain, get up, ice my shoulders, and, since sitting at the computer was out of the question, I would make myself as comfortable as possible with pillows and cushions in the recliner in front of the television.

Daytime television was one of those things that I have always absolutely abhorred, but since I was unable to go outside, days and nights had blurred into one. In the basement, any time looked like nighttime. All my efforts were spent trying to find the position, whether lying or sitting, that generated the least amount of pain. Reminded by a note in my agenda that I was scheduled to sponsor a Dr. Christiane Northrup talk on PBS, I tuned in to the station a couple of minutes early only to catch the tail end of a show called *Yoga for the Rest of Us: Back Care Basics*. How fortuitous! This was exactly what I needed. I'd take up yoga and heal myself. Firing off an e-mail to my contact at the network, I asked how I might get a copy. Since there seemed to have been a mix-up with my sponsorship, they'd send me a complimentary copy of the DVD. It was a sign, the reason I had been guided to watch daytime television!

If one sign wasn't enough, another came when, not long after, again, flipping through the TV Guide on my television, I came across a show entitled *Waiting for God*. I could hardly believe there was a comedy with the title of my new book. Disappointed, but at the same time grateful for this bit of information, I understood that I was to find another title for my book.

I have forgotten what I really am, for I mistook my body for myself. Sickness is a defense against the truth. But I am not a body. And my mind cannot attack. So I can not be sick. (W-pI.136.20:3–7)

My inability to work was becoming a concern; while I may have been indisposed, the bills certainly were not. Fortunately for that week, I had phone consults, so I was able to stand up and move around while working. I would not have been able to sit at my desk for the full hour and a half I needed to prepare and complete a consultation.

While trying to understand why this was happening, it occurred to me that my ego might have been rebelling against my Course studies. I was already aware of how fearful and threatened that part of my mind was; perhaps I was punishing myself for getting too close to the truth, for threatening the existence of my ego identification. In my current condition, it was clear that I identified with my form in a body, and not with my being as spirit. I was clearly separate and distinct from my Source. With the level of pain I was experiencing, there was nothing in what I had learned in *A Course in Miracles* that could convince me otherwise. As many times as I repeated—I am as God created me, I am not a body, I am spirit—the fact remained that I was entirely identified with the pain in my body.

Since nothing I had tried so far was working, I took my brother's advice and called his chiropractor. Fortunately, he graciously accepted to drive me to her office. She recommended her own blend of homeopathic remedies, which of course I took, then I scheduled a second appointment two days later. As I was leaving her office she warned that the pain might increase while the body healed itself. That night, I spent another hellish night of pain, but I sucked it in and took it as a positive sign. It must be working!

Between uncomfortable naps, there was plenty of time to think, and one subject that preoccupied me more and more was money. Over the past few weeks, I had been chasing a client for an unpaid bill, a rare occurrence in my practice. Struggling with feelings of frustration and resentment, I tried to remind myself of the principles of the Course as they relate to relationships. It was difficult for me to see her as innocent. In fact, as far as I was concerned, if I let myself think with the wrong mind, the woman was anything but.

I also felt some resentment for the person who had referred her, for he apparently had been aware of her habit of bouncing cheques. If he had told me about this in advance, I could have made provisions. In short, despite my best efforts, it was difficult to think with the Holy Spirit rather than with the ego.

I think it was the middle of the afternoon when I awoke with a very clear question on my mind. As usual, it was the pain that woke me, but the words rose above the pain, loud and clear: "Are you ready to get to work now?" I understood this to mean: Was I ready to apply forgiveness to the situation at hand? At that moment I felt ready. I was open for guidance and I would learn to apply forgiveness.

Taking a break from DU, I picked up Gary Renard's second book, *Your Immortal Reality*. It was actually the third time I was reading it and, coincidentally, I was at a section in which his teachers remind us of the importance of relinquishing all grievances in the process of forgiveness. I thought it might be a good opportunity to apply what I had learned in the situation with my client.

> Love holds no grievances. You who were created by love like itself can hold no grievances and know your Self. To hold a grievance is to forget who you are. To hold a grievance is to see yourself as a body. To hold a grievance is to let the ego rule your mind and to condemn the body to death. Perhaps you do not yet fully realize just what holding grievances does to your mind. It seems to split you off from your Source and make you unlike Him. It makes you believe that He is like what you think you have become, for no one can conceive of his Creator as unlike himself. (W-pI.68.1.1–7)

Lying on my bed propped up by pillows in a relatively pain-free, perhaps at least moderately codeine-induced, moment, I thought about the client with the rubber cheques. I looked for a way to change my mind about how I perceived this situation, to look at it with the Holy Spirit rather than with the ego, to experience love rather than resentment.

I began to meditate on how we are all really fighting the same battle, the battle to protect our separate and individual existence in a made-up world, the battle to cover up our thoughts of sin, guilt and fear. While thinking of our common struggles, I relaxed, allowing myself to drift into a profoundly restful state, all the while remaining fully conscious. Soon, an image began to form in my mind, like a memory from long ago, where I saw myself in a trench dressed in dirt-covered battle gear, my fellow infantrymen nearby. It was wartime; WWI came to mind. In the fear-filled darkness of the night, we sought out each other's eyes, looking for the tiniest spark of solidarity that would confirm that we were fighting the right battle, looking for the strength and motivation that would help sustain us through another day of combat and death.

> Truth does not fight against illusions, nor do illusions fight against the truth. Illusions battle only with themselves. (T-23.I.7:3–4)

Life in the dream is very much like a battlefield, and I thought of how, at any given time, I was very much at war on several fronts, from the basic struggle for survival to the struggle against aging and illness, to the struggle to ward off danger and the threats to my emotional well-being. All these struggles I shared with my client with whom I was engaged in battle. What I needed was to make a choice as to whether or not I wanted to continue to do battle. Did I really want to keep fighting the forces of attack in a world that was made up, a world that was of my own making in the first place?

The Course says that I don't really need to do anything;[3] I certainly don't have to do battle, and, in fact, all I need is a little willingness to see things differently, to make another choice. It was becoming increasingly clear that most of the time I was actually doing battle with myself—either punishing myself or causing myself pain—justifiable consequences of my guilt for the alleged original sin against God. In the end, my biggest forgiveness lesson would be to forgive myself for that one mistaken choice—the choice for separateness over oneness, a choice that could never be

---

3. I Need Do Nothing. (T-18.VII)

true, for how could anything exist outside of perfect oneness? That's all it was, I reminded myself, a mistake, and in counterbalance to that little mistake, I had great willingness to learn a different way of looking at the world.

Forgiveness is my function as the light of the world. I would fulfill my function that I may be happy. (W-pI.62.5:2–3)

I thought again of my insignificant battle with my client, imagining the spark in her eyes, as we recognized each other for what we really are in truth—Spirit—only dreaming we are bodies fighting for survival in a make-believe world. Seeing Spirit in her eyes, I was suddenly overwhelmed by a profound and complete love, knowing that we were as one, not separate at all, with no battle between us. Over the next few days, each time I thought about my client, I practised this kind of forgiveness. In looking for the sameness instead of the separateness, little by little the battleground faded, until all that remained was the love that had lain hidden beneath the grievance.

As a matter of course, I sent her another e-mail reminder, a polite note, and, this time, it really didn't matter whether I was paid or not. This was just routine business. The ego would have wanted me to continue to resent her for making me chase after her payment, but now I saw her as one of my angels, just another opportunity to practise forgiveness. In the end, I felt tremendous gratitude for the chance to put into practice what I was learning, and in my new way of seeing the world, she had become an instrument of the Holy Spirit.[4]

Trapped in my nightmare of almost constant physical pain, I did more thinking. There had to be something I could do to accelerate the healing process. With my mind thus preoccupied, the pain was less evident. I thought of my Course journey, and how I felt at a loss as to how to apply what I had learned to my own healing. I understood that I could not ask God to heal me from a condition I had created myself, of which He had no knowledge. This point

---

4. Interestingly, I received a cheque in the mail the following day.

was made quite clear in the Course. In fact, to have God interact in the world would make the world real, and if the truth is that only oneness with God is real, then the world cannot be real.

The thought that there existed something that was *not this*, that there was God—a state of perfect oneness and peace, everything that this world was not—sustained me through this trying period. It was becoming increasingly clear to me that this world could not possibly have anything to do with God, and in that knowledge, there was hope. The more I thought of it, the more I was relieved. This was a really good thing. Thank God He had nothing to do with this world, I repeated to myself many, many times. Thank God.

A week after my first visit to the clinic, I returned to have my prescriptions renewed. Although the pain in my shoulders was beginning to diminish, the pain in my upper back, the more unbearable of the two, hadn't changed. My new doctor sympathized with my situation, taking the time to recount her own experience with a shoulder injury. She strongly recommended physiotherapy, and following her advice, I went down the hall to schedule an appointment.

The following morning, I received a new diagnosis from the physiotherapist. "I'm not touching those shoulders," she said. "At least not yet." Then she explained that I had a radiculopathy at C7. My brain being already numb from the meds, I asked her to write down the diagnosis. Happy with this new information and hopeful that she would fix the problem, I scheduled another appointment.

The task of chauffeuring me to my appointments was shared by my brother, my sister-in-law, Bob and Veronica. Never having been a big fan of angels, seeing them as little more than big white fluffy imaginary things floating around in the heavens, I began to see these wonderful people as my angels. There was no doubt in my mind that their kind help was guided by the hand of the Holy Spirit. This is when I learned that it was okay to accept—and even okay to ask—for help from others.

Sickness is a defense against the truth. I will accept the truth of what I am, and let my mind be wholly healed today. (W-pI.136.15:6–7)

Another week of pain management passed with slight improvement in the shoulders, but none in the back. I think any improvement I experienced was more on the level of becoming accustomed to living with extreme pain. From what I had learned during brief Internet searches, my condition could take up to nine months before I would recover, and some even said the condition could leave me with chronic pain. "Not acceptable," I told myself. I needed some serious healing. Exhausted and desperate for healing, I cried out to Jesus, "Okay, I get it! I know I believe that I'm a body. I get it. Please help me! What should I do?"

I wasn't far along enough in my understanding of the Course to simply see the truth and be healed, but I knew who could help me. Unable to sit in anything that resembled a meditative position, I settled down for a nap, supported by pillows and cushions of various sizes and shapes to find that position with the least amount of pain. As Jesus was my favourite healer, I trusted that he would show me what it was that I needed to learn so that I could heal. When I lay my head on the pillow, it wasn't difficult to imagine myself laying my head on his lap, just as a child might seek comfort from an older brother. He would help me remove the blockages to my true identity as Spirit.

When I received my copy of *Back Care Basics*, I eagerly opened the package and headed downstairs to give it a try. Yoga could be very healing. *This will work for me*, I thought, as I pulled up a chair for the seated warm-ups. The average age of participants in the class was well over sixty. *Piece of cake*, I told myself as I began the gentle head and neck rotations, and though my range of motion was severely limited because of the pain, I remained optimistic. I felt encouraged; I was actually doing something. But my optimism was short-lived, since after a couple of days, I still had not progressed beyond the first ten minutes of the warm-up. Disheartened, I watched as the group of seniors moved into forward bends and other simple moves I could only dream of doing.

Having exhausted all my resources, I was beginning to lose hope. The days were turning into weeks, and although the inflammation in my shoulders was diminishing, the pain in my back remained the same. The Gary Renard workshop was just a few weeks away and, by the looks of it, I wasn't going to make it. Since driving was out of the question, I tried to imagine alternative scenarios like taking a taxi downtown to catch a couple of hours of the Saturday workshop or asking Bob for a lift. One thing was certain: I was going to miss the Berber evening.

Unable to work at the computer, go for my daily walks or read for more than a couple of minutes at a time, life as I knew it had pretty much ground to a halt. There were moments when I reminded myself that God had nothing to do with any of this and then I would feel tremendous relief. In fact, despite the almost constant gnawing pain, I felt intensely blissful, even forgetting that I was in a body. Thank God He has nothing to do with this world! Once again, I lay my head on Jesus' lap. He would help me get through this.

I suppose I shouldn't really have been surprised when out of the blue my friend Didi called to see if I would be attending a networking meeting the following morning. It had been a couple of months since we had seen each other and we had some catching up to do. I told her about my unfortunate situation, my reason for not attending the meeting.

"How interesting," she said, "I have an appointment with a healer this week. Maybe he can do something for you."

Her appointment was for Thursday and she was asking if I'd be interested in going with her. Would I? But at the same time fearful of anyone causing additional damage to my back and not ready to place myself in the hands of a quack, I asked if he was a "ramancheur."[5]

"Oh no, he's very gentle," Didi said, trying to reassure me. "My friend, who's a doctor, told me about him. She knows him quite well. Apparently he has a real gift."

---

5. A "ramancheur" is a French-Canadian expression for a folk healer, someone who resets bones, but who usually does not have any formal medical training.

"Okay," I said, and gave her a recap of my condition so she could ask him if he would see me.

Within minutes, Didi called back. "Oh yes, he'll see you. This is exactly the kind of work he's good at. But the appointment is for tomorrow. Can you still make it?"

It's not like I was going anywhere, and besides, sooner was even better. I needed relief. Not wanting to be negative, I couldn't help but be a bit skeptical, having been unimpressed with the healers I'd seen in the past. But I wasn't getting very far with my yoga practice and none of the other remedies were working. *What the heck*, I thought—he sounded harmless. Besides, Didi had called *me*, so I saw this as an offer of help from the Holy Spirit. It might be my answer. If it worked, I wouldn't need to spend the remainder of the year managing pain. Besides, I was at least a little intrigued at the prospect of meeting a real healer.

That evening, I pondered healing and healers, and I must admit I grew excited about this new opportunity to be with Jesus. For me, all healers were one. The Course teaches that there is only one dreamer, and when that one dreamer is healed, we are all healed. There is only one ego, one wrong mind split off into billions of separate parts. I had an image of a shattering explosion in reverse, imploding back into itself, to its one source, like bits and pieces of shattered glass returning to wholeness, like watching the big bang in reverse. One mind, one healer.

When Didi picked me up the following morning, it was cold and rainy. Sitting in the car would be painful. In my mind, I had registered that we weren't going very far, thinking that Sorel was just off the West Island, a short drive away. Wrong. The drive to the South Shore took over an hour. While Didi drove and talked, I managed my pain as best I could, keeping my gaze forward since I couldn't turn my head to acknowledge her conversation. Just when I thought I could no longer take the pain, we turned onto a long drive that led to a beautiful A-frame house overlooking the river. Had I not been in so much discomfort, I think I would very much have enjoyed taking a stroll on the property.

As I unfolded myself out of the car, a cheery woman with dark curls came out the front door followed by a man of small stature looking to be in his late fifties. They greeted us warmly, but as I reached out to shake Robert's hand, a frightful thought occurred to me and I panicked. While Donna was English-speaking, originally from the United States, he was French-Canadian.

"*Vous êtes un ramancheur?*" I asked as we shook hands, now wishing I had never agreed to this adventure. Not only had I misunderstood the geography, I was now placing my back in the hands of a quack.

Robert replied that he was, fifth generation, which was only small comfort. But there was nothing but kindness and humility in his expression and I felt momentarily reassured. *Jesus, if this man breaks my back, it's your fault!* Then I did some quick thinking; I hadn't gone after this, it had found me, he was recommended by a doctor and he did have years of experience. The Holy Spirit had a hand in this, I was sure.

It didn't take long for Robert to size up my condition, bent over myself where I stood.

"I guess we start with you?" he said.

As much as I wanted to be home, safe in my bed, I couldn't back out now. I followed him into the house—*Jesus, I'm in your hands.*

We chatted briefly about the unique architecture of the house he had built, of which he was clearly proud. Then I was ushered into a small room off the kitchen. There was a futon and a chair and a small dresser, all the conveniences of a guest room, but none of the usual items found in a clinic. I sat, as instructed, straddling the straight-backed chair. Thankfully, I wasn't asked to remove any clothes. In answer to his questions, I explained my condition and demonstrated the limited motion of my arms. At this point, I could barely raise the left arm more than a couple of inches from my side.

Robert ran his fingers up and down my spine, pressed a few spots, then instructed me to lie face down on the futon. All the while, I maintained the thought of Jesus by my side. I was, not to say the least, scared shitless. On the futon, he pressed a few more points along my back, making adjustments as would a chiropractor. To my surprise, the treatment had not been painful. In fact, I doubted that anything had been fixed. Perhaps this had been a big waste of time, I thought. When I got up, he looked at me, then at my left arm.

"You know what I have to do, right?"

Although I had never before witnessed this type of intervention, somehow, I knew exactly what had to be done. The treatment wasn't over. He didn't have to say anything; I just knew. And it wouldn't be very pleasant. This is what *ramancheurs* did. Resigned to my fate, I said, "yes."

"Because if you don't," he added, "in a few months you won't be able to move your arm at all."

"I know," I replied.

"Would you prefer doing this another time?"

Are you kidding! "No," I replied immediately. I couldn't spend another night with the pain.

"Okay," he said. "But let's take a break first."

Didi took my place in the treatment room. When they were done, we all sat in the kitchen.

"Would you like a shot of something?" Robert asked me.

I knew what he meant. "No," I said as bravely as I could.

"Are you ready?" He looked at me with genuine concern. I was terrified of facing the pain, but at the same time determined to fix my back.

"Let's do it," I said. But before I entered the treatment room, I turned to Didi. "You should go to the other end of the house or, better yet, outside."

She looked at me, concerned. "Trust me," I said. "You don't want to hear this."

Donna joined us for the second session. While I straddled the chair, she positioned herself in the same spot I visualized the Holy Spirit when I practised Reiki, at my right shoulder.

"You can hold on to me," she said.

When Robert took hold of my left arm, I began to pray to Jesus. Again, I focused on his presence in the room with us.

I took a very deep breath. "Okay, I'm ready," I told Robert.

Very slowly, gently, but steadily, he began to rock my arm back and forth, then side to side. It hurt like hell, but I tried to manage the pain with deep breathing. This is what had to be done, and with Jesus and the Holy Spirit next to me, how could I go wrong? When Robert began to crank my arm up, I yelped in pain. Slowly, but relentlessly, he manipulated the arm, up and down, back and forth, taking it further and further each time. My yelps turned into screeches as he worked the arm into a wider range of motion. Donna held my head against her chest, her woolly sweater and soft abdomen muffling the worst of my cries. Between shrieks I begged for him to stop, I couldn't take the pain anymore.

"We're almost finished," he replied. "Hold on, just a bit longer," he said as he cranked the arm way up above shoulder height, a level to which I had been unable to raise my arm for over a year.

"Stop, stop, stop! I can't take it anymore," I cried, breathing rapidly and on the verge of losing consciousness.

"Almost done," he said as he took my arm all the way up and down around the back. And then I felt it. Something snapped. When he brought my arm back down, I knew it was over.

"There," he said calmly. "We did it."

Whether or not I was healed, I couldn't tell. All I knew was that the ordeal was over and, by all appearances, I had survived. Instinctively I turned my head to the left and found that I met with no resistance.

"You turned completely white," Robert said.

Then I began to shake; I felt very cold. Not surprisingly, I was in shock. We returned to the kitchen where I was given a jacket to put over my shoulders and a cup of tea. Anything warm.

As we sipped our tea and chatted and the blood began to circulate once more through my veins, a beautiful boxer ambled into the room and nudged my legs. Robert told the story of how she had been hit by a passing truck and how he had reset her severely damaged legs and hips. Apparently she had stood at the door while I was being treated. She understood pain, I thought as I patted her head and smiled into her knowing eyes.

Before we left, Robert gave me instructions for my return home. I was to stop taking the prescription medication and should cancel my physiotherapy, but could take acetaminophen for the pain. He stressed that I should have someone massage my upper arm for about five minutes, once every day.

No problem, I told him. Then in answer to my unspoken query, to my surprise he replied that there would be no need to repeat the treatment. Thank God, I thought. I didn't think I could do this again. In fact, there was no way that I could ever go through this again. Ever.

On the drive home, I was surprised to find that I could easily turn my head while Didi and I carried on a conversation. The pain in my back seemed to be considerably relieved, and, although still skeptical, I felt very hopeful. That night, though exhausted, I resisted going to sleep for as long as I could, afraid to wake up in pain again. I shuddered as I thought over my adventure of the day. This was probably the most risky, the most dangerous thing I had done in a very long time, if not ever. The man could have been a quack. He could have broken my back or my neck. I was either very lucky, very guided or very nuts—probably all of the above! Furthermore, if I woke up the next morning with more pain, I'd have to return to the doctors and explain what I had done. They wouldn't take too kindly to my visit with a crackpot healer. I decided not to tell anyone about my healing excursion. The only person who knew about it was Bob. At any rate, since I wasn't one hundred percent better, it was best to not say anything at all.

As I lay in my bed fighting off sleep, I recalled the sense of closeness to Jesus and the Holy Spirit I had experienced during my session with Robert. This is a feeling I wanted to keep with me always, but I knew that it would pass, so I held on for as long as I could. I thought that even though God didn't have anything to do with this world, we had Jesus and the Holy Spirit as His representatives. I slept very well that night, the first time without pain in weeks, and, when I awoke, I found that I was lying on my left side, something I had not done in months.

This was great, I thought. It was working. I tried to raise my arms, and found that I had much more mobility than before. There was still considerable pain, but it would pass in a week or so, Robert had said. This was the best diagnosis and the most effective treatment yet. Over the following couple of days, I continued to enjoy the benefits of my treatment with Robert. Feeling optimistic, I decided to forego the recommended daily massages. I had imposed enough on the good will of others; I would take care of the remainder of the healing on my own. Every day, I did a bit of yoga, even making it beyond the warm-ups to some of the standing stretches.

To my dismay, after those first few days, the pain gradually returned, until by the end of the week, I felt I had regressed considerably. I was losing hope when Robert phoned to inquire how I was doing.

"I was okay for a couple of days," I explained, "but the pain seems to be coming back like before."

"Have you been getting your daily massages?"

"Uh, no," I replied guiltily.

"The massages are important for the healing," Robert said. "Do them exactly as I showed you. Five to ten minutes a day. That's all you need."

After I hung up the phone, it dawned on me that my prayer for help had been answered, but I hadn't had sufficient trust to follow through with simple instructions. Instead, I had chosen to do things on my own, my usual way of doing things. I took this experience as a symbol of my stubbornness and resistance to following the teachings that were designed to help me reach my goal of awakening from the dream, the teachings I had vowed to follow. Message received, loud and clear, I immediately got on the phone and scheduled daily massages, alternating duties between my angels, Bob and Veronica.

As I prepared to go to sleep that night, I thought about how the world is an outside picture of an inward condition. My cats Maggie and Bubby had just taken their usual spots on the bed, one on either side of me, symbols of the duality embodied by my existence. She was female, he was male; she was dark gray with charcoal streaks, he was white with touches of gold. She was aloof and independent; he was my office mascot, often soliciting my clients for attention and head scratching. Yet there they were, every night, curled up one on either side of me, coexisting, yet never really living together in harmony. They were a symbol of my lifelong spiritual conflict, the tension between my inner and outer life, my desire to be a distinct, special individual, and my desire to return home to that place of eternal peace.

The following day I prepared a treatment bottle with the Bach Flower Remedy Scleranthus.[6] I felt pulled between two irreconcilable forces: the will to return home, where there is nothing but an experience of oneness, wholeness and peace, and the ego's will to remain a separate individual body. The battle that raged in my body was a symbol of the one that raged in my mind. The struggle between the right mind and the wrong mind, the struggle between the desire to choose with the Holy Spirit and go home, and the ego's ferocious desire to survive. My desire for oneness and peace was opposed to my desire for separation and specialness.

It took only a few days for the massages to take effect. They were working; the pain in my upper back was finally subsiding. Each day I added a couple of moves to my yoga practice. Bit by bit, my life started to return to normal. By the end of the week, I was even able to drive myself to Veronica's for my massage.

The following weekend, I attended one of the monthly dances put on by our dance club. This is where I met the lady Bob had been dancing with during my absence. The moment I saw them together, I knew they would one day become a couple. It was just one of those hunches. I teased Bob about it later that night, but he

---

6. Scleranthus is the remedy for states of duality and indecision.

rejected any possibility of romance. They were just dance partners; besides, she was in a relationship. But just as spring follows winter, I knew they would become more than dance partners, and I wondered if part of the reason for my illness was just so they could meet. Bob could then move on, even if it meant that I would no longer have a dance partner.

Days later, I was well enough to drive my daughter and future son-in-law around town while they looked for a reception hall for their wedding. The weekend after that, I attended another dance and this time I was able to dance the whole night without any problems.

Less than three weeks later, I attended Gary Renard's workshop. We did go out for Moroccan cuisine, complete with tagines and belly dancing. It was phenomenal. To cap off the weekend, I was asked if I wouldn't mind taking Gary and Cindy for a day of sightseeing in Old Montreal. Would I!

In another twist of fate, two weeks earlier, no doubt guided by the Holy Spirit, my mom had decided that I needed a new car. Instead of driving my guests in an aging and uncomfortable two-door coupe, it was in a brand new four-door sedan that I picked them up the following morning. What a blessing. We discussed visiting Saint Joseph's Oratory, but thought we might not have time to do both Old Montreal and the Oratory in one afternoon. The first place Gary chose to visit was Notre-Dame Basilica. Of all the places to be visiting, so soon after I had written the chapter on my churchgoing days—it was eerie! It felt very strange to be standing in that church after thirty years. We spent the afternoon strolling along the cobbled streets of Old Montreal and ended the day with a lovely dinner.

I took the events of those very intense few weeks—the help from my angels, the unexpected call from Didi, my surprisingly rapid recovery, the outing with Gary and Cindy—as symbols of the guidance that can result from a condition of openness and surrender. But more importantly, this was a lesson in trust—trust in my new teacher—a lesson I would never forget.

Chapter 14

THE SPECIAL RELATIONSHIP

The holiest of all the spots on earth is where an ancient hatred has become a present love. (T-26.IX.6:1)

*I*t wasn't long before I was able to resume my daily walks and shortly after that I picked up my nightly habit of playing solitaire while listening to Ken Wapnick lectures. While my recent experiences had brought me closer to Jesus and the Holy Spirit, I did miss my daily lessons. Although I felt that I had gained more than a gist of its teachings, I had no illusions about my progress with the Course: it was slow and steady, but there was still very much to learn. After more than two years of study, it was clear that reading the text and doing the lessons was quite different from applying them in my daily life. It was one thing to connect with the material in a lecture or to catch a glimpse of peacefulness and oneness with God in meditation, it was a whole other matter when the stuff of life got in your face. Ultimately, my goal was to reach a point where I would choose with the right mind all of the time and under any and all circumstances. This would require a little practice—okay, a whole lot of practice—and certainly a fair dose of patience, especially with myself.

It was in the area of relationships that I would find my greatest opportunities for learning, especially given that my trademark way of dealing with relationship issues was to isolate myself. As much as Ghanshyam's characterization of my personality as monkly years earlier had troubled me, I had grown to thoroughly enjoy the quiet of my solitude. Business and professional relationships were easy to handle, as they imposed no close ties and could remain respectfully distant, if I so chose. I had a growing public life, met hundreds of people each year, but, at the end of the day, I returned home to my quiet monkly life of reading, writing and seclusion. This cleverly devious design of my ego ensured sufficient tranquility to keep me content and lulled into a false sense of grace. The result was a lifestyle that was relatively peaceful and quite comfortable, but it was not going to lead to the lasting peace of God, the peace I yearned for.

> *There is no peace except the peace of God,*
> *and I am glad and thankful it is so.* (W-pI.200.11:9)

In my early attempts to apply the Course's teachings in situations that troubled me or threatened my peace of mind, I reminded myself that the world was not real, that it was just an illusion, and that I should not make a big deal out of whatever it was that confronted me. If I made a big deal out of it, I made the situation more real than it needed to be, trapping myself further in the illusion. While this thought process was often sufficient to deflate the conflict and return me to a relative sense of contentment, I came to understand that peace in this world could never last since this world is built on a false premise: that anything other than perfect oneness can exist. The feeling of peace was always relative to the conflict; it was never lasting. Although a fuller and deeper grasp of the cause of the impermanence of peace was yet to come, as often as possible, I tried to steer myself toward experiences of peace.

I want the peace of God.

To say these words is nothing. But to mean these words is everything. If you could but mean them for just an instant, there would be no further sorrow possible for you in any form; in any place or time. (W-pI.185.1–3)

I clearly saw the cost of the loss of peace when, one day I tried to help my mom with a computer problem. She hadn't been receiving her e-mails for a while, including some I had sent, so I thought

I would try to fix the problem. I had a clever idea, an *I can do it myself* idea for setting up an account in her name with my service provider. *Piece of cake*, I thought, having done it before for Bob. I created the alias, gave her a password, then began to walk her through the process of setting up her mail program, all of which was being done over the phone. Her mail client was different from mine, but similar enough for me to figure out the user interface on her side. My mom, bless her soul, was as knowledgeable about software configuration as was my cat Bubby.

After about half an hour of unproductive, yet patient instruction, it became clear that we were not looking at the same picture on our monitors so I decided to install her mail client on my computer. That took about a minute. Good, I thought. This will be a snap. Nearly an hour later, we had a partially functional e-mail configuration; mail was going out, but it wasn't coming in. Or was it the other way around? Fortunately, throughout all of this my inner peace remained intact. But time was marching on and at some point I needed to get back to work. So I called my computer-savvy brother who lived upstairs from my mom, and asked him to take a look at my set-up.

Minutes later he was telling me that I could not set up the account as I thought, which was news to me since I had successfully created one in the past, or at least, I believed I had. Then all of a sudden, I lost it. From a separate place in my mind, I watched myself explode into a rant about how computers were supposed to make our lives easier, how my mom wasn't getting the e-mails I had sent her and on and on for about a minute. In an instant, I had chosen frustration and anger over peace. It wasn't a big deal, but it cost me my peace. I thought about that seemingly insignificant event several times throughout the day and decided that from that point forward I would do my utmost to not lose my peace again.

I am never upset for the reason I think. (W-pI.5)

Though sincere, this decision to keep my peace was going to prove to be more challenging than I thought. It would take well over a year before I could begin to fully appreciate the deeper issues at work in this, and all my experiences of conflict or upset. Although it appeared as though I had gotten upset because I couldn't make things work the way I wanted, especially after having spent what I considered to be valuable time trying to find a solution to the problem, the truth was that the non-functioning e-mail was not the real cause of my distress.

Upon taking a closer look at the dynamics at work in that situation and applying what I was learning from the Course, it became clear that my upset was partly due to my decision to do things on my own, a symbol of my unconscious decision to be separate from God. But it also reflected my conflict with authority: Someone who claimed to know better (my brother) was telling me that I couldn't do what I wanted to do, a symbol of my deeper conflict with the ultimate authority (God), who, according to my made-up myth of existence, I had managed to prove wrong by accomplishing the impossible (separating from perfect oneness), the same God who no doubt will come after me and prove me wrong. On this deep, and unconscious level, one thing was clear, the last thing I wanted was to be proven wrong, since this would put my very existence into question. If I was wrong about the computer, I might very well be wrong about this existence in which I very much believed. Being right was therefore very important, and I would do whatever it took to prove myself right.

Another opportunity to practise what I was learning with a little more success arose not long after Gary Renard's workshop, when, while in consultation, the front doorbell rang. When I couldn't figure out who the four strangers at my door were, the short round man introduced himself.

"Hi, my name is Martin and this is my granddaughter Laurie."

Evidently, I still appeared baffled.

"We're here to pick up the couch."

Of course, I thought. "Oh yes, please come in." It all came together. The young woman was the daughter of a client and she was settling into an apartment downtown where she would go to university and I was very happy to be able to help her out.

The grandfather had nothing but gentleness and love in his expression, perhaps even a little pride in being able to help out his granddaughter. The other man and woman were there to help out.

Engrossed in my work, I had completely forgotten that I had made arrangements for them to pick up some furniture that I no longer needed. For some time, I had been planning to convert the spare room into a guest room and, with my daughter's wedding fast approaching, I was motivated to get it done. Quite happy to have found someone to donate the furniture to, I purchased the paint, cleared the room and plastered and sanded the walls. This was all the more pleasing as it happened barely two months after sustaining my back injury. Since I generally enjoyed painting and decorating, I was looking forward to the removal of the couch and large TV cabinet so that I could get to work.

After an unusual amount of fussing and discussing, the couch was finally carried out of the room, down the hall and out the door. There was a long pause before Martin knocked on the door to advise me that they had decided to not take the TV cabinet, as it appeared to be too large for the small apartment.

"Oh, no problem," I said politely. I'm always polite with my words, even though my thoughts might not be. He appeared genuinely concerned when he asked what I would do with it. I shrugged and said that I would probably put it in the garbage. I smiled politely, despite the fact that my plans had been compromised. Reassuring him that it was not a problem, I saw him out the door. Fortunately, I had been in the process of wrapping up my consultation, for after that incident, I found it difficult to focus on my work.

Although I had reassured the man that everything was all right, my inner dialogue indicated that things were not exactly all right. In fact, I clearly felt annoyed at having been stuck with the cabinet. I had made it clear in the ad on my website that both pieces were to be sold as a pair, and here I was giving them away, and they were being split. Digging into my Course knowledge, I saw this as an obvious symbol of the original split mind, and my own inner dichotomy.

> I will not value what is valueless. (W-pI.133)

After my client left, I stopped to observe my line of thinking, recognizing that I had lost my sense of peace and was beginning to generate thoughts that would prolong this unpleasant state of mind for more than a passing moment. I realized that I was allowing myself to be annoyed by "those people" who had not respected their end of the deal and had stuck me with a huge piece of furniture that I was hoping would be gone so that I could get on with my decorating project.

Then it occurred to me that my vested interest in this guest room was causing me to reinforce the idea of separateness in a *myself versus them* scenario. It also served to obscure the oneness that we shared in the form of our common source in God. Clearly, I had switched tracks and was now looking at the situation from the perspective of the ego. Deciding that I didn't want to pursue this wrong-minded thinking any longer than necessary, I asked the Holy Spirit for help in looking at the situation with the right mind. While awaiting the Holy Spirit's answer, I simply chose to no longer follow that line of thinking. If anything, I did have a choice in the matter; I could choose to not give it further thought.

Although I understood that the purpose of the Course was not to obtain or fix specific things in the world, I had observed that in working with the Holy Spirit and Jesus to change *how I see* the world, some pleasant and at times unexpected results sometimes occurred. Later that evening, I proceeded to dismantle the large heavy cabinet. During that time, I focused on the task at hand, removing bolts, collecting hardware, never once allowing thoughts of resentment to enter my mind—basically, succeeding in maintaining my sense of peace. I simply did what had to be done: dismantle a cabinet.

When finished, to my surprise, I noticed that the heavy wooden top I had removed from the unit fit perfectly over my small sewing cabinet, adding nearly twenty inches to its width. The pale wood finish blended in very nicely with what I had in mind for the room. The following morning, while I prepared to paint my guest room, I noticed that the heavy green cabinet that I had for months wanted to rid myself of was but a faint image in my memory. Instead, what I retained was the clear image of one sweet grandfather's face, the spark of love and pleasure in being able to help his granddaughter, and my small part in helping them out. This was a far more pleasant thought with which to begin the day than I would have experienced had I chosen to pursue thoughts of frustration and resentment.

Sometimes, wisps of understanding would bubble up to my awareness unexpectedly. One Sunday morning, I was listening to a Ken Wapnick CD while walking to the grocery store. It was a perfect late September morning, sunny and warm. I felt very much at peace. As I neared the parking lot of the Tim Hortons across from the store, I heard a loud voice, somewhere between a cry and a song. I couldn't tell what it was until I looked out and saw what was happening. I smiled as a big bear of a man, perhaps in his late thirties, walked gaily by me, singing *laa… laa… laa… laa…* He sang freely, without any hint of melody in his song, and, if there had been a melody, it certainly would have been completely off-key. With one thumb tucked into the suspenders that held up his ample trousers, he appeared completely content and carefree—lost in a world of his own making, oblivious of anything outside himself.

It was impossible not to smile, but what surprised me was the sensation of complete love and oneness that overcame me as I watched this wonderful simple man walk by me. *Yes, you are just like me and everyone else, lost in your separateness, making noise just to be heard, and in being heard, your seeming existence is made real.* Maybe he was intellectually handicapped ("retarded" is actually the word that came to mind). It didn't matter. He was no more, no less insane than the rest of us. His behaviour made him appear different, but that's where the difference ended. On the deepest level, since our existence is based on one single error—the mistaken thought that the separation from God could actually occur—at our source, we are essentially one and the same. In our mistaken thought, we are all equally insane.

That sunny fall morning, I understood that it does not matter whether a person is a brilliant scientist, a poet or a truck driver, each one clings to that which defines him, each one uses his voice to assert his existence. Now, whenever I hear someone going on about something that bothers them—or even something that they are happily passionate about—I hear *laa ... laa ... laa ... laa ...* There is no disrespect, nor malice in the thought, only a gentle reminder that we are all the same. I often catch myself validating my separateness through meaningless noise of my own, like in my writing.

While it had been easy to not judge a simple-minded stranger and to even share with him a moment of joyful oneness, it was a bit more difficult to reach that same level of non-judgment when someone was pushing my buttons. At a busy intersection, in my least favourite mall, it was my turn to go—at least that's the way I saw it. As I put the car into first and began to make a left turn, a woman on my right gunned it across the intersection. Being cut off on the right is one of my pet peeves, but since I was peaceful, I stopped just in time and smiled, but immediately slipped into ego mode mumbling most ungraciously between clenched teeth—*Go, bitch, bitch, bitch ...*

As I drove away, I reproached myself for my un-Course-like behaviour and called on my friend Jesus to help me look at the situation differently. The first order of business was to forgive myself. I was a newbie with this thought system. *It will take time ...* lots of it, I reminded myself, *I'd better be patient with myself.* I thought of the woman who was evidently in a hurry, lost in her own thoughts and obviously believing that she had the right of way. That's on the level of form. On a deeper level, she was, like all of us, really in a hurry to go home but, fearing punishment for that mistaken thought of sin, was also running to escape retribution for that sin, in essence, she was in a perpetual state of inner conflict. Is this not really what is going on when we are rushing through our lives?

Then I looked at purpose, a key to understanding the teachings of the Course. If the world is made up by *me*, I asked myself, why would I put someone on the road that day to push my buttons and cause me to lose my peace? Hadn't I already determined that I preferred peace to conflict? Then it occurred to me that I didn't need to be disturbed by someone outside myself; I in fact had already lost my peace the moment I chose to leave the safety of my true home with God and identify with the ego.

Since this was my dream, what was being played out was a reflection of the inner drama that lay hidden from my awareness. I needed that *bitch*, and so many others out there, so that I didn't have to see the real cause of my lack of peace, which was inside of me. I would continue to lose my peace in such situations for as long as I chose to identify with this dream. The reason I wanted to stay here in the dream is that I liked being an individual, separate from God, having forgotten that my true Self is Spirit, as God created me, safe at home with God. When I return home, I will lose this little self that I erroneously believe to be me and my peace will be everlasting. At the end of this line of thinking, I saw myself for the foolish child that I was, pretending to be a separate person, imagining all sorts of things in the little playground I call my life. Having forgiven myself, I returned to my state of relative peace.

Much as I had managed to delay the matter for as long as possible, if I was to make real progress with my Course studies, I would have to take a closer look at those situations that caused me to really lose my peace, in particular the conflict situations that continued to arise in my very special relationship with Bob. Although the dream of our past life connection had been helpful in explaining the nature of our present relationship, it had not brought about its healing. For that, I needed to delve more closely into the cause of my made-up world.

The Course states that, in truth, there is no world, the separation never happened and therefore there is no sin, no foundation for guilt and no need to fear punishment. But the truth is buried beneath a colossal made-up story that has us convinced that the impossible has actually occurred. How could anything be separate from perfect oneness? If that were possible, then perfect oneness would not be perfect. Nonetheless, enamoured with the idea of separateness, we continue to choose with the wrong mind—the ego—the result of which is a seeming state of duality.

Since oneness is perfect and whole and cannot coexist with separation, we must choose one or the other, but not both. Having chosen with the ego, it appears as though we have destroyed God, but in reality nothing happened. Yet, we believe that something has happened, since we appear to be here in the world. This world, a clever device of the ego, serves not only to keep us looking outwards and away from the truth that lies within, it also provides a hotbed of opportunities onto which we can project our deeply buried guilt. What has been repressed must be projected. It is an ingenious set-up.

This mythological depiction of the foundation for our existence really comes alive in our relationships, especially our special relationships. On the metaphysical level, since only perfect oneness is true, the seeming separation and our ensuing existence as separate beings must be false. This means that there is not really anybody *out there*. To engage in any form of significant exchange with another person or thing outside oneself, be it combat, attack, judgment, defence, competition or even love is to say: *That person or thing out there is real.* The only meaningful experience between separate beings is an expression of pure love, a love that is devoid of attachments or expectations, a love that is a reflection of our true state of oneness.

Special relationships are the ultimate symbol of separateness and duality and serve to consolidate our choice against perfect oneness at the cost of the peace of God. The more intense the relationship, no matter whether it causes joy or pain, the more is the idea of separateness reinforced and the more is our individual identity strengthened. Special relationships, when used for the ego's purposes, delay our return home. By their very nature, they imply specialness and uniqueness, special feelings—whether positive or negative—for one person over all others, and represent the rejection of the all-inclusive love that is the natural expression of the oneness of God.

When we seek to obtain what we lack, or what we believe we need or want from somebody, we are making scarcity real. When we seek love, we are seeking to replace the missing love of God. When we defend ourselves, we are making attack real, a reflection of our original attack on God. If we are resentful of a person whom we perceive to be in a position of authority, it is a reflection of our fear of God's wrath. Hatred is an expression of the viciousness that lies in hiding deep within, the result of our original murderous, though mistaken, thought of separation. Anger hides the unbearable fear on which is based our individual existence and is the only emotion that can manifest once perfect oneness has been rejected.

Fear and love are the only emotions of which you are capable. (T-12.I.9:5)

In our dualistic state as separate bodies, we maintain a balance between our special enemies and our special allies, both of which are needed in order for us to sustain our existence, like a cast carefully selected to carry the plot of the play. Our enemies are the scapegoats onto which we conveniently project our various negative emotions. Everyone has enemies; everyone has a favourite public personality, performer or relative that they love to hate. We need to get that hatred *out there*, otherwise we could not live with ourselves. What we do not know is that this deeply buried hatred is really a reflection of how we feel about ourselves for having killed off God and, as a result, lost our true home.

Special relationships serve another very important function in our dream life. We need someone or something *out there* to blame for our misery, thus ensuring our innocence. It's my astrology chart or my genetics or my terrible childhood, it's the economy, it's the government, it's the weather. We attract those special people and circumstances in our lives that are tailor-made to push our buttons, to ensure our innocence and justify our need to defend ourselves and, in turn, attack, if necessary. Focused on the outside world and unaware of our part in the making of the world, we continue to believe in our innocence.

Everyone has allies—those special friends or family members who we know will always side with us and tell us we are right, sympathize with us, love us, support us and encourage us. Our natural response is to love them in return. We are loved, admired and cared for, and therefore must be innocent of any wrongdoing. Our allies also serve to satisfy our various emotional, physical and material needs, filling the void left by the thought of separation. *See, I don't need God; I can get what I need from my partner.*

Throughout our lives we juggle this cast of characters—allies and enemies, some close, some distant, brief encounters and lifelong relationships—replacing them as needed, always maintaining that balance that keeps the plot moving. While each character plays his assigned function, the unfolding of our story of specialness is ensured. If all cast members were to suddenly assume the same role, our plot would soon fall apart and we'd have nowhere to act out our tale of separateness.

This relationship dynamic became increasingly evident in my work with clients, where, with the tools of astrology and numerology, I was able to easily identify a person's particular scenario. It helped explain how and why people made the relationship choices they did, needing specific actors in the play of their life in order to project guilt, maintain innocence, reinforce specialness and generally keep from looking at the deeply buried cause of the pain in their life. It also explained why patterns—especially unhealthy ones—were so difficult to break, given that they serve such an important and well-hidden purpose in maintaining the scenario.

As distressing as the Course's perspective on special relationships at first seemed, I grew to appreciate their potential for healing. The good news was that, as much as we need these special characters to sustain our individual stories and keep us mired in the dream, we also need them to undo the illusion. If we are to awaken from the dream and return home, the story must be undone, and just as each plot line in a story must be tied up in the final chapter, our relationships need to be released and forever healed. The Course's principal instrument for healing relationships—and by extension ourselves—is *forgiveness*. In fact, the practice of forgiveness is the heart and soul of the Course's teaching and it finds its most powerful expression in special relationships. This is where the journey home begins in earnest.

> Forgiveness recognizes what you thought your brother did to you has not occurred. It does not pardon sins and make them real. It sees there was no sin. And in that view are all your sins forgiven. (W-pII.1:1–4)

Like many other terms used in the Course, "forgiveness" carries an entirely different meaning from that to which we are accustomed. Normally, we forgive someone for what they *have* done, but now we are being asked to forgive someone for what they have *not* done. This new kind of forgiveness consists of a process of looking at the person or circumstance from a wholly different perspective, a sort of stepping back deep within the mind, allowing us to look at the *purpose* as well as the cause of our response to a given situation.

> [T]here is only one problem and one answer. In this recognition are all problems resolved. In this recognition there is peace. (W-pI.79.9:3–5)

Essentially, the Course teaches that there is only one problem—the thought of separation—and one solution—acceptance of the atonement, the principle that states that the separation never occurred. It does not say that there is one problem for this circumstance, a different problem for another and a variety of solutions from which to choose. What makes the Course simple and unique is that it states, unequivocally: one problem, one solution, and forgiveness is the means for correcting and undoing the error. The miracle chooses with the right mind and forgives, leading to healing. This means that *all* of our experiences as a unique individual in a body in a world reflect one of two possible choices: either for the ego or for the Holy Spirit. Not two million, two hundred or twenty—only two choices—and only one of these leads to the real solution. Forgiveness makes use of the full power of the mind through choice: the choice between the right-minded, or the Holy Spirit's alternative, and the wrong-minded, or the ego's way of looking at things. It's all rather quite simple—in theory.

On a more immediate level, one of the benefits of forgiveness is that it generally leads to a release from conflict and a return to a relative state of peace. That fact alone should be sufficient incentive for its regular practice. However, given that conflict actually serves an important function, there is very real resistance to the application of any practice that will alleviate it altogether.

> Forgiveness, on the other hand, is still, and quietly does nothing. It offends no aspect of reality, nor seeks to twist it to appearances it likes. It merely looks, and waits, and judges not. He who would not forgive must judge, for he must justify his failure to forgive. (W-pII.1.4:1–4)

While it may be easy to forgive a passing stranger for a minor annoyance, it certainly is a whole other matter when it comes to forgiving those special people in our lives who seem to know best how to get us riled up. Now we have *laa… laa… laa… laa…* with lyrics! Words with meaning have far greater impact than meaningless sounds. In special relationships, there are expectations and established patterns of behaviour—all of which are designed to elicit specific responses. In a special relationship, what is said or done has far more significance and is much more difficult to *overlook*—or forgive—than in a passing encounter.

> This tiny spot of sin that stands between you and your brother still is holding back the happy opening of Heaven's gate. How little is the hindrance that withholds the wealth of Heaven from you. And how great will be the joy in Heaven when you join the mighty chorus to the Love of God! (T-26.IV.6:1–3)

While I sincerely wanted to experience the peace of God, it was becoming increasingly difficult to ignore the fact that most of the time my choice was for the ego, and therefore contrary to my desire. The reason for this choice was that I liked being an individual and

I enjoyed very much my specialness, particularly my uniqueness. As long as I continued to identify with my separated self, I needed something or someone out there onto which I could project my inner sin and guilt, and my busy lifestyle provided ample opportunities for projection.

Now and then, I would wonder what it might be like to relinquish this ego identification, sensing just how much work and how exhausting it was to maintain this illusory self. I would catch momentary glimpses of a relief so complete and so profound that the world around me seemed to disappear, like a television station suddenly taken off air, leaving nothing but total peace and quiet. But as quickly as the world disappeared, it reappeared. Life as I knew it returned, situations arose, stress mounted and, sooner or later, something or someone would push my buttons and the cycle was once again renewed.

I could not help but notice that it was not only the negative experiences that reinforced ego-identification, but also the many exciting and fortunate situations of my life. These were much easier to live with than the conflict situations and, for that reason, more insidious in that they more cleverly disguised my specialness needs. Anything that reinforces identification with the ego's thought system is part of the illusion, the good with the bad, the seemingly important along with the most insignificant.

The practice of forgiveness is universal and can be applied to all circumstances, whether present or past, immediate or distant. Since all thoughts that prevent peace must be released before a complete healing of the mind and the return home can occur, I found this process to be very helpful for healing old wounds.

In my early attempts to apply forgiveness, I learned that if I allowed myself to get emotionally sucked into a situation, especially if I fell into experiencing strong emotions such as defensiveness, anger, resentment or fear, then it was much more difficult to put into practice. When this happened, I needed a time out to recover my perspective, after which I could examine the situation more closely. Although just as effective, the disadvantage of having to go back over the situation later was that I remained in a state of conflict or discomfort for longer than I liked.

In those situations when I did manage to catch myself before being completely overcome by the emotion, I simply "reeled it back in," as I came to see it, and proceeded to apply forgiveness right away, reminding myself that *I* had put it out there, that I no longer wished this experience, then I left it in the hands of the Holy Spirit. Generally, this was not a difficult process to apply, but I did notice that there were times when I didn't quite want to reel it in and give it up to the Holy Spirit.

That fall, Bob and I signed up for yet another year of dance. Once again, I seriously considered quitting, but since we were now in an advanced class, it would be difficult for him to find a partner and I knew that he did not want to start at the beginning with someone new. We were also in the process of renovating the basement and, if I quit dance, I was concerned that the job might not get finished.

On a deeper level, I still wanted to uncover the reason for our neurotic relationship, and I also wanted very much for it to be healed. I hoped to reach a point where, when conflict arose, I could simply look beyond it, go straight to that place where we are one mind—equally insane in our belief in separation—beyond that thought to that place where we are one with God. Many times I had asked the Holy Spirit to help me with this relationship. I wanted to feel the same love I had occasionally felt for complete strangers, but for some reason with Bob it wasn't happening. Although we continued to be good friends, an undercurrent of conflict simmered just beneath the surface, always ready to rear its ugly head and upset my sense of peace.

It was after the fourth or fifth dance class of the session that I finally saw the deeper dynamics at work between us. We had moved up to an advanced class that was made up of couples who had been dancing a long time, some well over ten years. Always competitive and eager to catch up, Bob wanted to learn as many steps as possible, which meant learning up to three new steps in each class. Not as competitive and forever a slow learner, I preferred to focus on one step at a time and making it look good before moving on to something new. It often took me two to three classes before I was comfortable with a new step.

While struggling with one of the new steps that day, I watched myself make a comment to Bob who was beginning to grow annoyed with my inability to learn my step. I probably said something about not being able to do my move properly because he wasn't holding me correctly. The actual words don't matter, but their effect does. I knew that my comment would set him off on a tirade of accusations about my not paying attention or my lack of willingness to learn or some such retort. When he stormed off leaving me in the middle of the dance floor looking stupid and feeling embarrassed, I saw our special pattern all too clearly.

It would have been simple to keep the peace; I could have kept my mouth shut or asked for help. But I didn't, and now I felt like crap. I saw his frustration as my frustration, his anger as mine, his impatience as my own. For years I had been trying to leave this relationship and I felt trapped. I wanted to blame him for my frustration, but I knew I couldn't. I wanted to make him the cause of my upset, but at the same time, I also saw that I owned it, that I was the cause. Yet, I didn't know what to do with it.

Not a word was said on the drive home after class. That evening, I thought long and hard about my special relationship with Bob. The coffin had long been nailed shut; I was exhausted and really tired of the conflict. In fact, I was at my wits' end. Dance, renovations—nothing mattered anymore. This was the end of the line. Before going to sleep, I shared my feelings with Jesus. I no longer wanted this experience, I told him. I wanted to know how to look at the relationship differently so that, once and for all, it could be healed. I asked if he could show me the way, help me look beyond the conflict. I was ready to see.

> You do not realize how much you have misused your brothers by seeing them as sources of ego support. (T-15.II.4:1)

Taking a look deep inside, it suddenly became shockingly clear. It seemed that my willingness to look at the truth that lay behind my conflicted relationship with Bob had disturbed the beast that lay in quiet waiting. An angry inner presence arose, making it clear that it did not want me to experience peace in my relationship. I saw how I was quite purposefully holding on to this conflict, that I, in fact, did not want to let it go. I *wanted* Bob to piss me off. I *needed* him to abuse me and embarrass me and disturb my peace of mind. If I forgave him and let it go, then there would be nobody out there that I could blame for my upsets. As long as he was there to cause me pain, I was able to continue to plead my innocence.

I was horrified to see how this relationship had served the purposes of my ego. As I stood back and relinquished my need for this conflict and sought instead our true condition of oneness, the years of conflict manifested in my relationship with Bob suddenly began to fade. In that release, I felt a very deep love for Bob, deeper than I had ever felt for him. I also saw that I had very little understanding of the true meaning of love, and that the love of God, which we all seek, is really not the same as the love of this world. At that moment, I realized that I no longer needed this conflict with Bob.

Chapter 15

THE SHADOW OF DOUBT

A blindfold can indeed obscure your sight, but cannot make the way itself grow dark. And He Who travels with you *has* the light. (T-31.II.11:8–9)

*A*fter nearly three years of working with the Course, instead of feeling more at peace with myself and with God, to my dismay, I began to feel agitated, even concerned about my new spiritual path. Again, on the surface, things were going very well, in fact, it was an exciting time. I was in a number 5 Personal Year of change and expansion, my practice was growing well, I was picking up radio interviews across the U.S., and *The Power of Time* was gathering great reviews. As had been the case in the past, the problem was on a deeper level. It was a malaise with which I was all too familiar, but also of which I had grown very weary. The shadow of doubt was beginning to creep into my awareness, threatening the tender peace I had begun to foster. The moments of extreme joy I had experienced when I first began to study the Course were now a rare occurrence, replaced by a vague feeling of unsettling.

No one created by God can find joy in anything except the eternal; not because he is deprived of anything else, but because nothing else is worthy of him. (T-8.VI.3:2)

Occasionally I would go through a process of reasoning, which I thought was fairly logical but suspected might not pass academic scrutiny. I would start with the idea that there *had* to be something other than this world. That being true, what was *not this*, as I had come to think of God and Heaven, must be the opposite in nature to this world, which is imperfect and finite. This is a world of multiplicity, a world where nothing lasts. What is *not this world* must be unlike this world and therefore must be whole, eternal and perfect. If a world that is whole, eternal and perfect exists, how can anything else exist? This world can *not* then be real. This thought process would keep me going for a while, but then doubt would once again resurface from another angle.

> The Kingdom cannot be found alone, and you who are the Kingdom cannot find yourself alone. (T-8.III.6:1)

Having listened to hundreds of hours of lectures by Ken Wapnick and read Gary Renard's books multiple times, I had acquired what I thought to be a good grasp of the metaphysics of the Course. But even this understanding wasn't enough to chase away the clouds of doubt that were beginning to darken my vision. I was aware that I could call on Jesus and the Holy Spirit for help as I had during my illness, but I hesitated to call on them for help with all my little issues, thinking I should not bother them with trivialities. Looking back now, I realize that this was a cleverly disguised ploy on the part of my ego designed to keep me from progressing with my studies. I had managed to convince myself to *not* ask for help, while if there is one thing Jesus asks of us throughout the Course it is to ask for his help in looking at the situations we encounter on a daily basis.

> Trust not your good intentions. They are not enough. But trust implicitly your willingness, whatever else may enter. Concentrate only on this, and be not disturbed that shadows surround it. (T-18.IV.2:1–4)

While, as with all things in my life, I had a fair amount of willingness to pursue this radical new path, occasionally, my faith faltered, causing me to doubt the wisdom of my choice. Everything I had ever believed in over the span of my life, from my naive faith in the teachings of the Catholic Church to my later more contemporary but no less naive New Age beliefs, had suffered a severe beating.

One thing was clear: if only for lack of logic and consistency, the old belief systems no longer worked for me.

For most of my life, I had maintained the conviction that we were given everything that we needed not only to resolve our problems and issues and to overcome obstacles, but also to thrive and grow. I had believed in a sense of fairness and justice, a sense of proportion, and that we were each given the skills that we needed to reach our unique potential. Furthermore, I believed that we were never given more than we could handle. I think these ideas were the only way I could make sense of a world that was filled with inequity. That way of looking at the world, though born of a need to make sense of it all, was little more than an attempt to make sense of something that could never be made sense of in the first place, essentially, a world designed by an insane mind.

My old beliefs taught that *something* or *someone* had given us skills, tools and opportunities and a life in which to use them. By extension, it would logically follow that that same *something* or *someone* must also have given us the struggles, problems and issues in our lives. If that same causative force were also supposed to be all-loving, how could it assign struggles and pain and devastation? This didn't make sense. I simply could not believe in an intelligent plan that was unfolding the way it was meant to, nor could I accept that things were as God wanted them to be. I was now beginning to see the world for what it was: an outward projection of an inward condition. In one fell swoop, the world—in fact, the entire universe—became *de-spiritualized*.

But be you thankful that only little faith is asked of you. (T-25. VIII.2:7)

Despite the fact that the teachings of *A Course in Miracles* made a whole lot more sense than anything else I had ever studied, my mind managed to churn out a few more doubts. What proof was there that the message of the Course was the Truth? More specifically, how did I know that oneness was true? These teachings were diametrically opposed to those of the shaman whose extensive spiritual and metaphysical knowledge had so completely seduced me years earlier. I could well imagine what he might say about my new choice of spirituality given his stand on the spiritualities of oneness, the core message of *A Course in Miracles*. Had I been lured by the promise of peace into a regressive spirituality at the cost of my individuality?

> It is impossible that the Son of God lack faith, but he can choose where he would have it be. Faithlessness is not a lack of faith, but faith in nothing. (T-21.III.5:1–2)

One night, while turning over cards for my solitaire game, I pondered the question once more. In certain esoteric teachings, the zodiac is seen as a series of archetypes depicting the various stages of the human experience. It begins with the simplest manifestation in Aries—representing emerging self—to the most complex in Pisces—the symbol of universality. Since it is the last sign of the zodiac, the one with the broadest scope and potential for learning, did this mean that the Age of Pisces was our best chance for uncovering the truth? The historical Jesus was associated with the dawn of the Age of Pisces and the foundation of Christianity. It seemed fitting that it was at the end of this era that he brought us his Course. Since this age was in the process of being supplanted by the Age of Aquarius, what did this mean in terms of *A Course in Miracles*? Would its teachings become outdated?

Since I knew better than to look for answers outside myself, I laid down my cards, closed my eyes and began to meditate. I imagined going to the altar where I thought about God. When I meditated, I was never alone, with the Holy Spirit always there by my side ready to help, only if I was ready to listen. Thinking about the coming Age of Aquarius and its promise of enlightenment, I wondered if the teachings of the Course belonged to a passing time, and if what it was teaching might be wrong. Although I had my doubts about some of these ideas, the popular belief was that we were progressing toward a better age, leaving behind the darkness and the hatred and the violence. Troubled by these thoughts, I asked for help in sorting them out before drifting off to sleep.

I woke up suddenly, in the middle of the night, my mind filled with a clear insight on the question. Since the ages progress backwards through the zodiac, from Pisces (the principle of oneness) to Aquarius (the principle of individuality), we may very well be progressing into a climate of increased separateness and specialness. Since the thought of separation from God is at the root of all of our experiences of conflict, perhaps we are deluding ourselves into thinking that the world is automatically evolving toward a better future. There was the distinct possibility that the Age of Aquarius, in which so many New Agers place hope, might not bring the progress anticipated. In fact, it might very well take us a step backwards. And, just as each sign has as much potential for good as for evil, since the dark side of Aquarius is very selfish and cruel, the potential for regression was staggering.

As disturbing as this thought might once have been, with my new perspective on life and the world, it made sense. The more we progressed and the more we learned about the universe and about ourselves, the cleverer we became at disguising the truth, for this world was designed to cover up the truth. In the end, it didn't really matter which way we seemed to be progressing along the zodiac, whether backwards or forwards, the truth was that it is all still just a dream. Sure, things in the world appear to be progressing, but are they really? Are we not simply more adept and better equipped to do what we have always done?

As I continued to meditate, I saw clearly how any way I looked at it, there was really only one thing that stood between me and the truth, and that was my profound fear of looking inward and finding my way home. My fear was of losing my separateness, my specialness, my individuality. It was understandable that I would have been seduced by Arthur's philosophy of specialness and individualism and profoundly frightened by the Course's teaching of oneness with God.

Salvation, perfect and complete, asks but a little wish that what is true be true; a little willingness to overlook what is not there; a little sigh that speaks for Heaven as a preference to this world that death and desolation seem to rule. (T-26.VII.10:1)

Although this revelation did considerably alleviate my concerns, I still needed to further examine the matter of my faltering faith. Everyone believes in something, even if they do not believe in God. Believing in *nothing* is a belief in itself. I am entirely free to choose how I will look at the world, I am in fact entirely free to believe in whatever I choose. I can choose to believe in what the Catholic Church teaches or I can choose to believe in the latest New Age fad. However, because I choose to believe in something, it does not necessarily make it true.

Even though I had no proof, why not choose to look at the world through the lens of the thought system of the Course? What did I have to lose? From what the Course was teaching, I had everything to gain and nothing to lose. But to look at the world and to see my life consistently through this new lens required so much training, so much practice. Was it not a form of brainwashing? But then, were not my previous beliefs various forms of brainwashing? These lines of questioning were frustrating, and part of me just wanted a clear sign of sorts.

Normally, whenever doubt arose, a small event would occur, something to reassure me, an e-mail from one of our study group members, a call from a client wanting to talk about the Course, a comment in a Ken Wapnick lecture, a passing word from a stranger—small things, and then I would be reassured. What I knew I lacked, and very much longed for, was that profound faith that seemed to sustain the journey of accomplished spiritual seekers like Thomas Merton. Ken Wapnick had his moment when Jesus *showed up* for him,[1] and Gary Renard was given his own special message about renouncing the world.[2]

---

1. *Absence from Felicity*, page 324.
2. *The Disappearance of the Universe*, page 90.

I knew it was childlike, but I wished for a sign of my own so that I could experience the comfort of knowing with certainty, but at the same time, I felt divided on this matter. If I received a special message, would that not only reinforce my sense of specialness? Would it not make my question and my doubt, hence my separateness, real? Since specialness is part of the root cause of this world from which I wish to awaken, would this not be counterproductive? Lord knew I was already special enough! This was a fire to which I clearly did not want to add additional fuel!

It had been nearly three years to the day since my father passed away when I saw him in a dream one night. I missed him. I felt there were so many things we might have talked about. He stood chatting casually with friends, appearing very happy and peaceful when he turned and looked at me. "Everything is going to be all right," he said. Though I wasn't quite sure what his words meant, looking back, it appeared to be a message of hope in preparation for challenging times to come.

When not musing over the meaning of life, I still had a life to live. Typical of a number 5 Personal Year, I had to deal with unexpected and sudden change, not something I was overly enthusiastic about. My life had settled into a relatively peaceful pace over the last year and I wasn't looking for more change than was necessary. Things were simple, uncomplicated and relatively stress-free. This is the lifestyle I had set up for myself and I was quite comfortable with it. I worked, wrote and lived like a monk. In fact, if I could have, I think I would have taken a small room in a Tibetan monastery. I was losing interest in the things of the world, and had begun to withdraw even from my business networking activities.

Then a very clear thought occurred to me: *You won't get very far with your goal of waking from the dream by living in isolation. You need to be with people.* I immediately understood what this meant. In order to awaken from the dream, I needed to apply the teachings of the Course. Making up a safe, peaceful little life, with limited opportunities for forgiveness would reduce my opportunities for learning and healing, ultimately delaying my awakening—clearly another ego-based device.

Right on the heel of that thought, I learned that my brother was moving out of the upstairs rental and my mom was putting her duplex up for sale. This meant that our plans for her to move in with me *one day* suddenly moved up the calendar considerably. Over the next few weeks, my house became chaotic as we began to move some of my mother's things over, and also started work on a huge closet in the basement. My mom also decided it was time to renovate my walkway and driveway, both of which were crumbling and in desperate need of reconstruction. In the process, I had to part with my ancient crab apple tree and all my flowerbeds, since we also decided to do the window wells and a new patio. This was a lot of change for me!

It was springtime and Bubby was shedding by the handful. He had enough fur for five felines! It was nearly a full-time job just sweeping up the plaster dust and the balls of long white silky fur that piled up in all the corners of the house. A couple of times, I had thought of asking my mother if she would like me to give him up. I thought I might find a good home for him, save her the agony of dealing with his fur—she was forever plucking hair off my clothes. This was by far not a thought I relished, but I accepted that I needed to be practical. Unfortunately, this was yet another hunch.

It was a Saturday night, and we had just finished another family dinner, this time the theme had been the cuisine of Mali.[3] The food was wonderful, and as usual everyone had done their best to portray the unique flavours of the West African cuisine in their dishes. When everybody had gone, I finished cleaning up the kitchen and prepared for bed. That's when Bubby fell ill. He had vomited a few times in the past couple of weeks, and had been a bit clingy and lethargic, but I chalked up the vomiting to plaster dust and cat hair, and the clinginess to my going out more than usual. That night, Bubby didn't take his usual spot on the bed with his head on my

---

3. See *The Power of Time* (page 79) for the story of the origins of our family dinners.

leg while I laid out my cards for my nightly ritual of solitaire and Ken Wapnick. When he continued to be sick, I gave him Reiki and some Bach Flower Remedies and settled him on a towel on the dining room floor before heading off to bed.

I had trouble falling asleep, and when I did finally doze off, it was an uncomfortable sleep. I woke up several times, and a couple of times went looking for him. Guessing he'd gone downstairs to find a comfortable spot to sleep, I decided to let it go until morning. My daughter and son-in-law were asleep on the futon downstairs and I didn't want to wake them.

Back to bed I went, for a fitful sleep, waking and thinking about my life, and the big changes that were coming up and wondering if Bubby was okay. I held off going downstairs for as long as possible, since my guests had expressed a desire to sleep in. Just after seven, I finally decided to get up and go look for Bubby. My worst fears were confirmed.

It was a Sunday morning, and the only place open was the emergency twenty-four-hour veterinary clinic. It was early when I arrived, and there was only one other pet owner in line. When I stepped up to the counter, the minute the technician looked at Bubby, she called for an immediate examination. She would see him before the dog that was ahead of us. It took over two hours before the vet finally called me into the exam room. The prognosis wasn't good. When I understood that he was going to die, I cried. He was nearly completely dehydrated, had an irregular heart murmur and was in extreme pain. Of course, there were options. They could stabilize him and, after a few days, open him up to identify the mass in his gut, but there was no guarantee that he would get better, let alone survive, and never mind the thousands of dollars it would cost to find out what was making him ill.

It all came together quickly. In a way, it was an answer to my question of a few weeks back. It was time to let him go. He'd had a good life, though terribly short, being not even five years old. I cried some more, and then made my decision, wishing the doctor could have made this decision in my place. The attendant brought Bubby in, wrapped in a towel, an IV taped to his leg. I held him one last time. I cried a lot, then I gave the okay. The procedure took all of two seconds. He was at peace. I held him a couple more minutes, all life gone from his big green eyes, and then I let him go for good.

I was in shock as I drove back home that morning. I cried some more when I told the kids what had happened. Hiding my grief was impossible; denying it would have been silly. Bubby, who had spent his days napping on my desk while I worked and his nights curled up next to me, was no more. I spent most of the rest of the day vacuuming the house, getting rid of white fur balls, doing laundry and washing the floors where he had been ill. I put a plant on the small table he used for climbing onto my desk, and removed the small footstool he used for climbing onto my bed.

A Ken Wapnick lecture played in the background as I did my chores, but the words faded into background noise. I felt not only the loss of Bubby, but also lost in the house I had grown to cherish. I tried to apply what I had learned from the Course. I knew very well that my house was a pale substitute for my true home in Heaven, but my ego was very attached to it. My peace was profoundly disturbed by the chaos of half-finished rooms and construction work. I felt loss everywhere I turned.

I reasoned that the loss of my favourite cat was a clear symbol of the idea of separation from God. This was the true cause of my feelings of devastation. I had trouble falling asleep that night. My mind wandered in every which direction, trying to make sense of this unexpected turn of events. I looked for clues as to Bubby's condition. It is often very difficult to tell that a cat is ill, the vet had said. Yet, I tried to blame myself. I should have sensed something. He had been more clingy than usual, and had a lot of trouble jumping up onto his footstools and chairs. He slept most of the time and had lost his appetite. I should have detected the changes sooner, but I was too busy with my little worldly life. I could also have blamed it on the dust and dirt from the ongoing construction in the house. My guilt was palpable. Then I looked for the positive side. No more fur balls. No more worrying if someone had let him out. No more brushing hairs off my clothes. I could wear black. It would make life easier for my mom when she moved in.

Recalling my actions following Bubby's death, I found it interesting to note that I was naturally inclined to tell someone of what had happened. It was as though I needed to share my grief, even though talking about it would stir it up and bring it to the surface, causing me to cry again. It was a strange pattern of behaviour, as though I cherished my grief. And, in a way, it was clear that that was the case. My grief over my cat's, or anybody's death, was proof that there was something that could actually be separate. Death was permanent. It was proof that separation was real and that I did not have control over life or death. I was a victim of loss. However, it also pointed to the thought that this could not be the world that I was meant to experience, for, how could a kind and loving God make a world in which there could be such a thing as death? How could there be permanent loss?

I wanted to understand what had occurred in the perspective of the Course. The decision for separation is the cause of the world I see. It occurred to me that with my thought of giving him up so my mom would not have to deal with his fur balls, I had effectively killed Bubby. Besides, since I wrote my own script, I must have chosen to kill him. Any way I looked at it, I killed him, a symbol of my inherently murderous nature.

I asked the Holy Spirit to help me see this difficult situation differently. I avoided asking Jesus, because I was growing overly concerned about making him very special in my life. The last thing I needed was more specialness, whether inside or outside myself, since specialness was opposed to oneness. Several times it had occurred to me that it was probably a very good thing that I had never heard the voice of Jesus, as my ego would certainly have revelled in the specialness. Somehow, I sensed that what I needed would be there when I needed it. I would practise trust instead. My real goal was to return home, not to become more special.

Still, I thought of Jesus, and wondered what it must have been like for Helen Schucman and Bill Thetford, and even Ken Wapnick, to have been so close to him. Tired, and in desperate need of a good night's rest, I took a dose of Rescue Remedy[4] and was soon fast asleep. But before long, I was awake again. I thought about how my life seemed to be in a tailspin and how uncomfortable I was with all the change. One of my concerns was, given my propensity for isolation, would I be able to get along with my mom once she moved in with me? My mother and I are very different in character, style and personality; in fact, in most things, we don't see eye to eye, nor do we do things in the same manner. Both fiercely independent and individualistic, headstrong and passionate in our opinions, we are quite set in our ways. I know she loves me, and I love her too, but our differences keep us at a respectable distance from each other. Once again, I asked for the Holy Spirit's help in seeing clearly into this issue.

Deep into the night, between bouts of analysis and semi-conscious sleep, I found myself drifting and falling back in time to another place until I had a clear impression of myself as a young girl of maybe ten or eleven, hiding my identity beneath layers of clothing, hugging a rough cloak over my head. I knew I wasn't supposed to follow the others—my older brother had scolded me a number of times already, but I couldn't help myself. I was curious. I wanted to see more of the incredible man who sat and talked to the small group of men along the roadside. There were other children running and playing nearby, mostly boys, and the man seemed to like them very much, but I wasn't allowed to be there.

"You must return home to help Mother prepare the bread," my brother had told me. "This gathering is for grown-ups. Go home now." But the man fascinated me. He was kind and gentle and had a smiling look in his eyes, and he seemed to love everyone. Jesus, they called him. Everyone seemed to like him. When they rose to walk on down the road to the farther reaches of town, I wanted to follow too, like my brother, but I dared not lest he find that I had disobeyed. So I stayed behind and watched until I could no longer

---

4. A Bach Flower Remedy typically used in times of crisis or emergency.

see him. I knew he would be doing something special; I had heard that he could heal the sick. One day, I told myself, one day, I will be older and I will go with him too.

The image disappeared as I became more fully awake. It was hard to tell whether what I had experienced was a dream, since I was sure I had been awake. There was also no way of verifying whether or not this had been an accurate recollection of an actual past life, or the projection of an unfulfilled childhood wish. What I got was a very strong sense that there was a connection between my mom and the older brother in the dream vision. It was possible that my mom and I had experienced a similar relationship in a past life. In many ways, the images made sense. My mom had been a strong authority figure in my life, and I did have a childhood fascination with Jesus.

> The secret of salvation is but this: that you are doing this unto yourself. (T-27.VIII.10:1)

The week passed, and my grief gradually subsided. I know, he was just a cat, but I had made him very special. The fact is that it would take nearly six months before I fully understood the real cause of my grief. My cat Bubby had been for me a symbol of innocence, the innocence I had lost when I had committed the ultimate sin against God. I had projected this innocence outside myself, and it was symbolized in my dream by my cat. Since there is not really anyone or anything out there, and since everything I believe I see is really a picture of what is buried deep inside of me, the true cause of my grief over the loss of my cat was my belief in the loss of my own innocence.

Following the death of Bubby, I focused on work, my favourite anaesthetic. When people inquired about my next writing project, I hesitated to talk about *Making Peace with God*, still struggling with my uncertain faith. While my difficulty in making time for writing was evidence of this inner conflict, it also spoke of my anxiety about bringing this work into the world. As long as the manuscript remained on the computer, everything was fine. I was writing, an activity I thoroughly enjoyed, while I continued to deepen my understanding of the Course. I had come to accept that not very many people would agree with my new spiritual views, and some might even think that I had gone over the deep end. I rationalized my concerns away by reminding myself that this was a self-study program, and no one need know what I was thinking. I could continue to be vigilant for my thoughts and practise forgiveness without anyone's knowledge. It was my dream, and I wanted to awaken from it.

Many times, I recalled my mom's troubling words, a clear echo of my own doubts: *If only there was proof.* Intellectually, the Course made sense. But it was so completely different from anything else and so impossible to talk about with someone not on the journey that I often felt lost and alone. In truth, I was beginning to miss not having someone with whom to share my concerns. In a way, I felt shame for my weakness, but I needed to be honest with myself: *If only there was proof.*

Life eventually did return to normal. Since I was spending a lot of time at the computer, I made a point of doing yoga stretches at least once a day. Clearly, sitting at a computer for hours at a time was not good for this body. If I didn't stop to stretch, it wasn't long before I felt tension in my back and shoulders. Following a relaxing evening yoga session, I pressed the play button for my meditation music. Settling on the Zen bench, I felt content and looked forward to spending a few minutes making peace with God. The temperature had been unusually cold for the end of April, and the basement was cool. I grabbed the tattered old bedspread I used to curl up in when I watched television and quickly threw it over myself, but it was lighter than I expected, and it flew up and landed over my head. Chuckling playfully as I tugged and wrapped it around myself, I snuggled my head deeply into the soft cotton folds.

Closing my eyes, I took a couple of deep breaths, and, with my mind calm and clear, as was my custom after yoga, I sat quietly, peacefully. Suddenly, I lost awareness of my basement yoga room. Wrapped up in the old bedspread, I became the young girl from the dream-vision, clutching the dusty shawl about myself, trying to be as inconspicuous as possible. Hiding behind a group of men who were having an animated discussion by the roadside, I craned my neck to catch a glimpse of the man who stood just beyond them talking to passersby. Then he turned and spotted me where I was certain no one could see me. He smiled, and, for one transcendent moment, I knew that the waiting had not been in vain, for, in that briefest of moments, I knew that I had seen the Face of Love.

Be kind, he said without words. *Be kind*. The experience of love in that one single moment was so overwhelming that I doubled over in child's pose[5] and wept. His gaze held a kindness filled with the purest love I had ever seen and I understood that this was my answer. *Be kind to others, but above all, be kind to yourself.* This was the way. As I wept some more, I felt the lifting of huge burdens and soon I was overcome by a most profound sense of peace. From that moment on, I was certain that I would never again travel alone. From that moment on, I was certain that I would never again doubt.

> The grace of God rests gently on forgiving eyes, and everything they look on speaks of Him to the beholder. He can see no evil; nothing in the world to fear, and no one who is different from himself. And as he loves them, so he looks upon himself with love and gentleness. He would no more condemn himself for his mistakes than damn another. He is not an arbiter of vengeance, nor a punisher of sin. The kindness of his sight rests on himself with all the tenderness it offers others. For he would only heal and only bless. And being in accord with what God wills, he has the power to heal and bless all those he looks on with the grace of God upon his sight. (T-25.VI.1:1–8)

---

5. Child's pose is a yoga posture of rest and surrender.

Chapter 16

THE JOURNEY BEGINS

The journey to God is merely the reawakening of the knowledge of where you are always, and what you are forever. It is a journey without distance to a goal that has never changed. (T-8. VI.9:6–7)

*B*e normal, Ken Wapnick admonishes in his talks—*be normal!* It has been four years since I began the *Course in Miracles* leg of my spiritual journey, and, for the first time in a long while, I feel I can be normal, well... almost. Where, at least for a little while, I found it difficult to live my everyday life and do ordinary things without feeling as though there was something more important I should be doing—study the Course, meditate or move to a cave in Tibet—things have finally fallen into place. Move over Ken Wapnick, bossa nova is back!

In the end, my experience of the Course hasn't changed my life much, at least not outwardly. I am still the same person, with the same tastes and preferences and, fortunately or unfortunately, depending on the perspective, the same personality. Some people care for me; others don't. That's the nature of a world that is fundamentally dualistic. I still enjoy the same foods, dress the same way and basically do the same things as before. While I continue to listen to Ken Wapnick lectures, I also take the time to enjoy my favourite music, especially while driving along a country road on a beautiful summer day with the windows rolled down—certainly among my favourite things to do.

The house has changed a lot, but I've settled into my new life-style. The new garden did very well last summer, and the lilies, my favourite flowers, were absolutely fabulous. My mom and I bought a hibachi, and we made some of the best BBQs ever. In the spare office, I installed a wireless card in the old desktop computer so my mom could have e-mail and browse the Internet. I'm hoping to teach her enough about the computer so she can help me with some of my projects—but shhh—just don't tell her ...

In the fall of '07, when I became very busy with the launch of *The Power of Time*, Bob and I agreed that it was time to end our dance partnership. Not long afterwards, he started to date the lady he had danced with while I had been ill. He did help me finish renovating the basement, and now I have a beautiful room where I can practise yoga and hold workshops. He gives me a hand with little projects now and then, and I continue to make batches of oatmeal muffins for his breakfasts. Bob and I will remain always the best of friends.

I have gained a whole new level of respect for the Course, no longer treating my copy of the book with special reverence, often piling my headset and MP3 player on top where it usually lies on the dresser next to my bed. The book with the navy blue cover and its contents are also part of the dream. Although I may not catch all of the nuances and references in the text, or in Ken Wapnick's lectures, I do have a profound appreciation for its teaching. Each time I read a passage, I am blown away by its all-encompassing message. It is literally bursting at the seams with incredible wisdom, knowledge, guidance and helpful tools for whomever seeks to awaken from the dream. *A Course in Miracles* truly is a phenomenal work!

If anything, the change has been an inner one, the greatest impact being on the level of thought. Clearly, I do not look at the world as I used to; I couldn't if I wanted to. Sometimes it feels as though I am living another life, a stranger's life. Sometimes, I don't recognize who it is I see in the mirror, or who it is that is thinking my thoughts or speaking my words. I have come to accept that I will live out my life as it was scripted, continuing to do the work I have been doing for nearly twenty-five years, but I will make the best use of it by applying what I have learned through my Course studies. Besides my normal job, I now have an inner function: practise forgiveness, undo the ego's thought system and accept the atonement for myself. That, I must admit, is the biggest job of all.

There are many other spiritualities out there, but this is the one for me; of that, I have no doubt. Having settled on *A Course in Miracles* as my path, I am now officially no longer in the spiritual buffet line, bringing to an end a very long quest for truth. Gone is the nagging sensation that there is something I need to see, that there is something missing. Gone is the struggle with unsatisfactory answers and spiritualities that don't make sense. Gone is the confusion about the nature of this universe, which was and always will be a place where the insane come to dream awhile.

I can imagine that *A Course in Miracles* is not likely to be a popular spirituality, at least not any time soon, since it requires serious study and sincere application. For most of its students, this path is a lifelong process. It also is not designed to solve problems in the world; instead, it addresses the source of the problems of the world, a decision made in the mind. For someone looking to feel good about the world, this may not be the best path. For someone looking to experience peace of a lasting kind—the peace of God—this is the path.

I am also very relieved to know that the real God is not the God of my childhood. The God of our religions is judgmental and biased, kind and loving one day, wrathful and vengeful the next. He commands some people to kill other people. He sends plagues, disease and pestilence onto his own creation. He lets his children suffer. In short, he is as insane as the delusional mind that made him up. Thankfully, the real God has nothing to do with this world; thank God there is *not this*, otherwise, there would be no hope.

My life is my classroom not because God wants me to grow and learn and develop my talents and abilities—I've already established that my true Self is Spirit, perfectly whole, as God created me and therefore not in need of any learning. My life is my classroom only because I have fallen asleep and am having a foolish dream in which I believe I am a separate, special individual—anything but what God has created. I am convinced that remaining in the dream is preferable to awakening, for in waking, this separated self will no longer exist. But since this dream state keeps the peace of God from me, I have decided that I would rather go home. Jesus gave us a Course that was designed to gently awaken us from this dream. With his help, when I am ready to let go of this dream self, I will return to my true home.

Although for a while I harboured doubts about continuing with my profession, even wondering if I should mortgage my home and buy a flower shop, I have come to accept that my function in this life is to continue with my practice. Astrology and numerology do work, within reason, but they will never be absolute, like everything else in this dream universe, and, for me, that's okay. I find comfort in knowing where the absolute truly is.

> If you have made it a habit to ask for help when and where you can, you can be confident that wisdom will be given you when you need it. (M-29.5:8)

In my practice, my approach has changed somewhat. Before each consult, I repeat the wonderful little prayer from Chapter 2 of the Text, reminding myself that *I am here only to be truly helpful,*[1] then I am confident that I will be guided to say whatever needs to be said. When working with clients, I have a far clearer picture and deeper understanding of their life stories, sometimes catching glimpses of past lives. I also have a fairly good grasp of the nature and purpose of their special relationships. I sense their pain, their fears and their anguish as though they were my own, and, in a way, they are my own, for on the deepest level, we share one mind.

I see how each person's script is an effective blend of the various forms of expression that are the result of the original mistaken thought of separation and the resulting sin, guilt and fear. Some

---

1. T-2.V.18:2–6.

will express anger, fear or specialness more easily; for others, it is guilt, hatred, resentment or victimization. Some are particularly sensitive to the feelings of loss associated with the idea of separation and spend a lot of time trying to fill the void either with special love relationships, food, alcohol or other addictions such as work, shopping or even incessant activity. While other people spend a lot of energy projecting their inner guilt outward, some choose to punish themselves instead.

Of course, we all have our lovelier qualities such as the ability to cherish and care for the special people in our lives. We boast various forms of intelligence, skills, talents, good intentions—in fact, just enough nice traits to make our separate selves tolerable to ourselves and to others. Each person's script contains the perfect blending of good and bad, of opportunity and challenge. Sometimes we are victims, at other times, victimizers; we are happy, then sad; we gain and we lose; we heal and fall ill again; we love and we hate; we attack and we defend. It all seems to make sense because there are usually some plausible reasons and explanations for each aspect of our story. And if there are no plausible explanations, we make some up, like, *It's God's plan for us*; *It's what the universe wants*; *It's all good…*

The apparent plausibility of the nature of the universe and our existence attenuates our need to probe for the deeper meaning of life. If we were to probe deeply enough, we might discover the truth, which is not what the ego thought system is designed to do, since the truth will show us that there is no sin, there is no need for this dream and our life here in this world is not our true life. In the end, what we all have in common is the one problem: we believe we have separated from God; and the one solution: acceptance of the atonement for ourselves.

Looking back, I can see the various themes weave themselves together to form the symphony of my own life: themes of specialness, independence, adventure, and sufficient abundance and opportunity to make it a rather fine life. Most of my decisions, actions and lifestyle preferences can be attributed to my early childhood experiences, from my fondness for isolation and the quiet life to my all-pervasive *I can do it myself* attitude. I could say that I pushed away love throughout my life because of my early experience of isolation. I could also say that my *I can do it myself* attitude is a result of a lack of trust no doubt due to the same cause. I could go on analyzing all aspects of my life and probably even make a whole lot of sense. Yet it would still not give me the truth, since the Course tells me that I am seeing with eyes that cannot see and I am thinking with a brain that can only falsely interpret, since it was designed to keep me in the dream, away from the truth.

From the perspective of the Course, the various themes of specialness and independence of my life can be seen as reflections of the original mistaken thought of separation from God. The *I can do it myself* theme reflects the thought that I don't need God, that I can exist on my own, separate from God. The choice for isolation over intimacy is really a symbol of the fear of the perfect oneness of God. Physical and emotional pain and pleasure—all perceptual experiences—are proof that I exist, in a body. In fact all my choices, responses and decisions can be traced back to that one mistaken thought: that it is possible to accomplish the impossible—to separate from my source. The metaphysics of the Course simplifies all questions that relate to the meaning of my existence to the one simple error—not even a sin—just a mistaken choice, thus eliminating the need for complex and sometimes endless analysis and justification.

While thinking about the popular trends in what passes for spirituality today, it occurred to me that the practice of tapping into the power of the mind to accomplish specific goals such as acquiring a new house, attracting a loving relationship, securing a better job or attracting wealth is a bit like being in the middle of the desert with a handful of dried beans and learning that you can magically manifest a bucket of fresh water. Excitedly, you plant your seeds, add a little water and, before you know it, you have healthy little seedlings growing at your feet. Encouraged by your success, you use the fledgling power of your mind to manifest a little creek, and now you have enough water to nurse your plants to maturity. With a little more practice, your mind grows to be so powerful that you are able to manifest a flowing river, and your garden grows into a flourishing oasis. Now you are able to feed your family and friends, which all seems very good, except that, no matter how abundant your flow of water and how many beans you grow, the fact remains that you are still in the desert. Although this may be satisfactory for many people, clearly, I have no interest in remaining in the desert any longer than necessary.

> A desert is a desert is a desert. You can do anything you want in it, but you *cannot* change it from what it *is*. It still lacks water. This is why it *is* a desert. The thing to do with a desert is to *leave*.[2]

Despite my initial misgivings, I know that I am not dim-witted and, although I may have struggled in my youth while juggling two languages, I don't believe I'm dyslexic. What I *am* is extremely resistant to learning and especially to applying the teachings of the Course in my life. On a number of occasions, Jesus says that this is a simple course, and I can just imagine that he might have been chuckling to himself when he made those statements. He no doubt knew that it would be very difficult for us to learn his Course, not because the teachings are complicated, but because of our stubborn resistance to accepting the truth. I have seen the beast that lies between me and the peace of God, and I know it isn't about to give up the battle any time soon. But that's okay; I forgive myself. I have a brilliant and compassionate teacher in Jesus and the wisdom of God in the Holy Spirit and every confidence that they will help me find my way home.

A couple of people have asked if I have awakened from the dream, a question that always makes me laugh, as though awakening from the dream was a competition of sorts. The fact that I am even addressing this question should be a clue. Ken Wapnick's wonderful workshop called *Climbing the Ladder Home*, which I have listened to many, many times, describes step by step the process

---

2. *Absence from Felicity*, page 236.

of returning to our true home in Heaven. Let's just say that I now know that there is a ladder and I can, at least most of the time, manage to keep one hand on the bottom rung. If I forget where the ladder is, I know which workshop will help me find it again.

> Your chosen home is on the other side, beyond the veil. It has been carefully prepared for you, and it is ready to receive you now. You will not see it with the body's eyes. Yet all you need you have. Your home has called to you since time began, nor have you ever failed entirely to hear. You heard, but knew not how to look, nor where. And now you know. In you the knowledge lies, ready to be unveiled and freed from all the terror that kept it hidden. There *is* no fear in love. (T-20.II.8:1–9)

What I have now is a wonderful teacher in whom I can fully place my trust, a teacher who is sensitive to my resistance to learning the Course and uncovering the truth, and brilliant enough to know how to help me overcome that resistance. In Jesus, I have found the teacher I really needed. In *A Course in Miracles* I have found a thought system that is logical, simple and absolute, an ontology that is consistent and intelligent, a teaching in which I can have complete faith. I no longer wonder whether what it says is true; it makes too much sense to not be true. I do not wonder whether it will take me home; I know it will.

For my efforts, I have received some invaluable gifts, the first and perhaps the dearest among them being trust. No matter what happens, I know I can put my trust in the Holy Spirit and in Jesus and sooner or later I have the understanding I need to deal with the situation at hand. Day by day, one forgiveness opportunity at a time, I am removing the blockages to the truth that lies within. But the gift that will remain with me always is the memory of the Face of Love, a ready reminder to be kind not only toward others, but also toward myself.

> Truth can only be experienced. It cannot be described and it cannot be explained. (T-8.VI.9:8–9)

The Journey That Never Was

But for a little while
The journey grows certain
Then as darkness is brought to light
As form loses its value
As illusion loosens its grip
And its need is undone,
The journey fades.
For in truth the journey has ended
For a moment only we seemed to travel
A voyage that was but a buffer
Against the healing light of truth
Against the fear of what awakening brings
Where nothing is exchanged for everything
Indeed the journey was never begun
For I am at home in God
In truth the journey never was.

PAULINE EDWARD, 2008

APPENDIX

*I*n late 2007, one of our *Course in Miracles* study group members sent me a frantic e-mail. "HOW DO YOU DO IT?" Dale shouted in the subject line of her message, clearly desperate to find solutions to the issues that had been troubling her for some time. I understood that she was looking for ways to resolve her problems in the world, and, much like myself just a couple of years earlier, she hoped that the Course would give her the answers she needed. Dale was just beginning her Course journey, and, naturally I sympathized with her anxiety. However, in replying with a quote from the Course, I doubt very much that I adequately answered her concerns, given that at the time I was experiencing doubts of my own. So, better late than never, in answer to your question, Dale, I am happy to share with you some of the things I have learned.

For any given situation, there are a number of teachings I can draw upon to help me return to a peaceful state and, most importantly, make a better choice not only for myself, but also for whomever else might be concerned. Now I know that there is an alternative to the thought system of the ego—the Holy Spirit's thought system, and choosing with the Holy Spirit invariably leads to a far better experience for all. In no particular order, here are a few of my favourite lessons.

A SENSE OF HUMOUR

> In gentle laughter does the Holy Spirit perceive the cause, and looks not to effects. (T-27.VIII.9:1)

Above all, no matter what is going on, I try to keep a sense of humour; otherwise, it's easy to get discouraged. The Course teaches us to look at the situations in our life from a unique perspective, identifying the root cause of our upsets, desires and reactions while showing us how to release them through the practice of forgiveness. Seeing that the cause is a decision we made in our mind can be distressing, especially as we begin to see it on a regular basis. In a way, by not taking things too seriously, I can treat myself like the child that I am, which is how Jesus treats us in his course; then I can more readily forgive the situation and, of course, myself.

TWO DISTINCT LEVELS

> We have referred to miracles as the means of correcting level confusion, for all mistakes must be corrected at the level on which they occur. Only the mind is capable of error. (T-2.IV.2:3–4)

One of the most important aspects of the teachings of *A Course in Miracles* is that it speaks to us on a very deep level; in fact, much of the time, Jesus is not even speaking to me, Pauline Edward, the author of this book. Pauline Edward is just a figure in a dream, and all the other people in Pauline Edward's life are players in the dream. The Course says that we made the dream. But if Pauline Edward is a player in the dream, then, who is the dreamer?

When I identify with Pauline Edward, I am identifying with a dream figure. Jesus speaks to that part of the mind that has until now remained hidden from our awareness; he is speaking to the dreamer. As much as this might at first seem frightening, I see this as a really good thing, because it means that despite everything I have learned and done in my life thus far, there is a whole other level that remains to be uncovered. This gives me hope.

A Course in Miracles is designed to uncover that part of the mind that we are not even aware exists and therefore it speaks to us on two very distinct levels. Without an understanding of the Course's metaphysics, I was confused about how to apply its message in my life, especially at the beginning, when I was looking for a way to resolve my relationship issues with Bob. It was only once I saw my less-than-glorious ego-investment in maintaining the conflict in that relationship that I was able to look at it with Jesus and let it go. Acknowledging *why* I needed this conflict in my life as well as knowing that I could make a different choice, and then asking for help in making that choice, is what ultimately led to the healing of our bond.

ON ASKING FOR HELP

If it helps you, think of me holding your hand and leading you. And I assure you this will be no idle fantasy. (W-pI.70.9:3–4)

I no longer expect the Course to fix my problems in the world. That's not what the Course is about, and if it did claim to fix things in the world, then it would be no better than any other spirituality already in existence. My life and all its big and little circumstances are all part of a dream. If the Course were to address these, then it would be making the error—the dream—real. Thank God this is not the case; otherwise, we would be in serious trouble. If God were to intervene and fix things in the dream, then there would truly be no hope, for there would be no way out.

While not expecting the Course to fix my life, I do finally make very liberal use of the help offered by my new teacher, Jesus. I have accepted that even though I can do lots of things on my own in the world of form, one thing I cannot do is to wake myself from the dream I am having, a dream that was deviously designed to keep me from choosing my true reality. However, when I do ask Jesus to help me see things differently, within a short period of time, situations usually get resolved, an added bonus for placing my trust in the right teacher.

I do not ask Jesus for help each time I take a breath or each time I need to make an everyday decision. That would be putting emphasis on the dream, and if there is one thing I do *not* need, it is to reinforce my identification with the dream figure. What I *do* need is to get in touch with the dreamer. The Course does not ask me to change the dream figure, because it is only a dream figure.

While the Course asks that I be vigilant for the deeper, hidden part of my mind, it does not ask that I give up my personality, my preferences or even my autonomous and independent nature. Being able to do lots of things on my own is not a bad thing, and the Course certainly does not require that I stop being resourceful and productive. What I can do is place my skills and resourcefulness in the service of the Holy Spirit. Then, whenever guided, I know that what I do will be kind, loving and helpful for all.

STUDY

> This is a course in mind training. All learning involves atten-
> tion and study at some level. (T-1.VII.4:1–2)

It wasn't until I had gained a sufficient understanding of the metaphysics of the Course that I was able to begin to apply its teachings in my life on a daily basis. Having a gist of its message was enough to get me started, but I needed to see the sin, the guilt and the fear that lay buried deep beneath the complex script of what I knew as my *self* and my life. In fact, *A Course in Miracles* is called *A Course in Miracles* not as a matter of course, but because it actually is a course, and, like any subject worth learning, it requires study and application.

If I wanted to build bridges, I would go to school and become an engineer. The day of my graduation, I doubt very much that I would be assigned the task of building a bridge across the St. Lawrence Seaway. I might get a job as an apprentice in order to practise my newly acquired knowledge in the field. Depending on my efforts and dedication to my work, I might eventually become a good engineer, perhaps even a great one.

The same holds true for *A Course in Miracles*. The willingness to learn a new way of looking at the world and the amount of time devoted to applying its principles as situations arise on a day-to-day basis will be directly proportional to my growing understanding and eventual release from the dream. The Course is not one of those books to be read once, or opened at random in search of spontaneous inspiration for how to fix things in the world. On a number of occasions, I have heard people say things like: "Yeah, I read it. I can relate to it. It's a really cool book," while they go on and on bitching about how horrible such and such a person is, or how much someone or something pisses them off, or how unfairly they have been treated. Clearly, they haven't really studied the "really cool book."

No one can fail who seeks to reach the truth. (W-pI.131)

When I finished reading the Text and doing the Workbook lessons, I was very relieved to have completed such a challenging undertaking. In fact, I think I might have even promised myself *never again*. That's how relieved I was. But since this is a course, and I really do want to master its teachings, I came to terms with the fact that I would probably have to read it again one day.

Well, that day did come, and, to my astonishment, when I picked up the big book with the navy blue cover and began to reread the first chapter, I found that I actually understood much of what I was reading. I didn't fall asleep, I didn't have to reread each line ten times, and I didn't feel intellectually handicapped. What was most encouraging is that I realized that I can do this—*I can learn this course*. At the same time, I also decided to do the workbook lessons again. This time around, I was surprised to see how each lesson is in itself filled with the entire essence of the teachings of the Course. I can now more fully appreciate the brilliance and depth of the Workbook.

IT'S ABOUT THE MIND

[S]eek not to change the world, but choose to change your mind about the world. (T-21.in.1:7)

I understand now that it's not what I do in the world that will get me home. I could be practising astrology or I could be managing a flower shop—it wouldn't really matter. It is what I do with my mind that matters. By the same token, what other people appear to be doing in the world is not necessarily a reflection of what is going on in their mind, which makes a case for withholding judgment. So, in the end, it does not matter what another person is doing or thinking; it's what's going on in my mind that matters!

ALL OF IT!

> There is no order of difficulty in miracles. One is not "harder" or "bigger" than another. They are all the same. All expressions of love are maximal. (T-1.I.1:1–4)

One of the most challenging teachings of the Course is that it says that I am the cause of the whole world I see. It's my dream. All of what I see is of my own making, since the world is nothing more than an outward picture of an inward condition. Furthermore, it says that not only did I make the parts I like, I made *all of it*, the good and the bad, the beautiful and the ugly, the joy and the sadness. As difficult as this concept may be to accept, it makes the job of forgiving a whole lot easier. I don't have to question whether or not I should forgive one person over another, or wonder whether or not it might be okay to judge someone for doing something particularly nasty. The Course is unequivocal in its teachings: forgive all of it because it is all part of the same dream, my dream. Jesus even tries to motivate us to practise forgiveness by pointing out that we will feel a whole lot better when we practise his teachings. And guess what? He's right!

FACT VERSUS INTERPRETATION

> Perhaps it will be helpful to remember that no one can be angry at a fact. It is always an interpretation that gives rise to negative emotions, regardless of their seeming justification by what *appears* as facts. (M-17.4:1–2)

Although at first reading—and despite Jesus' claims to the contrary—this did not seem like a practical course, with continued study, I began to see that it is indeed a very practical course. When facing a situation that stirs up anger, fear or resentment, when I feel judged or criticized or when I become defensive, when I experience anything that takes away my peace, I try to remember to stick to the facts at hand. This requires that I stand back a little, look at what is happening objectively and, in the process, perhaps save myself a trip down judgment lane.

For example, on the highway, someone might drive up my right side and cut me off, causing me to blurt out a few choice expletives. I could justify my irritation by pointing out that the idiot invaded my driving space, something I highly value, and perhaps even put my life in danger, something I value even more. My driving space is really a reflection of my personal space, which defines and protects my existence in a separate body. The ego part of my mind revels in the opportunity to blame something outside of me for my upset, thus reinforcing the notion that there is danger and threat outside and that there is also a *me* that is in danger, not to mention an *innocent* me who was simply driving along in my lane minding my own business until this jerk came along.

Recognizing that I have wandered *off Course* (the pun was impossible to resist!), I then call on Jesus to help me look at the situation with the Holy Spirit's thought system instead of the ego's. I separate out my interpretation of the situation—an interpretation that invariably suits the needs of my ego—from the facts. In this example, from the perspective of the ego, it appears as though the guy cut me off and pissed me off in the process, while the fact of the matter is that a guy drove up the right lane and merged in traffic ahead of me, and the whole thing looks rather silly. It is my *interpretation* of the situation that led to an experience of anger.

THE PRICE OF BEING RIGHT

Do you prefer that you be right or happy? (T-29.VII.1:9)

When I see myself insisting on being right, I stop, examine my motives and look for my ego investment. Wanting to be right almost invariably leads to conflict, since it usually occurs in a competitive situation. If I am right, someone else must be wrong. Separate interests are being served; shared interests have been sacrificed. When I ask for help, I am reminded that I can always choose to disengage from the conflict even if there is no doubt in my mind that I am right. The joy derived from proving myself right in the world is a false joy, masking an inner need to prove that I am right about my existence, and God is wrong, a belief that is founded on an error. Choosing with the Holy Spirit leads to a deeper and far more satisfactory joy, since it leads to an experience that is based on my true nature, an experience of peace and oneness. Specialness and separateness belong to the ego's script; shared interests and oneness are of God.

DOES IT REALLY MATTER?

Recognize what does not matter, and if your brothers ask you for something "outrageous," do it *because* it does not matter. Refuse, and your opposition establishes that it does matter to you. (T-12. III.4:1–2)

A helpful way to determine whether I am thinking with the ego or the Holy Spirit is to look for *purpose*, a very important concept in the teachings of the Course. What is my investment? Why do I want to do a particular thing in a particular way? If someone asks me to do something that I don't want to do, or if a situation arises in which I become upset because things are not going as expected, I know that I have responded with the ego. If I think there is something important *out there* that I should be doing, if I feel that my plans have been thwarted, if I think that my will has been challenged, I know that the ego is involved, for an investment in the world is an investment in nothing.

Of course, this does not mean that I should go out and kill if someone hands me a gun with a request to shoot their wicked mother-in-law. That would be silly, and the Course is anything but silly. It does not mean that I should do everything everyone asks of me either; that would be just as silly. It does mean that I should look for any ego investment in my response. If I respond with judgment or defensiveness, for example, I know I have chosen with the ego; if my response is kind and loving, chances are that I have chosen with the Holy Spirit. The only worthwhile investment in the world is in being vigilant for my thoughts so that I can make a different choice.

A CALL FOR LOVE

I have said you have but two emotions, love and fear. (T-13.V.1:1)

Jesus says that there are only two emotions, love and fear. When I am in the presence of someone who is lashing out at something they claim is bothering them or perhaps they are getting in my face about something I have done, it can be very helpful to remember that what I am seeing is usually a call for love. A call for love is very often a mask for fear; what is not love is fear, the Course says. Love is an expression of oneness, while fear is an expression of separation and can manifest in many forms such as anger, attack, resentment, judgment, comparison and specialness. If someone appears to be calling for love, my response is simply to love. If they appear to be expressing love, my response is simply to love.

Sometimes, as a way of avoiding becoming drawn into situations of conflict and judgment, I remind myself that this is the other person's part of the dream of separation that we all share, and I do not have to get sucked into it. To do so would not only cost me my sense of peace, it would also reinforce the choice for the wrong mind, the thought of separation. By not jumping in, whether or not I say or do anything, I can at least show that there is another way of looking at a situation. Sometimes, I may even come up with a helpful solution. Again, my response would simply be kind and loving.

A SIMPLE TEACHING

This is a very simple course. (T-11.VIII.1:1)

For a spiritually undisciplined person like me, this is a really cool spiritual path because it does not impose any outwardly challenging rules or austere practices such as abstinence, fasting, never-ending rituals, flagellation or the wearing of long orange robes. Thank goodness, because orange is definitely not my colour!

Jesus asks only that we be willing to look. That's all. Actually, not quite. We need to be willing to look at what lies buried deep in our mind with honesty and a fair amount of courage. As it turns out, this is probably the most difficult of spiritual paths since it is not about feeling good about the world or making the world a better place, it is about looking at the true cause of our seeming separation from our true Source, our predicament as figures in a dream—our choice for the ego.

> The ego is therefore capable of suspiciousness at best and vicious-ness at worst. That is its range. (T-9.VII.3:7–8)

The ego's thought system is all-pervasive, profoundly anchored, determined to survive at all costs and very uncool. It is filled with specialness, fear and judgment and invariably leads to conflict and lack of peace. Peace in this world is always temporary, a respite of sorts between dramas, and serves only to keep us from looking for the truth where it really lies—buried deep inside our mind. This is really not a very nice thought system, but it is the thought system we adhere to, so a fair amount of patience is required when it comes to observing our responses and choices.

Another great aspect of this spirituality is that, while it does not ask me to change anything in my life, at least not in the world of form, what it does ask of me I can do at any time, under any circumstance and without anybody ever knowing what it is I am doing. It requires only that I be vigilant for my thoughts. I observe the situation, acknowledge that the world was made up by me, I declare that I do not wish to continue this way and I give it up to the Holy Spirit—and voilà!—He does all the heavy lifting, and peace soon returns.

Since, like most people, I am a doer, switching gears, becoming an observer and handing over the reins is not always easy. However, when I do take the time to stop and look at the situation with Jesus, I can generally recognize my ego at work, and by practising forgive-ness, I can save myself the aggravation of experiencing a surge of negative emotion such as resentment, impatience or anger. Each time I practise forgiveness, I know I am one step closer to going home.

One of the early Workbook lessons (Lesson 23) describes forgiveness in a simple, three-step process. The first step requires that I acknowledge that I am the cause of what I perceive, that, in fact, the world is an outward picture of an inward condition. *I* am the one who put it out there so that I wouldn't have to deal with it inside myself. The next step is to decide that I no longer want the experience and to let it go. The third step belongs to the Holy Spirit. By letting go, the Holy Spirit takes over and completes the process. It really is quite simple!

PEACE IS A CHOICE

I could see peace instead of this. (W-pI.34)

Over the last couple of years, I have learned the tremendous value of peace. Any sentiment, response or reaction that diminishes my experience of peace is worthy of my undivided attention. In fact, the loss of peace has become my biggest red flag. Even happy events can fall into this category, especially those that serve to reinforce my specialness. With what I have learned from the Course, when I take the time to be aware of my thoughts, I can usually see which thought system I have chosen. It is then a simple matter to make a different choice, for I do wish to experience the peace of God. When I take the time, I look at the situation with Jesus, and then choose the Holy Spirit's alternative. It's all in the choosing; this is where true power lies.

Knowledge is not the motivation for learning this course. Peace is. This is the prerequisite for knowledge only because those who are in conflict are not peaceful, and peace is the condition of knowledge because it is the condition of the Kingdom. (T-8.I.1.1–3)

BIBLIOGRAPHY AND RESOURCES

All references to *A Course in Miracles* are from the Second Edition, 1992. Published by the Foundation for Inner Peace. P.O. Box 598, Mill Valley, CA 94942–0598.

Renard, Gary R. *The Art of Advanced Forgiveness*. Video DVD. Kiel WI: Pathways of Light, 2005.

————. *The Disappearance of the Universe: Straight Talk about Illusions, Past Lives, Religion, Sex, Politics and the Miracles of Forgiveness*. CA: Hay House, Inc., 2004.

————. *Secrets of the Immortal: Advanced Teachings from A COURSE IN MIRACLES*. Audio CD. Boulder, CO: Sounds True, 2006.

————. *Your Immortal Reality, How to Break the Cycle of Birth and Death*. CA: Hay House, Inc., 2006.

Wapnick, Ph.D., Kenneth. *Absence from Felicity: The Story of Helen Schucman and Her Scribing of A COURSE IN MIRACLES*. CA: The Foundation for *A Course in Miracles*, 1991.

————. *The Journey Home: The Obstacles to Peace in A COURSE IN MIRACLES*, CA: The Foundation for *A Course in Miracles*, 2000.

————. *The Message of A COURSE IN MIRACLES, Volume One: All Are Called*. CA: The Foundation for *A Course in Miracles*, 1997.

————. *The Message of A COURSE IN MIRACLES, Volume Two: Few Choose to Listen*. CA: The Foundation for *A Course in Miracles*, 1997.

NON COURSE-RELATED

Edward, Pauline. *The Power of Time: Understanding the Cycles of Your Life's Path*. Woodbury, MN: Llewellyn Worldwide, 2007.

Merton, Thomas. *The Seven Storey Mountain*. Orlando, FL: Harcourt Brace Jovanovich, Inc., 1976.

WORKSHOPS BY KENNETH WAPNICK, PH.D.

(CDs available from the Foundation for *A Course in Miracles*)

Asking the Holy Spirit, 2003
Be Kind, for Everyone You Meet Is Fighting a Hard Battle, 2006
Classes on the Manual for Teachers of *A Course in Miracles*, Vol. I and
 II, 2001-2002
Classes on the Text of *A Course in Miracles*, Vols. I-VIII, 2001-2002
Climbing the Ladder Home, 1996
The Experience of *A Course in Miracles*, 1998
Learning from the Holy Spirit, 1996
The Lifting of the Veil, 1999
Living in the World: Prison or Classroom, 2003
No Man Is an Island: Our Common Purpose, 2005
The Pathway of Forgiveness, 2001
The Quiet Answer, 1999
Rules for Decision, 1993
Special Relationships, Parts I and II, 1985
The Web of Specialness, 1992

INTERNET RESOURCES

A Time for Success, www.atimeforsuccess.com
Foundation for *A Course in Miracles,* www.facim.org
Foundation for Inner Peace, www.acim.org
Gary Renard's website, www.garyrenard.com
Pauline Edward's website and blogs: www.paulineedward.com

THE POWER OF TIME
Pauline Edward

Don't wait around for life to just "happen." Develop a solid, successful life plan with guidance from astrologer-numerologist Pauline Edward. Whether your goals are personal or professional, *The Power of Time* will help you take advantage of the powerful natural cycles at work in your life. Simple calculations based on numerology reveal where you are in each nine-year cycle and what to expect from each year, month and day. With your life path clearly mapped out, it will be easy for you to pinpoint the best times to start a new job, focus on family, launch a business, take time to reflect, make a major purchase, complete a project, expand your horizons and more. By reading this book, you will:

- Gain a deeper understanding of your life purpose
- Learn how to focus on your needs and opportunities given your trends
- Learn how to make your action plans even more effective
- Identify and learn how to deal with potential obstacles
- Gain the knowledge and confidence you need to achieve your goals

Mostly, you will feel much more in tune with your natural cycles and will experience increased confidence, greater success and an overall sense of satisfaction.

NOTABLE FEATURES
- A powerful guide to personal and professional planning using your unique life cycles, based on easy-to-use principles of numerology
- Includes practical worksheets to calculate your life path, personal years, months, and days
- Features helpful exercises for tailoring goal-setting and planning activities to your personal timetable

ASTROLOGICAL CROSSES IN RELATIONSHIPS
Pauline Edward

For the first time ever, here is an astrology book that focuses on astrological crosses (the cardinal, fixed and mutable aspects of the signs of the zodiac) and their impact on people's lives, behaviour, actions and motivation. Crosses are so important to truly understanding a chart that you will wonder how you ever completed an astrological analysis without this essential component. *Astrological Crosses in Relationships* explores the strengths and challenges of each cross, using many real-life stories taken from the author's consulting practice. Crosses revealed in the birth chart provide the best clue to personal energy style:

- Cardinal energy dreams and initiates
- Fixed energy desires and creates
- Mutable energy communicates and analyzes.

With this innovative guide, you can learn to identify crosses in everyday life experiences, mend star-crossed relationships and balance a lack or overemphasis of crosses in your birth chart.

"Pauline Edward has written the best book yet about the nature of Cardinal, Fixed, and Mutable. Her readable, insightful work can help both beginning and experienced astrologers gain much understanding about life's processes. Highly recommended."
—Michael Munkasey, PMAFA, NCGR-IV

Made in the USA
San Bernardino, CA
13 August 2013